The Modern Greek Language in It's Relation to Ancient Greek

E. M. Geldart

Copyright © BiblioLife, LLC

BiblioLife Reproduction Series: Our goal at BiblioLife is to help readers, educators and researchers by bringing back in print hard-to-find original publications at a reasonable price and, at the same time, preserve the legacy of literary history. The following book represents an authentic reproduction of the text as printed by the original publisher and may contain prior copyright references. While we have attempted to accurately maintain the integrity of the original work(s), from time to time there are problems with the original book scan that may result in minor errors in the reproduction, including imperfections such as missing and blurred pages, poor pictures, markings and other reproduction issues beyond our control. Because this work is culturally important, we have made it available as a part of our commitment to protecting, preserving and promoting the world's literature.

All of our books are in the "public domain" and some are derived from Open Source projects dedicated to digitizing historic literature. We believe that when we undertake the difficult task of re-creating them as attractive, readable and affordable books, we further the mutual goal of sharing these works with a larger audience. A portion of BiblioLife profits go back to Open Source projects in the form of a donation to the groups that do this important work around the world. If you would like to make a donation to these worthy Open Source projects, or would just like to get more information about these important initiatives, please visit www.bibliolife.com/opensource.

Clarendon Press Series

THE MODERN
GREEK LANGUAGE

IN ITS

RELATION TO ANCIENT GREEK

BY

E. M. GELDART, B.A.
Formerly Scholar of Balliol College, Oxford;
Modern Language Master at the Manchester Free Grammar School.

Oxford
AT THE CLARENDON PRESS
M DCCC LXX

[*All rights reserved*]

PREFACE.

In sending out into the world the present volume, I have little else to say by way of prefatory remark than to express the sense of the obligations I am under to those who have helped and encouraged me. Foremost among these must stand the name of F. W. Walker, Esq., late Fellow of Corpus Christi College, and Head Master of the Manchester Free Grammar School, my kind friend and instructor, who is the cause, in a sense which he will sufficiently understand, of the publication of this work.

My best thanks are also due to Professor Jowett for looking over a portion of the same while it was yet in embryo, and for most valuable suggestions which I have attempted to follow out; and to my friends S. Versés and A. Pantazides for the loan of various works which have been of indispensable service to me in the preparation of the final chapter of this book. Nor can I refrain from expressing my indebtedness to the learned lectures, and ever-ready willingness to communicate information with which all who have attended the public instructions of the Professor of Comparative Philology are so well acquainted, and which have had no unimportant influence in moulding the views hereinafter set forth. From Professor Gandell, and Dr.

Hessey, Grinfield Lecturer on the Septuagint, I have also obtained valuable information.

To Professor Blackie of Edinburgh my thanks are due for very kind and unexpected encouragement. He will easily discover where I have derived help from his interesting treatise on Greek Pronunciation.

Last, but not least, I must tender my warmest thanks to the Rev. Hermann Eduard Marotsky, Minister of the German Church, Wright Street, Manchester, without the encouragement and confirmation afforded by whose critical knowledge, my concluding essay on the dangerous domain of theology would hardly have been hazarded.

I have no right however to be silent on other obligations of a less personal nature in themselves, though in one case at least proceeding from a personal and esteemed friend, the Rev. George Perkins, M. A., author of the lucid and able article in the Cambridge Journal of Philology for December, 1869, entitled 'Rhythm versus Metre,' to which I am much indebted.

Other works which I have advantageously consulted are Schleicher's 'Compendium der Vergleichenden Grammatik,' Renan's 'Eclaircissements tirés des Langues sémitiques sur quelques points de la Prononciation grecque,' Mullach's 'Grammatik der Griechischen Vulgarsprache,' Lüdemann's 'Lehrbuch der Neugr. Sprache,' Prof. Telfy's 'Studien über Alt- und Neugriechen und die Lautgeschichte der Griechischen Sprache,' Sophocles' 'Modern Greek Grammar' and 'Glossary of Later and Byzantine Greek.'

Finally, I would take this opportunity of thanking the Curators of the Taylorian Institution at Oxford for their great kindness in granting me the use of the room in which

I delivered a course of lectures which form the foundation of the present treatise.

If I have passed over any in silence I hope it will be understood that such silence is unintentional.

In conclusion, I will give some account of the best books to be used in the study of modern Greek, especially in its relations with ancient Greek. The most instructive works on the subject with which I am acquainted are Professor Mullach's 'Grammatik der Griechischen Vulgarsprache,' Sophocles' 'Modern Greek Grammar,' and his 'Glossary of Later and Byzantine Greek.' All three of these works contain some account of the development of modern from ancient Greek; and each supplies in some measure the deficiencies of the others. Professor Mullach's work is, on the whole, the most scholarly and exhaustive. His account of the Greek dialects, ancient and modern, is specially valuable. All would have been better for a larger and wider recognition of the discoveries of modern philology in the region of comparative grammar. Sophocles' works, especially his Grammar, require to be used with caution. For the headings 'Ancient' and 'Modern' which he places over his various paradigms, should be read, in nearly every case, 'Language of Polite Society' and 'Language of the Common People,' or 'Cultivated' and Vernacular;' for the so-called ancient forms never died out, but may nearly all be found in the more cultivated modern Greek of the middle ages. Where, however, the so-called modern form has completely supplanted the classical, as in ἐγράφεσο for ἐγράφου, γράφεσαι for γράφει or γράφῃ, the fact should be noticed. Again, in other ways truth is sacrificed by Mr. Sophocles to system, as when he gives τοῦ πατέρα, τοῦ ἄνδρα, as the modern Greek for τοῦ πατρός, τοῦ ἀνδρός. These forms occur no doubt, but the classical forms are more common even in the vernacular, in which however the metaplastic nominatives πατέρας and ἄνδρας have supplanted πατήρ and ἀνήρ. For the study of the popular language as contained in the Klephtic ballads, &c., Passow's 'Carmina popularia Greciae recentioris' renders all other collections superfluous. For the history of modern Greek literature Peucker's 'Neugriechische Grammatik' contains some valuable contributions, which may be further supplemented from the Νεοελληνικὴ Φιλολογία, a work lately published in Athens, and forming a biographical history of mediaeval and modern Greek literature.

CONTENTS.

CHAPTER I.

Introduction.

Causes for the neglect of the study of modern Greek. Antiquarian prejudice; counteracted by utilitarianism. Political insignificance of Greece: hopeful signs. Obscurity of modern Greek literature: actual but unmerited. Direct practical utility of an acquaintance with the language. Reasons why it should be studied by scholars and theologians. The obstacle presented by the Erasmian system of pronunciation, pp. 1–7.

CHAPTER II.

On the Pronunciation of Greek.

The opinion of Schleicher. What is meant by the general identity of modern and ancient pronunciation. Modern pronunciation either barbarized or legitimately developed. Difficulties of the former alternative. Examination of evidence regarding the original pronunciation of each letter. I. Vowels. II. Consonants. III. The aspirate. General conclusion, pp. 8–40.

CHAPTER III.

Accent and Quantity.

Their connection in the law of accentuation. All modern Greek vowels not isochronous. Syllables not necessarily lengthened by stress. Real explanation of the supposed conflict between accent and quantity traced to our use of the Latin accent in Greek. Erasmus and the bear. Insular character of our prejudice. Stress brings out, but does not obscure quantity. How is emphasis given? View of Mr. W. G. Clark. Dominant importance of rhythm in poetry. Opposition of accent and quantity as the foundation of verse not absolute. Importance of quantity in accentual verse. Accent heard in quantitative poetry. Musical rhythm. Error of ignoring the importance of *ictus*. Significance of accent in ancient poetry. The rhythm of ancient Greek prose destroyed by ignoring the accent, pp. 41-67.

CHAPTER IV.

On the Origin and Development of Modern Greek Accidence.

Origin not one, but various. Connection of grammar, logic, and metaphysic. No rigid line of demarcation. Mere accidence independent in a sense of the progress of thought. Levelling tendency. Tendency to metaplastic formations: common to ancient and modern Greek. Many apparent metaplasms not simply such. The preservation of archaisms in the vulgar language. Analogies in English. The Grinfield lecturer on the Septuagint. The principle of extended analogy. Phrynichus and modern Greek forms. The mixed declensions. Dialectic influences. Archaisms and dialectic forms of the Septuagint not artificial. The Macedonian dynasty and the κοινὴ διάλεκτος. The disappearance of the dative case, pp. 68-84.

CHAPTER V.

The Origin and Development of Modern Greek Syntax.

Difference in modes of expression between modern and ancient Greek. Compound tenses. Tendency to waste words, pp. 85-90.

CHAPTER VI.

Modern Greek Phraseology.

Euphemism. The influence of philosophy; the Ionic philosophers. The Eleatics, Sophists, and Rhetoricians. Modern Greek particles more explicit but less expressive than ancient. Socrates. The Cyrenaics. The Cynics. Plato. The Stoics, pp. 91-100.

CHAPTER VII.

The Historical Development of Modern from Ancient Greek.

Hellenistic Greek. The Macedonian age. The language of the Septuagint and the New Testament not simply Hebraistic. Modernism of the Septuagint: of Polybius: and of the New Testament. New religious meaning of certain words. The age of Diocletian. Nubian inscriptions. The Byzantine period. Apophthegmata Patrum. Theophanes. Malalas. Leo the philosopher. Porphyrogenitus. Theophanes Continuatus. Specimens of popular language in Scylitzes and Anna Comnena. Close of the mediaeval period. Theodorus Prodromus the first modern Greek writer, pp. 101-113.

CHAPTER VIII.

Dialects of Modern Greece.

Asiatic. Chiotic. Cretan. Cyprian. Peloponnesian. Dialect of the Ionian Islands. The Tsakonian dialect. Its Doricisms. Its declension: and conjugation. Traces of Semitic elements. Tsakonian probably a lingua franca. Specimens of Tsakonian. Albanian considered as modern Graeco-italic. Its alphabet partly Greek and partly Latin. The infinitive mood. Conjugation. Pronouns. Prepositions. Numerals, pp. 114-137.

CHAPTER IX.

Modern Greek Literature.

Ptochoprodromus. Sethos. The Book of the Conquest. Belthandros and Chrysantza. Gorgilas. Chortakes. Scuphos. Kornaros. Rhegas. Cumas. Coraes. Oekonomos. Nerulos. Angelica Palle. Christopulos. Klephtic ballads. Belief in genii. Analogies in the Old Testament. Cultivated Literature of the present day. Tricupes. Roïdes. Asopios. Rangabes. Zalacostas. Valaorites. Conclusion, pp. 138-177.

APPENDIX I.

On the Greek of the Gospels of St. John and St. Luke.

Preliminary considerations. Greek of the New Testament popular, but not vernacular. Luke and the Acts somewhat artificial. Frequency of modernisms in St. John. List of striking modernisms. The Revelation. The Gospel according to St. Luke. His modernisms. The Acts. Agreement with the results of German criticism, pp. 179-188.

APPENDIX II.

A Short Lexilogus, pp. 189-208.

Index of Greek and Albanian Words, pp. 209-216.

CORRIGENDA.

Page 33, line 9, *for* ζμερδάλεοs *read* ζμερδαλέοs.
 „ 35, „ 7, *for* ἦνθα *read* ἦνθον.
 „ 130, „ 26, and elsewhere, *for* ἴδε *read* ἰδέ.
 „ 141, „ 14, *for* περιβοητοῦ *read* περιβοήτου.

CHAPTER I.

Introduction.

THE present spoken and written language of Greece is one of the most remarkable phenomena in the whole field of philology, and none the less remarkable, perhaps, is the small amount of notice which it has met with.

It is a strange and unparalleled fact, that one of the oldest known languages in the world, a language in which the loftiest and deepest thoughts of the greatest poets, the wisest thinkers, the noblest, holiest and best of teachers, have directly or indirectly found their utterance in the far-off ages of a hoar antiquity, should at this day be the living speech of millions throughout the East of Europe and various parts of Asia Minor and Africa; that it should have survived the fall of empires, and risen again and again from the ruins of beleaguered cities, deluged but never drowned by floods of invading barbarians, Romans, Celts, Slaves, Goths and Vandals, Avars, Huns, Franks and Turks; often the language of the vanquished, yet never of the dead; with features seared by years and service, yet still essentially the same; instinct with the fire of life, and beautiful with the memory of the past.

Yet it is perhaps still stranger, that while the records of its youth and manhood form the lifelong study of thousands in England, France, Germany, and the rest of Europe; nevertheless, almost the first symptoms of sickness and decay were the signals for us all to forsake it, few of us waiting to see whether its natural vigour had carried it on to a green old age, or whether, as most of us too easily assumed, it was buried in a quiet grave, and had given place to a degenerate scion, or had at best sunk into the dotage of a second childhood.

It seems hardly too much to say that our conduct in this regard shows a kind of literary ingratitude which ought to shock our moral sense. Greece has in various ages preserved to us the succession of culture when the rest of the earth was overrun with savages. For us it has held the citadel of civilization against the barbarism of the world, and now the danger is over we have forgotten our benefactor, and trouble ourselves little how it fares with him. The case reminds us of the words of the Preacher, 'There was a little city, and few men within it; and there came a great king against it, and besieged it, and built great bulwarks against it. Now there was found in it a poor wise man, and he by his wisdom delivered the city; yet no man remembered that same poor man.'

The reasons for this neglect are many and various. With learned men of the old school it is due to a certain antiquarian bent of mind, amounting to a positive prejudice against everything modern. The manner of life which such persons lead is not inaptly expressed in the words of Southey:—

> 'My days among the dead are passed,
>   Around me I behold,
> Where'er these casual eyes are cast,
>   The mighty minds of old.
> My never-failing friends are they,
>   With whom I converse night and day.'

To those extreme devotees of the 'good old times' to whom Aristotle is the last of philosophers and Augustine the last of theologians, and with whom the fact that a language is dead is of itself almost the best reason for studying it, the discovery that the elder and nobler of the two sister tongues Greek and Latin is as really alive as it was in the days of Homer, can hardly be expected to prove welcome. This is, however, less and less the spirit of the learned in our own day. The study of Sanscrit and Comparative Grammar has opened a new field and awakened a new interest. Now all languages, new or old, have at least a certain value, even though they be as barbarous and destitute of literature as most persons suppose the language of modern Greece to be.

Again, from quite a different quarter a reaction has arisen against the exclusiveness of the old school; a reaction which forms part of the great utilitarian movement of this nineteenth century. The voice of the middle class, which has found a powerful spokesman in one of our most distinguished statesmen, himself a scholar of no mean attainments, has been heard to declare, in the words of a Wise Man of old, that 'A live dog is better than a dead lion.'

The remaining reasons for the general neglect of the language of modern Greece may be briefly summed up as follows:—the political insignificance of the nation; the obscurity of its literature; the small practical use of the language; and last, but perhaps not least, the prevalence, in our own land especially, of the Erasmian system of pronunciation. With reference to the first point, a few words may not be out of place.

The political insignificance of Greece cannot be of very long duration. A people which has made such rapid strides in education as the Greek nation, since its independence was established, must be worth something after all. The evils of place-hunting, national bankruptcy, squandered resources, and party strife, are inseparable for the present from a nation so suddenly called into existence, and composed of such very raw materials as was the Greek nation in 1828. They are evils deeply felt by the large majority of the people, and there are many signs that they are on the way to removal. As a hopeful symptom, I would refer to the appearance of a very ably edited illustrated periodical, now issued monthly in Paris, and supported by influential Greeks wherever the Greek language is read and understood. It is entitled 'Εθνικὴ 'Επιθεώρησις,' or 'National Review,' and contains articles, both original and translated, on every branch of Science, Literature, and Art. But the great importance and significance of the work appears to me to be the wholesome truth which it desires, as the chief object of its publication, to inculcate on the Greek mind. The 'Revue de l'Instruction Publique' for the 4th of November, 1869, thus comments on the periodical in question:—

'Les rédacteurs de l''Εθνικὴ 'Επιθεώρησις se proposent de faire pénétrer dans leur pays les notions scientifiques dont l'absence nuit, en Grèce, au developpement de l'agriculture, du commerce et de l'industrie. . . . Persuadés que la principale cause de l'abaissement de la Grèce est dans le manque de routes publiques, ils feront tous leurs efforts pour combattre l'institution ruineuse d'une armée inutile, qui, depuis la restauration de la nation hellénique, a dévoré plus de trois cents millions (de drachmes), et pour tâcher de faire couler dans le domaine de l'agriculture et de l'industrie ces flots d'or et d'argent dépensés sans raison.'

With regard to modern Greek literature, that it is obscure must be admitted, but that its obscurity is well merited is by no means so certain. To begin with the Epic poetry of modern Greece, 'Belthandros and Chrysantza' is without question a far more imaginative poem than the 'Niebelungenlied,' and I have little doubt that any one who would compare the two, would feel that the former is the work of a far superior genius. The popular songs of the Greek mountaineers are acknowledged by every one who knows them to be quite without parallel.

In lyric poetry there are few writers, ancient or modern, with whom Christopulos would compare unfavourably. The present polite literature of Greece has scarcely had time to ripen, but one poet at least, Zalacostas, has certainly the marks of genius; and the prose productions of Greece are already of sufficient importance to attract the notice of our best Reviews.

With respect to the practical usefulness of the language, I may remind those who are accessible to no other argument than that of direct utility, that a competent acquaintance with modern Greek will obviate the necessity of engaging an interpreter when travelling in Greece, Turkey, Egypt, and Asia Minor. Greek, as the language of the most thriving mercantile race, is the medium of communication between many of the various nations of the East.

The real importance of modern Greek is, however, rather a matter for the attention of the scholar, than the man of business or pleasure. I will briefly point out what I conceive to be the real advantages derivable from the study of modern Greek.

I. First, I will mention what scholars like Ross and Passow have already noticed, that great light may be thrown on the meaning of classical authors from the study of the modern Greek language. But this is of course especially to be looked for in proportion as the usage of the writers departs from the recognized classical standard. Hence the knowledge of modern Greek is of chief significance in the verbal criticism of the New Testament and Septuagint.

II. But this is not all. I believe, and I hope to be able to show, that the idioms of modern Greek may be employed in a manner hitherto quite unlooked for, in the criticism of documents of doubtful age, as for example the Gospel of St. John, with a view to determining the period at which they were written.

III. Comparative philology derives no unimportant light from modern Greek, because it preserves many archaic forms, which are *postulated* by philologers, but not actually to be found in any known ancient dialect.

IV. The relation between accent and quantity in poetry can never be fully nor fairly judged by any one who is not familiar with the sound of Greek read accentually, a familiarity which can hardly be acquired apart from a practical acquaintance with Greek as a living spoken language.

V. The pronunciation of Greek and the interchange of certain letters within the limits of the Greek language is a sealed mystery to those who are ignorant of the sounds which the Greeks of the present day give to the letters of their alphabet and their several combinations.

To prove and illustrate the propositions here advanced will be the main object of the following work.

The attention of the reader will be directed first of all to the question of the original pronunciation of Greek, partly on account of its philological importance, and partly because the prevalence of the Erasmian system of pronunciation in the West of Europe, and in England especially, where it may be said to have accomplished its own *reductio ad absurdum*, has built up a wall of partition between the Greeks themselves and those who make the Greek language their study, which completely severs us from one another.

How small the resemblance between our pronunciation of φυτεύσαντες and the Greek! How can we wonder that in our *fyootyoosántes*, he should fail to recognize his *philéph-*

sandes? Mutual disgust is the natural result of so great a disparity. When we hear Greek spoken by Greeks, we find it hard to believe that this jargon, as it seems to us, has any relation with the language we used to learn at school. On the other hand, the Greek who is not well acquainted with the origin and history of the controversy on Greek pronunciation, is liable to the mistake that a deliberate insult is intended by those who substitute for what are to him, at any rate, the harmonious sounds of his mother-tongue, a pronunciation which, however euphonious in itself, must sound to him at best like the hideous distortion, the ghastly caricature, of a familiar voice.

CHAPTER II.

On the Pronunciation of Greek.

'Εὰν οὖν μὴ εἰδῶ τὴν δύναμιν τῆς φωνῆς, ἔσομαι τῷ λαλοῦντι βάρβαρος καὶ ὁ λαλῶν ἐν ἐμοὶ βάρβαρος.—St. Paul.

Das Altgriechische nach Art des Neugriechischen auszusprechen ist ein Fehler, der auf vollständiger Unkenntniss der Sprachengeschichte und der Lautlehre überhaupt beruht.—Schleicher, *Compendium der Vergleichenden Grammatik*.

The αὐτὸς ἔφα of so distinguished a philologist as Schleicher, to the effect that to pronounce ancient Greek like modern Greek is a mistake founded upon complete ignorance of the history of languages and of the whole doctrine of pronunciation, will probably be enough to set this question at rest in the minds of most people. The writer of these pages ventures to dissent from this conclusion, which Professor Schleicher arrives at entirely on *à priori* grounds, betraying at the same time a very insufficient acquaintance with modern Greek pronunciation. It must however be acknowledged that the theory of pronunciation which Professor Schleicher rather leaves to be inferred, than states as the one to which he inclines, has the striking merit of consistency, and is far superior to any form of the Erasmian system.

Nor would we be misunderstood when we say that we favour the opinion of the general identity between the modern Greek pronunciation and that of ancient times. We do not mean to say, for example, that the diphthongs so called were never diphthongs in reality, or that φ was never pronounced like *ph* in *haphazard*. But all that comparative philology can prove, all that *à priori* reasoning requires, and, as I think we shall see, all that *à posteriori* evidence for the most part allows us to believe, is, that the above letters were so pronounced in some pre-historic period of language, when Greek was forming, when the elements of which it consists were in a state of fusion. This, however, has nothing to do with the question, How is it most reasonable to pronounce Greek as we find it for the first time in the pages of Homer?

From that time, and we know not for how many centuries earlier, the language, notwithstanding the changes which have passed over it, remained in all its essential features stereotyped and fixed, especially as regards the forms of words and the manner in which they are written. Now, how does it stand with the *à priori* argument? Is it most likely that the forms have been preserved, but the pronunciation utterly corrupted, or that both have been handed down to us together? To believe the first is to believe what is contrary to the whole analogy of what we know of other languages. Since Sanscrit was Sanscrit, who doubts that the pronunciation has been in the main preserved? Since German was German, who questions the fact that it was sounded as it now is? Or how can we believe that Chaucer, whose English differs from our own as regards the grammatical forms more than Homer from Romaic, if read by us in the present day, would be perfectly unintelligible to himself?

Again, the following argument must commend itself to

every one's understanding. If the modern Greek pronunciation be not the same with that known to the ancients, it must either be a legitimate development from it, unaffected by external influence, or it must be a corruption, the result of foreign admixture. If a legitimate development, then no one can fix *à priori* the limits of its first appearance; and it may just as well be as old as Homer as not. If it be the result of contact with foreign influences, then it will be possible to explain the peculiarities of modern Greek pronunciation from such external causes. Here we may at once eliminate Turkish, because we know that at the first appearance of the Turkish supremacy in Greece, hundreds of families fled to the West of Europe, bearing with them that very system of pronunciation which not only the Greeks still use, but which learned Europe universally allowed until the time of Erasmus. What then is left us? French, Teutonic, Slavonic, Roman. But none of these throw any light on the peculiarities of Greek pronunciation, as the sounds given to γ, β, δ, μβ, μπ, νδ, ντ, οι, ει, η, ι, which receive illustration mainly, and indeed almost exclusively, from Greek itself. Again, the general, though by no means complete uniformity of modern Greek pronunciation wherever the language is spoken, is another very strong argument for its antiquity, and against its being a corruption resulting from contact with other languages. The fate of Latin has been very different. In the Spanish dialect of modern Latin we clearly trace the influence of Arabic, in Italian of Teutonic, in France of Celtic sounds. In Greek, on the other hand, though the countries where it is spoken are as widely distant, and the foreign influences to which it has been subject as diverse, we find, with very trifling dialectic variations, the same universal traditional pronunciation among learned and unlearned alike. In Egypt, in Asia Minor, on the shores of the Euxine, in Constantinople, in Athens, in Crete, in the

Aegean, the pronunciation presents the greatest harmony just in respect of those letters on which the whole controversy turns.

We shall now proceed to notice, one by one, the peculiar features of Greek pronunciation, and collect the evidence on the subject supplied by MSS., ancient inscriptions, the notices of grammarians, transcriptions into Latin and the Semitic languages of Greek words, &c., as it bears upon each particular sound. At the same time we shall endeavour to show what we hold to be in itself the strongest proof of the general identity of modern and ancient Greek pronunciation, namely, that exactly the same letters appear to be interchangeable in ancient as in modern Greek. Had the letters in question altogether changed their force, this extraordinary coincidence, which would then have to be regarded as the result of mere accident, would be positively inexplicable. In order that this part of the evidence may present a more complete appearance, the corresponding changes in modern and ancient Greek will be given, even where there is no controversy with respect to the sound of the letters. We will begin with

VOWEL SOUNDS.

A.

This letter is pronounced by the Greeks as *a* in most languages, or as *ah*, or the *a* in *father* in English. It has never been doubted that this was the original sound of α. Schleicher, however, points out that besides the first intensification of *a* into *o, ā,* and *η*, and its further intensification into *ω*, an original *a* is often frequently represented by *ε* or *o*. Thus, besides the dialectic forms βέρεθρον ἔρσην for βάραθρον ἄρσην, we have κλέος for κλάτας, from *grávas*, πλέfω or πλέω from *plávámi*, ῥέfω from *srávámi*, φέρεσαι answering to *bhárasé*, &c. So too in modern Greek we get τίποτα for τίποτε, as in

Aeolic, κρεββάτιον for κραββάτιον, ῥεπάνι for ῥαφάνιον, εὐτοῦ for αὐτοῦ, ἀγγίζω for ἐγγίζω, from ἐγγύς.

As examples of a interchanged with o, we have in ancient Greek the Aeolic στροτὸς ὄνω ὀνεχώρησε = στρατὸς ἄνω ἀνεχώρησε, ἤμβροτον for ἤμβρατον, i. e. ἤμαρτον, ὅμως and ἅμα, ὄγκος and ἄγκος, ὀρρωδέω and ἀρρωδέω. In modern Greek we have, in like manner, καταβόθρα for καταβάθρα, ὁρμαθιὰ for ὁρμαθιά. Compare the classical βόθρος with βάθρον, ἐπιβάθρα.

Schleicher observes that the three terminations of contract verbs, άω, έω, and όω, were all originally but one, viz. άω. So in modern Greek έω is always represented by άω, at least in the language of the common people. As ζητάει for ζητεῖ, περιπατᾶτε for περιπατεῖτε, φοβᾶσαι for φοβεῖσαι, i.e. φοβῇ or φοβεῖ.

A in ancient Greek is seldom weakened into υ, yet this appears to have been the case in νύξ, ὄνυξ, κύκλος, μύλος, and a few other words, as μύσταξ, which also appears in the form μάσταξ, and βύθος, which is found side by side with βάθος. In modern Greek we get σκύφος for σκάφος or σκάφη. So, again, we have the diminutive appellation άφιον, as in χωράφιον, frequently represented by ύφιον, as ζωύφιον.

In ancient Greek a is often weakened into ι, as ἴσθι for ás-dhi, τίθημι for dádhāmi. Compare in modern Greek Ψιχάλα, ψιχαλίζει, with the classical ψακάς, ψακάζει. In modern, as in ancient Greek, we have η for a, μικρὴ for μικρά, πικρὴ for πικρά, and a for η, as βελόνα for βελόνη. A in Homeric Greek becomes αι, as αἰετός, αἰεί, διαί, παραί. So in modern Greek καταιβαίνω, ἀναιβαίνω, πιαίνω for πιάνω, καθισταίνω for καθιστάνω. Δίατα, a covenant, may be another form of δίαιτα, and probably an older one.

A is prefixed to many words more or less perhaps for the sake of euphony, as ἀβληχρός, ἀστεροπή, ἀσπαίρω, ἀσταφίς, in classical; Ἀβρύον, ἀβρότανον, ἀβδελλα, ἀβράμυλον for βράβυλον, ἀστάχυ, and many others, in modern Greek.

E.

Pronounced like *e* in *better*, only a little broader, more like the German *ä* in *Männer*. This sound has never been made the subject of dispute. As a representative of an original *a*, of which *o* is another, it is interchangeable with that letter, as ὀχθρὸς for ἐχθρός, in ancient; ὀχθρὸς for ἐχθρός, ὄξω for ἔξω, in modern Greek. Conversely, ἐδόντες for ὀδόντες, Ἀπέλλων for Ἀπόλλων, in ancient; and Ἔλυμπος for Ὄλυμπος, ἐψὲ for ὀψέ, in modern Greek. It is also prefixed, as κεῖνος, ἐκεῖνος, μέ, ἐμέ, in ancient; τοῦτο, ἐτοῦτο, σέ, ἐσέ, σύ, ἐσύ, in modern Greek.

H.

This letter is pronounced by the Greeks like ι, that is like *ee* in *see*, or *e* in *be*; while the followers of Erasmus pronounced it, and still pronounce it, as the Italian *e* long, i.e. as *ey* in *they*. Hence in the early days of the controversy concerning the original sounds of the Greek letters, Reuchlin and his adherents, who favoured the modern Greek pronunciation, were called the Itacists or Iotacists, while the Erasmians received the title of Etacists. The name is unfortunate, because just the one point in which the advocates of the modern pronunciation would be most inclined to make a concession to their adversaries, is with regard to the sound of the letter η.

That η was originally the representative of a sound distinct from ι is etymologically certain, inasmuch as in the Ionic dialect, and in certain cases in Attic, η stands for the doubly strengthened *a*, whereas ι is a weakened *a*, in the few cases where it represents it. At the same time there are cases where η represents a short *a*, as in τεσσαρήκοντα, διπλήσιος. In these instances η may perhaps stand for short ι.

E. Sophocles, in his Introduction to the 'Glossary of Later and Byzantine Greek,' London, 1868, adduces the authority of Dionysius of Halicarnassus, Aelianus Herodianus, Terentianus Maurus, and Sextus, to prove that the sound of η differed in their day from ι, and was like the long Italian *e*. Dionysius says, in pronouncing η the breath strikes the roots of the tongue, in sounding ι the back of the teeth. This, though a very vague distinction, is not altogether inapplicable to the difference between the sounds of *ay* and *ee*. Herodian simply says people are mistaken in saying νήστης for νῆστις. Here the difference implied may be very well one of quantity only. Terentianus Maurus says, distinguishing between ε and η, 'Temporum momenta distant, non soni nativitas;' and Sextus says much the same thing, viz. 'Καὶ συσταλὲν μὲν τὸ η γίνεται ε, ἐκταθὲν δὲ τὸ ε γίνεται η.' That is, long ε = η; short η = ε. This would seem to a casual reader to prove the point for which the Erasmians contend, viz. that η was sounded *ay*. A little consideration will serve greatly to modify the value to be attached to their testimony. In the first place, it should be remembered they are all more or less Romanized Greeks, in as far as they are Greeks at all, and they would therefore readily imagine that the η must or ought to be pronounced like the letter which they used to represent it; and as to them ε = ĕ, they naturally concluded η = ē. Again, etymologically they were right: η is not only the strengthening or lengthening of *a*, but also of ε. As ἐρωτῶ ἠρώτησα, ἐνέγκω ἤνεγκον, εὕρω ηὗρον.

Again, if η was considered by the ancients as a long ε, so was ει, for the old name of ε was εἶ, according to the principle which governed the original nomenclature of the Greek alphabet, and which was that each letter should be named by its long sound. So ο was called οὖ, yet no one supposes that ου was really the long sound of ο, because we know that ου was always transcribed in Latin by *u*. Equally certain is

ON THE PRONUNCIATION OF GREEK. 15

it that ει was almost invariably represented by the simple vowel *i* in Latin. Consequently we are led to the conclusion that ου and ει would be respectively the representatives of the English *oo* and *ee*, which are their exact phonetic parallels. For ου actually stands for οο in Greek, and ει for εε: e.g. χρυσόον = χρυσοῦν, φορέετε = φορεῖτε. In other words, as in English so in Greek it is plain, that certain long sounds corresponded actually to certain short ones, of which, according to *à priori* phonetic rules, they could not have been the representatives. An approximation to the English long *e* may be seen in the Dutch double *e*, and in the Hungarian *é*. That η and ει were very similar in sound is rendered highly probable both by the fact that they were each held to be the representatives of a long ε, and that they were interchangeable even within the limits of the same dialect. So we have not only κῆνος and τῆνος for κεῖνος, but also βούλει and βούλῃ, κλῆις or κλεῖς, κλειτὸς and κλητός. Nor does the Latin transcription of η by *ē* prove that it was sounded *ay*: for the Latin *ē* represented very often an *ei*, and on the other hand tended to become, and therefore probably closely resembled in sound, the simple *ī*. So we have *tristes* from *tristeis*, written *tristis; Vergilius* written *Virgilius*, &c.: and not only so, but in the Byzantine period *designatus* is transcribed in Greek δισιγνᾶτος: while, on the other hand, Plutarch writes *Palilia*, Παλήλια: where plainly η = long *i*. So that the transcription of η by *ē* in Latin inclines us to believe, not that η was sounded *ay*, but that *ē* in Latin was hard to distinguish from *ī*. When shortened, η tends to become ε, not only in ancient but also in modern Greek, as for example, Σερὸς, Ionic for ξηρός, ἀνάθεμα for ἀνάθημα; and in modern Greek, ξερὸς for ξηρός, θερίον for θηρίον, μερίον for μηρίον, κερίον for κηρίον.

Of the very close resemblance between ι and η in the time of Homer, that is between the sounds represented in later times by ι and η respectively, we have, Professor Mullach thinks, instances in the parallel forms ἧκω and ἵκω, ἐπίβολος and ἐπήβολος (where η seems to be simply ι lengthened by the combined force of the accent and the ictus), γίγας and γηγενής, which two forms we have together in the Batrachomyomachia,—

Γηγενέων ἀνδρῶν μιμούμενοι ἔργα γιγάντων,—

πίδαξ from πηδάω, ἠδὲ and ἰδέ. In many of these cases ι stands for long η, in others for a shortened η. Ross gives an inscription found at Carpathus in which ἰρώων stands for ἡρώων. The significance of this would depend greatly on the antiquity of the inscription. In the Cratylus of Plato, the obviously false etymology of Δημήτηρ from δίδωμι and μήτηρ, derives all its little plausibility from the resemblance between δη- and δι-. So in Aristophanes' Pax, 925, the point of a pun depends upon the resemblance in sound between βοῖ and βοηθεῖν, and again, 928, between ὐι and ὑηνία. Nor should the later parallel forms πρίστης and πρῆστις, σκήπων and σκίπων, with the Latin Scipio, which Plutarch writes Σκηπίων, be forgotten.

All the Semitic transcriptions, of whatever age, agree in representing η by ί, according to M. Renan, in his very learned and interesting pamphlet, 'Éclaircissements tirés des Langues sémitiques sur quelques points de la Prononciation grecque.' Thus in the Syrian Peschito Κηφᾶς = *Kifo*, Κυρήνη = *Kourini*.

In Hebrew we have *Tarschisch* for Ταρτησσός, *bima* for βῆμα, *diathiki* for διαθήκη, *listis* for λῃστής.

In Aethiopian, *paraclitos* = παράκλητος, *mestir* for μυστήριον. In Arabian, *Dimas* for Δῆμας.

In the eighth century after Christ, Theophilus of Edessa, a Syrian astronomer who enriched his literature by translations from the Iliad and Odyssee, introduced a system of vocalization, which M. Renan thinks must have represented a pronunciation reaching back to a very early age, and in which the letter ι appears as an H turned on its side.

In the New Testament, κάμιλος for κάμηλος, ἐλάκτησε for ἐλάκτισε, are no doubt errors in spelling, but they show the early prevalence of the confusion of η with ι: so too ἐξυπνίσω for ἐξυπνήσω.

It is not of much importance that η represents in Alexandrine and Hellenistic Greek the Hebrew ‎ֵ‎, as in Ἐμμανουήλ, Σαλαθιήλ: because η was the only letter left for this purpose, all the rest having been appropriated to the Hebrew sounds which they most resembled.

There is another passage in Plato's Cratylus, 418 c, bearing on the sound of the letter η, to the consideration of which we must devote a few lines, as it has been claimed both by the Itacists and Etacists respectively in support of their views. It is this:—

Οἱ παλαιοὶ οἱ ἡμέτεροι τῷ ἰῶτα καὶ τῷ δέλτα εὖ μάλα ἐχρῶντο, καὶ οὐχ ἥκιστα αἱ γυναῖκες, αἵπερ μάλιστα τὴν ἀρχαίαν φωνὴν σώζουσι. Νῦν ἀντὶ μὲν τοῦ Ἰῶτα ἢ Εἶ ἢ Ἦτα μεταστρέφουσι. ... Οἷον οἱ μὲν ἀρχαιότατοι ἱμέραν τὴν ἡμέραν ἐκάλουν, οἱ δὲ ἐμέραν, οἱ δὲ νῦν ἡμέραν.

Here it seems we must read, instead of ἢ Ἦτα, simply Ἦτα, the former ἢ connecting Ἰῶτα ἢ Εἶ.

The Erasmians are so far right in their interpretation of the passage, that we must agree with them in thinking that if Plato had not recognized a difference between ι and η, he would scarcely have distinguished the two as he has done; but if we are really to believe that he meant η to represent the sound *ay* in *day*, then the result is most alarming for the defenders of the Erasmian system, inasmuch as we have it on the authority of Plato that the pronunciation of ἦτα as ἰῶτα, so far from being an innovation as the Erasmians con-

C

tend, was the most ancient sound of that letter. The truth appears to be that Plato is thinking merely of the quantity of the respective sounds which he distinguishes. He speaks of η as a *grander* sound than ι or ε, μεγαλοπρεπέστερον: by which he can only mean that it is longer or fuller.

In any case he must have been wrong, at least as regards the general principle: for neither can we believe that the tendency to Iotacism was an archaism which has been revived quite lately in modern Greek, inasmuch as we can trace the tendency throughout the historical period of the Greek language, and find it more and more strongly marked as the language grows older; nor, on the other hand, can we believe that long vowels like η were originally represented by short ones like ε.

Plato knew of course nothing whatever of the now ascertained principles of philology, and he was led to his conclusions probably by the knowledge of the fact that ἡμέρα was found in ancient documents and inscriptions *written*, in default of the letter η,—which was not used as a vowel until the Archonship of Euclides, 403 B.C.,—ἐμέρα or ἰμέρα. If this view be correct, we may appeal to Plato in proof that the most ancient way of representing the letter η was by ι.

The Scholiast on Eurip. Phoen. 685 tells us expressly that before the time of Euclides ι was used for η, ο for ὠμέγα. Theodosius the Grammarian, who lived in the fourth century after Christ (?), assures us that η was formed by joining two ι's together. This is of course impossible, inasmuch as η was originally used as the sign of the aspirate, but it shows at any rate that by Theodosius η was considered as equivalent to a long or double ι.

The well-known line of Cratinus still remains to be noticed:—

'Ὁ δ' ἠλίθιος ὥσπερ πρόβατον βῆ βῆ λέγων βαδίζει.'

Everybody feels, it is argued, that to represent the bleating of a sheep by a sound equivalent to βῖ, βῖ, the vowel being sounded as *ee* in *see*, would be inadmissible.

After all, we must confess that the attempts to render the noises of animals by the articulate sounds of μερόπων ἀνθρώπων, are very diverse and very unsatisfactory. We do not understand their language, and it is hopeless for us to attempt to reduce it to writing. The German peasant hears his frogs say *acht, acht*, the Greek ear seemed to distinguish the mysterious syllables βρεκεκεκέξ. In English the very word *bleat* shows the possibility of associating an *ee* sound with the noise of the sheep. Yet we think our sheep say *bah, bah*, and I confess the Greek sheep seemed to me to say so too. But this may have been a Doricism.

As however the letter η could hardly have been in use as a vowel when Cratinus wrote, it is nearly certain that he must have written βεί, βεί, or perhaps simply βί, βί. This being so, the whole argument of the Erasmians falls to the ground as a 'demonstration in unreal matter.'

I.

Pronounced unquestionably as *ee* in *see*. The letters with which it is interchangeable have been, or will be, noticed under their respective heads.

O and Ω.

Both sounded nearly like *o* in *core, gore, shorn*, or like *aw* in *saw*. The distinction in quantity is rather felt than heard, and indeed ω at the beginning of a syllable sounds short, and ο at the end of a syllable, long. Λόγος sounds λώ-γος; πραγματικῶς, πραγματικός. That this was so in ancient Greek seems likely from the accent in πόλεως, μονόκερως, &c. It is almost impossible to preserve the pure sound of *o* when much lengthened. Our *o* in *note* is not strictly the *o* in *not* lengthened, but the sound ŏ rapidly followed by ōo, as in *boot*. Double *o* sounds in English as it did in Greek, simply ōo. Ου was one form of long *o*, and ὠμέγα was another, the latter used no doubt in those cases where the *o* sound was still preserved. Thus it is that we have ου as a strengthened form for ο: e. g. μοῦνος, οὐλόμενος, μοχθηρός, μουχτερός, modern Greek; μούργα for ἀμόργη, modern Greek, and many others.

Ου stands more frequently for ω, as γοῦν, οὖν for γῶν, ὦν: so in modern Greek, κιβοῦρι for κιβώριον, κουφὸς for κωφός, ψουνίζω for ὀψωνίζω, &c.

Υ as a vowel.

The modern Greeks generally pronounce this letter simply as a long *ι*. Schleicher says it was originally sounded like the German or Italian *u*, but soon acquired the sound of the German *ü*, or French *u*. The old sound is preserved in numberless modern Greek words, which may all be regarded as Boeotic forms, like γουνὴ for γυνή. Here follow a few examples, taken for the most part from Sophocles' 'Modern Greek Grammar:'—

Ἀγκύλος, ἀγκούλα, ἄγκυρα, ἄγκουρα, τυκάνη, δουκάνη (cf. in Homer δοῦπος for τύπος), στουράκιον for στυράκιον, κολλούρα for κολλύρα, τρούπα for τρύπα, σκοῦλος for σκύλος, κουλλὸς for κυλλός, ῥουκάνη for ῥυκάνη,—to which we may add κουτάλιον, undoubtedly a Doric or Boeotic form for κυτάλιον, i. e. σκυτάλιον,—μουρμουρίζω for μυρμυρίζω, μουρμῖγγι from μύρμηξ.

In Chios, Thessaly, and Macedonia, according to Professor Mullach, the *ü* sound is still heard.

The Tsakones at present inhabiting the ancient Cynuria, whose name Professor Mullach thinks may be a corruption of the ancient Καύκονες, have preserved to us another peculiarity of the pronunciation of *υ*, namely, its tendency to be sounded like the English *u*, viz. *yoo*. Thus in Tsakonian we have νοῦττα for νύκτα, i. e. νύξ.

So in old Boeotian inscriptions we have Διονούσιος, Λιουσίας, Ὀλιουνπίωνος. I suspect however, from the examples adduced, that both in the case of Tsakonian and Boeotian the ι represents the liquid sound of λ and ν before υ, as in modern Greek generally is the case whenever these letters stand before υ, ι, η and similar sounds.

In Syrian transcriptions υ is generally represented by ου (English *oo*), as *kindounos oksoúfafon* for κίνδυνος ὀξύβαφον. Similarly in the Chaldaean of Daniel, *Soumphonia* = Συμφωνία.

I may here remark, by the way, that to propose a Semitic origin for this and other Greek words in Daniel, is what no one could do, εἰ μὴ θέσιν διαφυλάττων. And not only so, but the words in question, both as regards their form and signification, are evidently *not earlier* than the Maccabaean period. פסנתרין ψαντέριν for ψαλτήριον is a natural form enough for the κοινὴ διάλεκτος which arose after the Macedonian conquests, but would be inexplicable before that time.

Coptic and Aethiopian transcriptions agree with the earlier Syrian in transcribing υ as ου, following, as M. Renan thinks, the Boeotic and Aeolic pronunciation which, it seems, largely prevailed among the Greek-speaking populations of the East.

In later Syriac however, as in the Peschito version of the New Testament, we find *i* as the representative of υ, according to the *prevailing*, though not universal, modern Greek usage: as *Evroclidon* = Εὐροκλύδων, *Didimos* = Δίδυμος, *clamis* = χλαμύς, *hili* = ὕλη. In *Sountico* for Σύντυχος the accented syllable preserves the *oo* sound, while the unaccented has lost it. That the unaccented υ was the first to become ι we may infer from the common occurrence of such words as μόλυβδος and μόλιβος, φιτύω and φυτεύω, βάρβιλος and βράβυλος, and such endings as -ηρός, -υρός, -υλός, -ιλός, -ηλός, used indifferently, and apparently without any distinction in meaning, as αὐστηρός, λιγυρός, ἀγκύλος, ποικίλος, ἐξίτηλος, στρόβιλος, αἴσυλος, ὑψηλός. Neither accent nor quantity seem to be very fixed in such words; yet ύλος seems most often paroxytone; when the accent is removed the tendency to become ηλος or ιλος would seem to increase. In Latin a short unaccented *u* also becomes easily *i*, as in *maximus*, *optimus*, for *maxumus*, *optumus*, another instance of the way in which the Iotacizing tendency in Greek is paralleled in Latin. There are many instances, however, of an accented υ becoming ι: witness βύβλος and βίβλος, βρί-θω and βαρύθω, βρύω, φίτρον, φύτρα, ῥύγχος and ῥίς, ῥύπτω and ῥίπτω: probably also πύθ- and πιθ-, πύστις and πίστις, μύσος (perhaps μῦσος) and μίσος, ψίθιος and ψύθιος, ὀδύνη and ὠδίν, ψιμμύθιον and ψυμμύθιον. E and υ are also interchangeable, as in μυκάομαι and μηκάομαι, κλυτὸς and κλητός, also κλειτός, στῦλος and στήλη, στήριγξ and στύραξ from στηρίζω, φληνὸς from φλύω = φλυνός.

In Arabic, Aethiopian, and Persian transcriptions υ is nearly always represented as *i*: *Kipros, asicriton, sizige, pilas*, and so on, for Κύπρος, ἀσύγκριτον, σύζυγε, πύλας. The Septuagint follows here, as in other cases, the Iotacist pronunciation.

In the Aeolic dialect ου sometimes stands for υ, as θουγάτηρ; but more often ι, as ἴψος, ἱπέρ.

The same three gradations are found in German: as *funf*, *fünf*, in the South pronounced as *finf;* so *nutzlich*, *nützlich*, and *nitzlich*. *Uber* stands in Martin Opitz, the founder of what is called the first Silesian School in German literature in the seventeenth century, for *über*, which in the South sounds as *iber*. Even in the written language, *Gebürge* and *Gebirge*, *gültig* and *giltig*, *Hülfe* and *Hilfe*, *Sprüchwort* and *Sprichwort* are used indifferently according to the taste and fancy of the writer.

ΑΥ and ΕΥ

are pronounced in modern Greek as *aw* and *ĕw* in German when the υ stands between two vowels or before a medial; in other cases as αφ or εφ respectively. The English letters *v* and *f* are only approximations to the German *w* = β, and the Greek φ. *F* and *v* in English, and in most European languages, are made by means of the upper teeth and the under lip, φ, β, and *w* in German, are formed by the contact of both lips. Any one who compares the two sets of sounds by pronouncing Αβ or Αυ-, and *Av*, Αφ, or Αυ and *Af*, in rapid succession, will see how much nearer the Greek β, or υ consonantal, and φ, are to the vowel sound *oo*, or even *u* (French), than the English approximations. The transition from *oo* (*u* Italian) to *w* (German) is marked by the English *w*.

It is worthy of observation that *v* never stands at the beginning of a word of Saxon origin; while in the middle of a word it generally represents either *b* or *f*; but very seldom, if ever, the German or Saxon *w*.

That αυ and ευ were sounded as αβ and εβ, if followed by a vowel, is generally admitted, and this is according to the analogy of Sanscrit.

In these cases the υ represents the digamma, which in its turn represents the Sanscrit or old Indian *v*, so-called, but what in reality is the consonantal sound of *u* = *oo*, into which the vowel sound is changed if followed by another vowel, as in *grávas*, *plávámi*, *srávámi* = κλεϝος, πλέϝω, ῥέϝω. The modern Greek forms πλεύω, ῥεύω preserve the ϝ, as υ consonantal.

But there are signs that at a very early period the consonantal sound of υ was heard even before a consonant.

In Syriac, αυ and ευ are rendered *av* and *ev*, as *Evroclidon*, *Pavlos*, *Avgoustos*; *evkaristia* = εὐχαριστία, *evtikis* = εὐτυχής.

It is true that *av* in Syriac represents also ω, as *Iavseph* = Ἰωσήφ, *Bariavna* for Βαριωνᾶ: and M. Renan suggests that *av* in Syriac was pronounced *au* (German), which is possible; but in any case there is the ευ = *ev* remaining. Αυ and ω, as well as the Latin *au* and *o*, are plainly nearly related, whatever may have been their pronunciation: as τραῦμα, τρῶμα, θαῦμα, θῶμα, *lautus, lotus, Claudius, Clodius, aut, o, amavit, amavi, amò*. So in modern Greek μαῦρος, Μῶρος, αὐτίον, ὠτίον, βαυκάλιον, βωκάλιον.

In modern Greek ευ also sometimes becomes ω, as ψεύματα, ψώματα, with which we may compare εὐλάκα, a Laconian form of αὖλαξ, and the form ὦλαξ, also Doric. In MSS. we have the double forms λαῦρος and λάβρος, λαύρα and λάβρα, καλαύρωψ and καλάβρωψ. In Homer ἄψ is, I cannot doubt, for αὖ + s = αὖs; s being added, as in οὕτως, εὐθύς, and other adverbs. Compare δέψω and ἕψω, the sigmated δεύω and εὔω, and in modern Greek ἐπίστεψα, κάψις, &c., for ἐπίστευσα, καῦσις. The Homeric word ἴφθιμος is derived by Liddell and Scott in a procrustean manner from ἶφι, θῖμος, notwithstanding the long ι and the θ, being a mere ending, while the last ι of ἶφι is violently, and contrary to all analogy, elided between φ and θ.

'Καίπερ οὐ ῥᾴδιον ὂν τοιούτοις ἀνδράσιν ἀπιστεῖν,' I must submit, first, that there is no such ending as θῖμος; and, secondly, if there is one thing certain about φθ, it is that no vowel has been dropt between the two letters. Let us, however, admit the identity of the Homeric and modern pronunciation, and we see at once that ἴφθιμος is but another way of writing ηὔθυμος, the Epic form of εὔθυμος. Here every single letter is accounted for, and the accent and quantity as well. In ἰθύς for εὐθύς it appears that the φ has been lost. Probably θένω, θείνω, θίνα are connected with φθίνω: as well as θέω, θοάζω, θύος, θᾶττον, Sanscrit *dhâvâmi*, with φθάνω, φθέωμεν, φθέωσι.

AI.

This combination as pronounced by the Greeks is not to be distinguished from ε. So we get in the grammarians ψέκας and ψαίκας, while γε- in the compounds seems to represent γαι-. Αἰπύς, *high, lofty*, seems (cf. ὕπατος, ὕψιστος, and ὑψηλός, from ὑπέρ) to be connected with ἐπί. Αἰ-άν becomes ἐάν. Φέγγω is from φαίνω, and probably stands for φαίγγω. Καὶ and τε for κε are, according to Curtius, but two forms of the same word. The interjections ἐ and αἰ suggest the same. Κεδνός for καιδνός, related to καίνυμι, ἑώρα and αἰώρα, μαίνομαι and μένος, μαιμάω for μεμάω, ἀμαιμάκετος for ἀμάκετος = ἀμάχητος, instead of ἀμεμάχετος, χαίτη from χέω, implying the verbal adjective χετός or χαιτός, are sufficient to show how often αι stands for ε. It invariably stands for the Sanscrit ê in the verbal termination αι, as φέρεσαι, φέρεται, for bhárasê, bháratê.

At the end of a word αι is short as a rule, both in prosody, as also before a following vowel in scansion, which renders it absolutely certain, that, in such cases at least, it could not have been sounded as a diphthong. Schleicher considers the termination of the second person plural passive -σθε, to stand for -σθϝε, which is short for -σθϝαι = -sdhvai. The diphthongal sound of αι, as of the other socalled diphthongs, was probably heard only when it was written with a diaeresis, as is the case at present in modern Greek.

In Latin αι was represented by *ae*, as Aeacus, Aeneas, Maenades, and *ae* was most undoubtedly a monophthong, so much so that if the metre required it to be diphthongal, its archaic representative *ai* was used, as *terrai frugiferai*.

In Greek inscriptions belonging to the Roman period we find ε representing αι, and *vice versâ*. When Plato, Crat. 412 d, is quoted as proof that δίκαιον was pronounced δίκαιον, because he derives it from διαΐον, it may be sufficient to reply that Plato knew how to spell. In Callimachus, 250 B.C., we have the following epigram:—

Λυσανίη, σὺ δὲ ναίχι καλός, καλός, ἀλλὰ πρὶν εἰπεῖν
'Ωδε σαφῶς, ἠχὼ φησί τις ἄλλος ἔχει.

Where ἔχει ἄλλος is supposed to be the echo of ναίχι καλός, the initial consonants disappearing, as we know they actually do in an echo.

EI.

This combination written without the diaeresis is, and no doubt was, sounded as ι. Ναίχι rhymes, as we have seen, to ἔχει. In Latin, ει regularly appears as i, and in Greek itself we have ἴρην and εἴρην, ἴλλω and εἴλω, ἴλη and εἴλη. Semitic transcriptions all point the same way, as well as the pun on ἀλλ' ἱμάτιον and ἀλειμμάτιον in Diogenes Laertius. In the Scythian patois, Aristoph. Thesm., ι stands for short ει, as ο for ω. Herodian, M. Victorinus, Choeroboscus, and Theognostus identify ει with ι, while Sextus says it had a sound peculiar to itself.

OI.

Now sounded like ει, η, ι, or υ, that is, equivalent to *ee* in *see*. Originally it was sounded apparently more like υ than any of the other letters or combinations, inasmuch as the name ὔψιλον was given it to distinguish it from υ δίφθογγος or υ διὰ διφθόγγου by the later grammarians. So in Boeotic we get τῦς for τοῖς. In the same way ἔψιλον was so called to distinguish it from αι or ε διὰ διφθόγγου. Thus John Lydus, a Byzantine grammarian, tells us, Ζητῆσαι δὲ ἀξιόλογον νομίζω τί μὲν σημαίνει [κυαίστωρ] διὰ τῆς διφθόγγου γραφόμενον, τί δὲ ψιλῆς; Κυαίστωρ τοίνυν ὁ ζητητής ἀπὸ τοῦ quaerere οἷον ἐρευνᾶν. Ὅτι δὲ μὴ δίφθογγος ἐν προοιμίοις ἡ λέξις, ἀλλὰ ψιλῇ γράφεται, οὐδέτερον μὲν τῶν εἰρημένων σημαίνει τὸν δὲ μεμψίμοιρον καὶ βλάσφημον διὰ τῆς γραφῆς ἐπιδείξει, ὅτι queror μέμφομαι.

Hence it is evident that the word ψιλόν, which means *simple* as opposed to double, is falsely explained *unaspirated* by Krüger and Buttmann, to say nothing of the inappropriateness, amounting to absurdity, of calling ε unaspirated, as though it had formerly been one sign of the aspirate, which it was not, as far as I know; or applying this designation to υ, the peculiarity of which is, that except in a few dialectic forms it is invariably aspirated at the beginning of a word.

The Semitic transcriptions of οι are very various: sometimes it appears as *i*, as *kirogrellios* for χοιρογρύλλιος: in Aethiopian sometimes as *o*, as *Phonix* for Φοίνιξ, probably a mere mistake; and most commonly by *ou*, i.e. *u* or *oo*, proving the similarity of the sound of οι to υ, which, as we have seen, is also represented by *ou*.

The Aeolians changed ου to οι, as Μοῖσα for Μοῦσα, which was probably very much the same thing as if they had written it Μῦσα.

Οι is short (as a rule) in prosody, and often in scansion, and that not only at the end of a word : witness Il. xiii. 275 (quoted by Mullach), οἶδ' ἀρετὴν οἷος ἔσσι : and again, Τοῖος ἐὼν οἶος οὗτις. It was then plainly no diphthong. Oeconomos, a Greek writer of the present century, thinks it was sounded in some dialects as ου = *u* Italian, and in some as υ passing into ι. This appears to us highly probable. In modern Greek we find προύκα for προῖκα, φλούδιον for φλοιίδιον or φλοίδιον, ἀτμόπλουν for ἀτμόπλοιον, as well as the ordinary ι sound. The Germans generally prefer ö (= *eu* French) as the representative of οι, and compare *oe* which invariably transcribes it in Latin, but we do not know how the Latin *oe* was sounded, although we do know that it was, like the Greek οι, monosyllabic, and, like it too, easily passed both into *u* and *i*: compare *foedus* with *fidus*, *moenia* with *munire*. If οι and *oe* were really like the German *ö*, then we may also compare such forms as *söhnen*, *sühnen*, and (according to Southern pronunciation) *sihnen*.

The account of the ambiguous oracle in Thucydides, ii. 54, clearly proves at least the close resemblance in sound between λοιμὸs and λιμόs. The sense which Mr. Sophocles obtains from the words is precisely the reverse; but he obtains it by sundry glaring mistranslations. He draws our attention to the fact that ᾄδεσθαι, ὠνομάσθαι, εἰρῆσθαι, and ᾄσονται all bear reference to the sound of the word, which is partly not the case, and partly nothing to the point.

He renders as follows: 'A dispute arose among men, some maintaining that the calamity mentioned had not been called (ὠνομάσθαι) λοιμὸs but λιμόs:' whereas Thucydides says simply 'that it was not plague that was spoken of, but famine.' 'Again, the opinion prevailed at this time that the word said was λοιμόs:' whereas all that the words will bear is, 'the thing spoken of was λοιμόs.' Again, τὴν μνήμην ἐποιοῦντο could not mean 'adapted their recollections,' but simply 'gave the account.' By such ingenious distortions does Mr. Sophocles adapt a passage, which is clearly a stumbling-block to his theory, into a bulwark of defence.

ΥΙ

sounds in modern Greek as ι simply. Homer nearly always makes υἱὸs two short syllables. In Syriac *oios* occurs for ὁ υἱός, which is the more remarkable as the usual Syriac representative of υ alone is *ou*.

Passing on to the consonants, we begin with

B = German *w*.

Liddell and Scott admit that it was softer than our *b*. It frequently stood for the digamma in dialectic forms, i.e.

ON THE PRONUNCIATION OF GREEK. 29

in those words where the digamma was still sounded; as βείκατι, βαλίκιος, for είκοσι, ἡλίκιος. So in modern Greek we have βάγγα, a *hollow*, compare ἄγκος and ἄγγος, &c.; βρίζα, as in ancient Greek for ῥίζα, in the sense of *rye;* βοῦρκος, etymologically the same with ὅρκος, βράχος, and ῥαχοῦλα.

It stands for the consonantal sound of υ in such transcriptions as Δαβίδ, Σεβῆρος, probably in the proper name Αγαβος for ἀγανός; and the word ἀπολαύω is only another way of writing ἀπολάβω. So in modern Greek we get ἀνάβω from ἀνάπτω, of which it is the root, in the sense of to burn; compare the ancient Greek αὔω, ἐναύω. In the middle of a word it thus preserves the digamma in modern Greek, and in such positions may be equally well written as υ; e.g. πλεύω, ῥεύω, πλέβω, ῥέβω.

If σέβας come from the Sanscrit *sev*, then it should properly be written σεύας; but it is possible that σέβομαι meant originally 'I move for a person,' the ancient sign of respect; and in that case it stands for σεύομαι, of which σοβέω is certainly the causative, written with β instead of υ, to preserve the sound of the last consonant in the root. Compare φοβέω, φέβομαι, φεύγω, i.e. φέβγω.

As a rule, however, β stands for the Sanscrit *g*, and thus in Greek it is interchangeable with γ, as βέφυρα, γέφυρα; βλέφαρον, γλέφαρον. So in modern Greek we have γλέφαρον, γλέπω, γούπα for βούπα, γούγουρας for βόρβορος (?): cf. γάργυρα, γαργαλέων.

Before ι, pronounced as *y*, it becomes, like γ and δ, ζ: as νίζω for νιβιῶ-; λάζομαι for λαβιῶμαι. I can find no instance of such a change in modern Greek, but even in ancient Greek it is very rare, and probably arose from the fact that a γ was heard in such cases after the β. Thus τρίζω and τρίβω are probably from the same root, τρίζω expressing the grating squeaking noise caused by τρίβω. The intermediate form would be τρίβγω, which occurs in modern Greek, as well as both τρίζω and τρίβω. So νίβω and νίβγω, for νίζω, are modern Greek forms. Cf. φέβομαι and φέβγω, i.e. φεύγω. The hard unaspirated sound of *b* is preserved when β follows μ, as ἐμβαίνω, ἐμβόλιμος.

B is interchangeable with μ, as μεμβράς for βεμβράς (ancient Greek); μυζάω, βυζάω; χήμη, ἀχηβάδα (modern Greek); with φ, as Βίλιππος, Macedonian for Φίλιππος (ancient Greek); cf. modern Greek Φιλαράς, Βιλαράς; ἀλείβω, ἀλείφω; βλησκοῦνι, φλησκοῦνι (modern Greek); with π, as βατεῖν, πατεῖν, πυτίνη, βυτίνη (ancient Greek); Ἀραπιὰ for Ἀραβία (modern Greek).

B, Δ are interchanged, as βελφίν, βλὴρ for δελφίν, δελεάρ (ancient Greek); κουνάβι for κουνάδι, from κίναδος (modern Greek).

Γ.

This letter is a guttural semivowel, like the German *g* in *Tag*: before ι and ε, however, it sounds like a very strong *y*; in other words, it sounds more palatal. The sound of the Hebrew ע, as preserved according to the most probable tradition, and most faithfully rendered by the Arabian *g* soft, as Professor Gandel informs me, corresponds exactly to the Greek γ. Thus we find in the Septuagint Γάζα, Γόμορρα, for עַזָּה, עֲמֹרָה: which proves almost to demonstration that the present pronunciation of γ must have prevailed in the time of the translators of the Septuagint. Only if we assume that γ was a soft semivowel, can we understand its evanescence, not only as a transcription of ע before an unaccented vowel, as Ἀμαλέκ, Ἠλί, but also in Greek words, especially before palatal vowels, as αἶα for γαῖα, ἴννος for γίννος; and in the middle of a word between two vowels, as ἰών, λίος for ἐγών, ὀλίγος; or before μ, as τμῆμα for τμῆγμα, as well as before σ in aorists of verbs, -άζω for -άγιω, aorist -ασα for -αξα. So in modern Greek we get the dialectic forms λίος for ὀλίγος, ἰὼν for ἐγών, λέω for λέγω, πρᾶμα for πρᾶγμα, &c.

With αἰα for γαῖα we may compare λαίνω for ὑγιαίνω. In ancient Greek ὑγιαίνω, ὑγιάζω, ἰάομαι are no doubt all connected; and in modern Greek it is hard to say in such forms as γιατρός, γαῖμα for ἰατρός, αἷμα, whether the γ is to be considered as prefixed to the one form or omitted from the other. In γούλια for οὔλια it may stand for ι, cf. οὖλος and ἴουλος, as in ἀγρέω, αἱρέω. In modern Greek, as in ancient, γ is often prefixed to λ, as γλυκοφέγγει for λυκοφέγγει, cf. λυκόφως, λακῶ, γλακῶ, λάρος, γλάρος; as well as before ν, as γνέθω for νήθω, γλείφω for λείχω.

Here we may compare γλαύσσω, γλήμη, γνόφος, for λεύσσω, λήμη, νόφος, i.e. νέφος: λεύσσω is probably but a sigmated form of βλέφω or βλέπω, standing for γλέφσω: compare γλέφαρον, and in modern Greek γλέπω, also the modern Greek σύννεφον, σύγνεφον.

The letter γ in modern Greek is often of etymological significance, in cases where it has disappeared from the classical form. Αὐγόν or Ἀβγόν, for ὠόν, preserves the original avján far more truly than even the form given by Hesychius, viz. ὤβεον, or the Latin ovum; as does μύγα for μυῖα, than the Attic μύα. Where two γ's come together the first is nasal. That this was so in ancient Greek, we know from the fact that ἀνγ-, ἐνγ-, &c. were always written ἀγγ-, ἐγγ-. In this position the second γ retains its hard sound, as is the case with β after μ.

The nasal γ is sometimes prefixed to a guttural in order to strengthen a syllable, as in Sanscrit so in ancient and modern Greek. Examples: Ἀκ΄, ank'ami, θιγγάνω from root θιγ-, ἀγκάθι from ἄκανθα (modern Greek), and δαγκάνω for δάκνω.

Δ

= Spanish d, or th in then, except after ν, where it sounds harder. Thus a lisped ζ = s, becomes δ. Accordingly we have Δεύς and Ζεύς, ἀρίζηλος for ἀρίδηλος, ζορξ for δορκάς. In modern Greek, ζορκάδιον for δορκάδιον, 'μαζί for ὁμαδεῖ. Most often this is the case when a palatal vowel has been absorbed, as πεζὸς for πεδιός, and in modern Greek Μπούζουνας for Ποδεών. Only on the assumption that δ = *th* in *then*, can we understand how σδ came to represent ζ in Doric, as μελίσδω, τωθάσδω, θαυμάσδω, or how ζ was accounted by the grammarians a double letter, compounded of δ and σ, whereas etymologically it is extremely doubtful whether ζ ever stands for δs, and certain that it never stands for σδ, the fact being that σδ and δs are ways of approximating the sound of ζ.

The sound of δ being so soft, it easily passes into γ before the half consonantal ι, so we have γιὰ for διά, &c. Thus we have reason to suspect that γέφυρα was originally διαίφυρα, perhaps Aeolic for διαίθυρα, although the accent and the earlier quantity are against this derivation. More certain is it that ιώκω stands for γιώκω, from διώκω; ιαίνω for γιαίνω, from διαίνω; the modern Greek γερὸς or γιερὸς for διερός; another form of ὑγιηρός. So we have too in modern Greek ιάκιον, διάκιον, γιάκιον, for *a rudder*. If ἱερὸς means originally *strong*, as some philologers think, διερός, ὑγιερός, γερός, and ἱερὸς are all different forms of the same word; ὑγρὸς is probably the result of metathesis. So we see little reason to doubt the identity of ὕαλος, *glass*, and γύαλον, γύαλαι from γυαλός, *hollow*. The earliest meaning of ὕαλον was a hollow transparent stone in which mummies were enclosed among the Egyptians (Herod. 3. 24). So αἰθέρια γύαλα, used of the heavens; not the 'vault of heaven,' as Liddell and Scott render it, so much as the hollows of heaven, i. e. the spheres in which the stars were supposed to be embedded, like so many flies in amber. The modern Greek for ὕαλον is γύαλον.

Z = *z* in English.

Schleicher himself completely discards the notion of pronouncing ζ as *ds* or *sd*. Etymologically, it stands for γι, δι,

ON THE PRONUNCIATION OF GREEK. 33

or βι followed by another vowel, as νίβγω, νιβιῶ, νίζω; τρίβω, τρίβγω, τρίβιῶ, τρίζω; Ζεὺς for Διεύς, ἁρμόζω for ἁρμόγιω. So in modern Greek we get διατάζω from διατάγιω, γαλάζιος for γαλάγιος or γλάγιος, τσούζω from τσούγιω, from the Latin *sugo*; Ζάβαλης for Διάβολος, ζάλον = ἴχνος, from γύαλον, shortened to γιάλον, i. e. the hollow print of the foot; ζαρίφης, better written ζαῤῥίφης, an extravagant dresser, from διαῤῥίπτω. The change of σ into ζ, mentioned by Liddell and Scott, is almost always before the letter μ, as Ζμύρνα, ζμικρός, ζμερδάλεος, ζμῆγμα, ζμυνή. In modern Greek, σ before μ always sounds as ζ. This fact is of itself enough to prove the identity of the sound of ζ in ancient and modern times.

Θ = *th* in *thin*, somewhat more forcibly pronounced than in English.

Θ originally stood for the Sanscrit *dh*, and it appears to be Schleicher's opinion that it was anciently sounded as *th* in *hothouse*. But this must have been in the pre-historic period of the language. Perhaps such forms as ἀτθικὴ for ἀττικὴ may be relics of such a sound. In modern Greek we have Γότθοι for the Goths. But that θ was very like the English *th* may be inferred from the fact that the Laconian dialect changes θ into σ, as σάλασσα, σεῖος, Ἀσάνα. In modern Greek we get ἀκαντσόχοιρος for ἀκανθόχοιρος. In Aeolic θ becomes φ, as φήρ, φλίβω, φλάω. So in modern Greek we have φλίβω, φλιβερὸν for θλίβω, θλιβερόν, φηκάριον for θηκάριον. In Doric χ sometimes stands for θ, as ὄρνιχος for ὄρνιθος, so in modern Greek ὄρνιχα for ὄρνιθα, and, *vice versâ*, ἄθνη for ἄχνη.

K.

Like the English *k* before the guttural vowels; before the palatals more nearly approaching the Italian *c* in *cività*, and with a very close resemblance to a palatal *t*. The best idea

D

I can give of this sound on paper is perhaps *tk*, as κεῖνος, κέντρον, κίτρινον, καὶ, pronounced approximately *tkeenos*, *tkéndron*, *tkéetreenon*, *tkĕh*; not that a *t* sound is actually heard, but that after forming a palatal *t* (and our English *t* is mostly palatal) the tongue is in the right position for forming κ. In Crete, κ palatal sounds just like the Italian *c* before *e* or *i*, or our *ch* in *chin*. In the same way the Sanscrit *ch* was formed from *k*, through the influence of contiguous palatal sounds. It is therefore probable that the Italian *c* palatal is also legitimately developed from the old Roman sound given to *c* before *e* and *i*, as in *cecidi*; while the French *c* dental and *ch* palatal, the Spanish *z* and *c* palatal = *th*, the German *z* and *c* palatal = *ts*, are more or less unsuccessful attempts to approximate the true pronunciation. The palatal sound of κ evidently represents the intermediate stage through which the guttural *k* must pass, and must always have passed, in order to become the palatal *ch*. In pronouncing κ *palatal* the tip of the tongue may be seen in a Greek's mouth coming right up to the ἕρκος ὀδόντων; not that the tip of the tongue is actually used in pronouncing the κ, but the upper part of the tongue is brought so far forward that the extremity necessarily reaches the teeth, and indeed protrudes a little beyond them. Κ palatal being thus so nearly allied to τ, we shall not be surprised to find them interchanged.

So we have in ancient Greek τίς for κίς, τε for καί, τύραννος for κοίρανος (for υ and οι see above, as well as for αι and ε), Κίμων for Τίμων, τῆνος for κεῖνος, πότε for πόκε from πόκα. So in modern Greek, especially in the Tsakonian dialect, κιμῶ for τιμῶ, σκιλβόω for στιλβόω, φκυάριον for φτυάριον, φκειάνω for φτειάνω, i.e. εὐθειάζω or εὐθειάνω. Conversely, τέριος or ταίριος, meaning suitable, or similar, is possibly for καίριος. Τινάζω and τινάσσω, the latter form common to modern and ancient Greek, are clearly connected with κινέω.

Π and Κ are also found interchanged in Greek. The

ON THE PRONUNCIATION OF GREEK. 35

original form of ἴππος was ἴκκος. So in modern Greek we have κοπέλα and κοκώνη, a girl; κώκα, an indentation connected with κόπ-τω, κοπῆναι. I much doubt whether ἀ-κωκή be not also connected with the root κοπ-, instead of being a lengthened form for ἀκή: and whether διοκωχή, &c., ought not also to be written διακωκή, standing for διακοπή.

Λ.

Interchangeable with ν, as in Doric ἦνθα for ἦλθα. So, in modern Greek, ἀνυφαντός becomes ἀλυφαντός, while ἄνθι in Tsakonian stands for ἄλφι.

Λ is also interchangeable with ρ: ἀμέλγω and ἀμέργω are originally the same word. Ἀμέργω is the older form, and is preserved in modern Greek for ἀμέλγω. Here we must say a word on νυκτὸς ἀμολγῷ. Buttmann is quite right in rejecting the translation 'milking time,' but plainly wrong in rejecting the derivation from ἀμέλγω or ἀμέργω. The form of the word is such that no other derivation is possible. Eustathius may also be right in saying that ἀμολγὸς is an old Achaean word for ἀκμή. A similar sense for ἀκμή is suggested by the word ἰκμάω, *to bruise out*, and ἰκμάς. But the sense and derivation are quite plain and natural. Νυκτὸς ἀμολγῷ means in the *dregs* of night,—a most fitting and poetical expression for the dead of night. Ἀμόργη or ἀμούργα, from ἀμέργω, means, in both modern and ancient Greek, neither more nor less than *dregs* or *lees*, the squeezings out; that is, what is left after the squeezing out of wine or oil. This is plainly the sense in which it is used to express clotted blood in Eur. Phaeth. 2. 2. 6, οὐκ ἀμολγὸν ἐξομόρξετε, εἴπου τίς ἐστιν αἵματος χαμαὶ πεσόν, where the cognate ἐξομόργνυμι, only another form of ἐξαμέργω, seems plainly used with a poetic sense of its identity in root. No more exact comparison could be used than the lees of wine for clotted blood. Compare Isaiah's well-known apostrophe, lxiii. 1–3, beginning, 'Who is this that cometh from Edom?' The modern Greek form for ἀδελφὸς is ἀδερφός, more archaic than the classical, inasmuch as it is derived from the Sanscrit *sagarbhjas*. In modern Greek the common form for ἦλθον is ἦρθαν; and ἔρχομαι appears also as ἔρθομαι, leading to the conclusion that ἔλθω and ἔρχομαι are not distinct but identical roots. For χ and θ, see above.

So, too, ἄλφιτον, ἄνθος, and ἄρτος are probably all identical, and are verbal participles formed from ἀλέω or ἀλέθω, standing respectively for ἀλ-θ-τον and ἄλτος with paragogic ι inserted in the first case, as in δολιχὸς in ancient, καπνιός in modern Greek. The θ in ἀλέθω seems to stand for φ, which represents the digamma: cf. ἄλευρα or ἄλεϝρα. I cannot doubt that ἀλθέω and ἀνθέω, ἀλδαίνω and ἄρδω, are all cognate words.

M.

With regard to the pronunciation of this letter there is no dispute: and the same may be said of

N.

When, however, the letters M and N are combined with π and τ respectively, μπ, ντ, these consonants become medials, instead of tenues, ἔμπορος = *émboros*, ἔντερα = *éndera*. In the same way the guttural nasal γ, when placed before κ, converts the κ into its corresponding medial, ὄγκος = *óngos*. Moreover, β, δ, and γ after μ, ν, and γ nasal, become simple medials instead of semi-vowels. With β and δ however this is not recognized by the educated, although it is universally prevalent in the mouths of the common people. This phonetic law may be most shortly expressed as follows:—μ, ν, and γ nasal take after them the corresponding unaspirated medial.

Exception: If γ be followed by χ, the latter preserves its

sound, and the same may be said of φ, θ after μ and ν: so that we may say, μ, ν, and γ are followed by their corresponding unaspirated medial, or aspirated tenuis.

In modern Greek therefore, as far as the sound is concerned, we may write indifferently, at least according to the popular pronunciation, ἐμβαίνω or ἐμπαίνω = embéno, ἄντρα or ἄνδρα = andra, ἄντρον or ἄνδρον = andron, ἄγκος or ἄγγος = ángos, ἐνδύνω or ἐντύνω = endýno. No one can doubt that this was the case in ancient Greek from time immemorial, who will consider such forms as πατέω and ἐμβατέω, Ἀμβρακία and Ἀμπρακία, ἐντύνω and ἐνδύω, ἐντέλεχεια and ἐνδελέχεια, ἄγκος and ἄγγος, θρίγγος and θρίγκος, ἔνδον and ἐντός, ἐνδόσθια and ἐντόσθια, ῥυντάκης and ῥυνδάκη.

Between μ and ρ, and ν and ρ, μλ and νλ, β (or π), δ, or τ respectively are inserted.

So we have in ancient Greek, μεσημβρία, ἀνδρός, ἀμβλακίσκω or ἀμπλακίσκω, ἤμβλακον or ἤμπλακον. In modern Greek, χαμπλός for χαμηλός, κορόμπλο for κορόμηλο, μπρέ, μβρέ, or βρέ for μωρέ.

Π = p
P = r.
Σ = s.

Σ is often prefixed, as σμικρός, ancient Greek; σμίγω, modern Greek.

Double σ in the later Attic dialect became ττ, as in κόσσυφος, κόττυφος; the intermediate stage must have been κότσυφος, which is preserved in modern Greek.

Σσ in terminations like -άσσω in φυλάσσω, κορύσσω, &c., stood originally for κj, or θj, but afterwards apparently also for γj instead of ζ, as in τάσσω and πράσσω. Schleicher imagines that in these cases ταγ- and πραγ- are softened from τακ and πρακ. So we get in modern Greek φυλάγω, φυλάζω, but φυλακή.

T = t.

Before this letter π and κ are sounded by the common people as φ and χ; while, on the other hand, after φ and χ, θ has more the sound of τ. This explains in ancient Greek the forms ὄχθη and ἀκτή, ὀπτὸς and ἑφθός, αὖθις = ἄφθις and αὖτις = ἄφτις, ἐντεῦθεν and ἐνθεῦτεν = ἐντέφθεν and ἐνθέφτεν, respectively.

Φ.

Has no exact representative in any European language that I know; but is like a labial *f*, and answers to β and the German *w*, as their corresponding sharp sound.

Χ.

Χ is like the German *ch* in *Bach*, but with this difference, that the German *ch* becomes palatal by the influence of the preceding vowel, while χ is affected only by the vowel that follows it. The same thing applies to *g* and γ. Thus the Greek says ἴ-χω, ἄ-χη, τα-χύς, the German ἔχ-ω, ἄχ-η, ταχύς.

Where the Greek says ἐ-γὼ the German says ἐγ-ώ, dividing the syllables differently. Thus to the Greek ear the German pronunciation of these Greek words sounds like ἔχιῶ, ἄχ-η, ταχ-ύς, ἐγιῶ. In the same way the German words *lach-en*, *mach-en*, would naturally be read by Greeks λά-χεν, μά-χεν, while *trag-en* would become τρά-γεν.

The prehistoric pronunciation of φ and χ as *ph*, and *kh* in *haphazard* and *inkhorn*, has left but the obsolescent relics, ἰακχή, Σαπφώ, ὀπφίς, βρόκχος, and these for the most part only when required by the exigencies of metre. In modern Greek *Khurdistan* is written [Κχονδιστάν] ⟨Κουρδιστάν⟩

Χ and κ are often interchanged, as δέχομαι δέκομαι, σχελὶς

σκελίς; so in modern Greek especially after σ, as σκίζω, σκόλασμα, σκολειὸ for σχίζω, σχόλασμα, σχολεῖον; but also καρκέσι for καρχήσιον.

Ψ

as the representative of πσ, φ (ν consonantal) σ, βσ, requires no further comment.

The Aspirate.

This is no longer heard in modern Greek, and we do not know that it was ever sounded as *h*, though it is not easy to conceive of its having been sounded otherwise. The fact is, the so-called rough breathing stood properly for some letter which had been left out at the beginning of a word, more especially for σ. Often too it was written where it had no etymological meaning, and often omitted where we should expect to find it. If it had any sound it was most likely that of *h*, and like that letter in Latin, extremely evanescent. The Latin *h* is a mere sign in all the modern Latin dialects, except in French, where a distinction is made between an aspirated and an unaspirated *h*. But even in French neither the one nor the other is sounded (at any rate so far as the English ear can detect); and the only difference between the *h* in *habit* and the *h* in *harpe* is, that it is the custom to cut off the vowel of the article before the one and not before the other. So, too, in ancient Greek the only difference between the rough and the smooth breathing may have been that it was the custom to turn κ, π, τ into χ, φ, θ before words which had the rough breathing, whereas before the smooth breathing they remained unaltered; while even this characteristic was effaced in the Ionic dialect.

In modern Greek, though the rough breathing is not heard, it affects the pronunciation of a preceding tenuis; and several compounds, as ἐφέτος for ἐπ'ἔτος, μεθαύριον for μεταύριον, show that the people have exercised their instinct in this matter quite independently of, because occasionally at variance with, grammatical traditions. They say too, ἀφ' οὗ, ἀφ'ὅτου, but κὅτι, ἀπ'ὅλους.

The law of compensation with regard to aspirated consonants, as seen in such forms as χύτρα, κύθρα, χιτών, κιθών, &c., also holds good in modern Greek; e.g. κοχλεάριον, losing its χ, becomes χουλιάριον.

The result of our comparison of modern Greek pronunciation with what appears to have been the pronunciation of classical times, is that even in the minutest particulars, so far as we can trace them, the same phonetic laws were at work in the time of Homer and of Thucydides as are at work now, and that they produced the same results. Can any one believe that anything short of a miracle could have produced so exact a coincidence, except upon the assumption that the pronunciation now prevailing is in the main at least identical with that of ancient times?

The consideration of the question is, however, incomplete until we have discussed, as we propose doing in the next chapter, the kindred subject of Accent and Quantity.

CHAPTER III.

Accent and Quantity.

QUANTITY, μέγεθος, was the foundation of ancient Greek verse, though, as we shall see, by no means its only regulating principle. In modern Greek, quantitative verse no longer exists, and therefore the quantity of syllables has lost the chief significance which it once possessed. That quantity was ever recognized in pronunciation apart from metrical considerations there is but small evidence to show; whereas we know that accents were introduced by Aristophanes of Byzantium about two hundred years before Christ, in order to preserve the true pronunciation of Greek at the time when it was becoming the vernacular of many Oriental races. The apparent influence which quantity had on accent is to a great extent, if not altogether, imaginary—the result of an artificial theory. The reason that ἀνθρώπου is not written ἄνθρωπου, is by no means that ου is a long syllable, but simply because ἀνθρώπου stands for ἀνθρώποσιο, ἀνθρώποιο, and the accent did not admit of being put further back than the last syllable but one. In πόλεως, ως is no contraction, but simply stands for ος; consequently the accent is not drawn forward.

With regard to modern Greek, it is neither correct to say,

with Sophocles, that all vowel sounds are isochronous, nor with Mr. W. G. Clark ('Journal of Philology,' p. 105), 'that the stress in modern Greek is exactly like our own, and is given by prolonging the sound as well as raising the voice. Thus λόγος, ὄνος, ἄνθρωπος are pronounced λώγος, ὦνος, ἄνθροπος.' The examples which Mr. Clark adduces are correct as regards the fact, while they sufficiently refute the assertion of Sophocles that all vowel sounds in Greek are isochronous. But Mr. Clark has been misled with respect to the true explanation of the lengthening of the syllables in question, and that not only as regards Greek, but equally as regards English.

Neither in Greek, nor in English, has the accent or stress any power to lengthen a vowel sound, although the absence of accent may in certain cases, and especially in English, tend to obliterate the sound of a vowel. In English as in Greek, and in almost all languages, when a syllable ends in a consonant, the preceding vowel is short; when in a vowel, that vowel is mostly long; a very simple and intelligible law of compensation, which in Hebrew is an established rule.

It is surely a strange thing that most scholars should have concurred in regarding the combination or simultaneous recognition in pronunciation of accent and quantity, as an insoluble problem; for we ourselves solve the problem practically in every sentence we utter. The accent continually falls on a short syllable, as *gétting, pícking, impóssible, crítical;* while a long syllable, whether long by virtue of the number of consonants heard, or by the long or diphthongal sound of the vowel, is perpetually found without the accent: *abnórmal, fināncial, fértĭle, pérfūme, pérfect, à priōri,* which is nearly always so pronounced, in spite of the fact that the first *i* is short in Latin. So that we may say of this, as of many an other imaginary difficulty, *solvitur ambulando.*

ACCENT AND QUANTITY. 43

Nobody will any longer believe in the reality of the supposed conflict between accent and quantity, who considers for one moment its origin, which is nothing but our application to Greek of the principles of Latin accentuation. In Latin it is a rule that the accent always falls upon the penultimate when long, and in words of more than two syllables, never when short. So that one may say that, wherever it is possible, the long syllables receive an accent, and the short ones are unaccented. Every language has its own law of accentuation, and this was the Latin law, as far as we know it from Quinctilian, and a very simple and natural law it was; but perhaps there is scarcely any other language on the face of the globe whose system of stress is so uniform and monotonous. Now, just because the Latin accent, however fallaciously applied to Greek, does in a remarkable manner tend to preserve to a great extent (though by no means completely) the quantity of syllables, the notion has arisen that it could not be otherwise preserved. That this notion is completely false is practically shown, first in our own language, secondly in Latin, in which we have to recognise, and do recognise, the length of the many long syllables which it is impossible even according to the Latin system to accent, and lastly in Greek as spoken in the present day, in which not only, as in every other language, are syllables containing several contiguous consonants long by the very nature of the case, but of the vowels some are always long, as υ, ι, οι, ει, and others common, as ε, αι, ω, ου, the latter being long or short according as they stand at the end of a syllable or are followed by a consonant. Besides this, it is to be observed that all the common vowels sound short before ρ. The accent, so far from altering the quantity, only tends to make it more distinctly heard. For instance, ουρ has the ου always short, but this is far more distinctly heard in φαγοῦρα than in οὐρά; so, too, αιρ is always short, but this is far more plainly heard in ἐξαίρεσις = ἐξέρεσις, than in αἱρετικός. Ωs, os, when belonging to one syllable, are always short, but this strikes us more forcibly in the pronunciation of πραγματικῶς, than in that of ὁσπήτιον.

Erasmus himself never recommended the disuse of the Greek accent in pronunciation, and very well draws out the distinction between accent and quantity as follows. He puts his lesson into the mouth of a bear, who is made to say:—
'There are some men so dense as to confound stress with length of sound, while the two things are as different as possible. A sharp sound is one thing, a long sound is another. Intensiveness is not the same thing as extensiveness. And yet I have known learned men, who, in sounding the words ἀνέχου καὶ ἀπέχου, lengthened the middle syllable with all their might and main, just because it has the acute accent, though it is short by nature, in fact as short as a syllable could be. Why, the very donkeys might teach us the difference between accent and quantity, for they, when they bray, make the sharp sound short, and the deep one long.' Yet Erasmus is wrong in maintaining that the syllable formed by the νε in ἀνέχου is as short as a syllable can be, if by that he means that the ε has the shortest possible sound, inasmuch as standing, as it does, at the end of a syllable, it is inevitably lengthened more or less. The followers of Erasmus in Germany, however vicious their pronunciation in other respects, invariably read Greek so that the accent shall be heard, and never dream that they are sacrificing quantity.

Our prejudice, then, against accents is for the most part insular, and deepened moreover by the insular peculiarities of our pronunciation. This is especially the case with respect to long and short υ, which we ordinarily pronounce in exactly the same manner, namely as *you*. The result

ACCENT AND QUANTITY. 45

of this is, that when we want to show the difference between long and short *v*, we have no other means open to us than that of laying a stress on the long *v* and leaving the short unaccented. In ηὐτύχει and ὑπεύθυνος we pronounce the *v* as *you*, i.e. really long, and we only distinguish between the long *v* in the one case and the short *v* in the other by flying in the face of the Greek accent, and reading the words respectively ηὔτυχει and ὑπευθύνος. In this case, so far from preserving the true quantity by the use of the Latin accent, we are only covering a false one.

The foregoing considerations must have made it plain to every one who has followed them, that the Latin accent is neither an indispensable nor an infallible means of marking the right quantity of Greek syllables. Such difference of quantity as is still recognised in modern Greek and other modern languages, so far from being obscured or altered, is only more strongly brought out by the accent. And although, as a matter of fact, the quantities of Greek vowel sounds at the present day no longer exactly correspond to the ancient quantities, yet it would be very easy to preserve and recognise the ancient quantities if there were any object in so doing. It is inconceivable that the difference between a long and a short α or ι in ancient Greek was ever anything but a very subtle and evanescent one, to a great extent artificial and based upon the usage of scansion; and one, as we know, singularly inconstant and varying.

The lengthening of *o*, however, seems plainly to have occurred subject to the very same conditions as in the present day. Ὅλος and οὖλος, βόλομαι and βούλομαι, μόνος and μοῦνος, οὐλομένην, Αἰόλου, νόσος and νοῦσος, all present us with cases of *o* lengthened by position, that is, because it stands before but one consonant. Why do we never find ποῦσος and τοῦσος, but always πόσσος and τόσσος, when the metre requires it? Simply because at that early period of the Greek language the σ was felt to be, as it etymologically is, really double; πόσος and τόσος standing respectively for πόσσος and τόσσος, i.e. (originally) πόσιος and τόσιος; of which the ι being consonantal, the σ belongs to the preceding syllable, making it impossible to lengthen the vowel. Thus we see that the greater the consonantal μέγεθος of a syllable, the less the μέγεθος of the vowel, and *vice versâ*. It is therefore incorrect to speak of the α in βλάξ being long by position; it is short by position, and that just because the syllable is consonantally long. In Αἰόλου, on the other hand, the ο is long by position, or at least has a tendency to become so, though short by nature.

Having established, then, the variable and uncertain nature of quantity among the ancient Greeks, and, except so far as it was of etymological significance or depended on syllabification, its arbitrary and artificial character, we will proceed to enquire what was meant respectively by accent, προσῳδία, emphasis, or stress in Greek, and how it was related to quantity and quantitative rhythm.

Mr. W. G. Clark, in his Essay on 'English Pronunciation of Greek;' quotes in answer to the question how emphasis is given, the words of Priscian: 'Vox tripartite dividitur, scilicet altitudine, latitudine, longitudine,' and remarks thereon: 'Thus a syllable may be emphasized in three ways—

1. by raising the note;
2. by increasing the amount of sound;
3. by prolonging the sound.'

'Emphasis,' he observes, 'may be given by employing each of these methods, or any two of them, or all three together.'

On this we have only to remark, that 1 and 2 usually go together. By raising the note we necessarily, if we employ the same quantity of breath, also increase the sound, inasmuch as we economize breath. So the shriller whistle of a steam-engine, *ceteris paribus*, is always the louder.

Emphasis by prolongation, though possible, is certainly very rare, if it ever occurs.

'What we blend,' Mr. Clark proceeds, 'both Greeks and Latins kept distinct,' meaning 1 and 3. This is not quite accurate. We, that is Englishmen, and certainly the speakers of most modern languages, do not, as we have seen, blend together 1 and 3, whereas the Latins did so far blend them, that while they never lengthened a syllable because it was accented, they did as far as possible accent it where it was long.

'In modern Greek the ancient tradition is so far preserved that the stress, as a rule, falls upon the syllable which in ancient Greek received the accent and in pronouncing which the voice was raised.' 'But,' continues Mr. Clark in the words already quoted and called in question, ' the stress in modern Greek is exactly like our own,' which is so far correct, ' and is given by prolonging the sound as well as by raising the note.' Even were it true that the accent sometimes contributes to lengthen the sound of a vowel, it would be obviously only an accident of the emphasis and not part of it. The many cases (and they are the majority) in which a syllable is accented without any lengthening of the vowel, were sufficient to show that emphasis is given in modern as in ancient Greek simply by raising the musical or quasi-musical note, and not by prolonging the sound. But Professor Max Müller, in one of his (I believe unpublished) lectures, has discovered an entirely new difference between ancient and modern accentuation, which, though nearer the truth on the whole than Mr. Clark's, is also very much at variance with what I am compelled to regard as the fact. He says that the ancient accent indicated a musical elevation of the tone, while the modern accent indicates simply stress. But what is 'stress?' Is it not an elevation of the tone? Mr. Clark and every one else has allowed *that*, whatever else they may suppose it to imply. Now the only difference between a musical and an unmusical intonation is this, that a musical tone consists of regular waves of sound, while an unmusical tone is a jarring irregular succession of unequal vibrations. That the ancients spoke more musically than we do, especially the ancient Greeks, may be readily admitted, but that they absolutely sang all their words will not be easily believed by any one, and would render completely nugatory the distinction between singing and speaking, which is as old at least as the literature and records of any known people. It is then, therefore, merely a question of degree as to the regularity, that is the music, of ancient and modern intonation. Of all cultivated languages, English is perhaps the least musical, except possibly Dutch. Then comes German as spoken in the north, after that German as spoken in the south. More musical are French, Welsh, especially in the pulpit, Spanish, and Italian. But the Greeks, especially when excited in preaching or public speaking, intone so melodiously, that something very like a tune is heard, of which the higher notes are always the more emphatic syllables. So that if musical intonation really was characteristic of ancient Greek accentuation, this feature has been most faithfully preserved. The written signs for Greek accents, as we have them, are attributed to Aristophanes of Byzantium, but some kind of notation for marking stress must have existed before his time. Not only does Aristoxenus, Aristotle's scholar, treat of accents, but a verse of Euripides has been discovered with accentual marks written on the walls of Herculaneum; and Plato himself used the word προσῳδία, the grammarian's term for a written accent. It is just possible that προσῳδία may mean in Plato only the accent as heard, and not also as written, but this is not very likely. The Greek system of accentuation bears a close affinity to that of Sanscrit.

Excepting isolated dialectic divergences, as κάλος for καλός, which for the most part have survived in various modern dialects of Greece, the general system of accentuation was, as its high antiquity would lead us to expect, everywhere the same, and there cannot be the smallest doubt that the Homeric poems were accented in the main as we have them.

Now in what relation did accent stand to quantity?

The usual reply is, that it had nothing whatever to do with it, and just in this very point is said to lie the difference between modern and ancient versification.

But this is not the case, for, in the first place, the word 'accent,' although the foundation of modern scansion, as the quantity of syllables was the foundation of ancient Greek versification, yet is by no means sufficient of itself to account for the run of a line. Both in ancient and modern poetry the ἀρχιτεκτονική, or sovereign science, as the Rev. G. Perkins well points out in the 'Journal of Philology' (vol. i. 253–263), is not metre, nor quantity, nor accent, but rhythm, to which the former are merely subsidiary.

The recognition of the dominant importance of rhythm is due mainly to Böck, and the verification and development of the theory to Rossbach and Westphal, who are followed with some modifications by Dr. Heinrich Schmidt in his work entitled 'Die Eurhythmie,' of which only the first part, 'Die Eurhythmie in den Chorgesängen der Griechen,' has at present appeared. The relation of rhythm to metre and quantity are so well expressed by Mr. Perkins in his essay above alluded to, that I can hardly do better than quote his words:—

'The master-science, that to which metric is subsidiary, and for which alone it exists, is the science of rhythm. The facts and details of the mere metrician are to rhythmic what shaped stones and carved timbers are to architecture, not dictating the character of the structure, but themselves liable to be altered in subordination to the builder's thought. And when we consider how strong and self-willed is the rhythmical faculty, how we can make a clock tick to almost any time, it would be strange indeed if man's own creation, language, refused obedience to this plastic energy. Well, one way, and a most important way, in which rhythm asserts its dominion over metre is, that while recognizing and dealing with the metrical feet, it strips them of their independent character and individual ictus, and makes them parts of new and larger groups (to which the old rhythmic still gives the name of *feet*), held together by one dominant ictus. Take for instance Tennyson's Locksley Hall. Assuming as we must that accent not quantity determines the relation of the syllables in English verse, the metre is trochaic tetrameter catalectic. Yet no one would think of reading it by single trochees, with an equal stress on the first syllable of each. There may be some arbitrariness, more or less diversity in our modes of grouping and accenting, but group them we do. Most readers probably break the line into two rhythmical feet, each of four trochees, allowing for the catalexis in the last half; though they might not be equally agreed about the syllables on which to place the ictus. The scanning of some of the classical metres by dipodiae instead of single feet, which is generally recognized as essential to the beauty of the verse, is itself a rhythmical rather than a metrical process.

'But rhythm does more than combine a succession of metrical feet into a larger rhythmical foot with a single ictus. It takes liberties with metrical quantity, and declares that under certain circumstances a spondee or a dactyl shall be delivered as a trochee, that the 2:2 relation shall for the time cease, and become, if not precisely 2:1, something sufficiently near to pass for it.'

The proof that the modern rhythmicians are right in their principle is, that they have reduced the seeming anarchy of Choric and Pindaric verse to order, law, and rhythmical harmony, appreciable even by our modern ears. What before was mere prose they have rendered into poetry. Quantity, then, is not all in all in ancient Greek poetry, neither is accent all in all in modern verse.

Here at once the absolute opposition between accent

and quantity is somewhat softened as soon as they appear but subordinate parts of a higher unity, namely rhythm. Again, the quantity of syllables is not wholly disregarded in modern poetry; it is impossible that it should be so. *Glanced* must be felt to be a longer syllable than *met;* the tongue cannot possibly get over the one in the same time that it gets over the other : and English verses in which the strongest ictus always fell upon the shortest syllables would be felt to be intolerably bad. If any one will compare Lord Derby's translation of the Iliad with that of Cowper, he must see that just in this respect the rhythm of the former is far superior to that of the latter. To illustrate the difference by an extreme and, as regards Cowper, merely fictitious case, let us suppose that where Lord Derby translates

'Prone in the dust he gnashed the brazen point,'

which (rhythmically) would have sounded still better had it been

'Prone on the ground he gnashed the brazen point,'

Cowper had rendered

'Upon a sod he bit a metal head,'

which is rather worse in point of rhythmical grandeur than

'Peter Piper picked a peck of pickled pepper.'

But how much worse still may the rhythm be made, by lengthening every syllable which has no ictus, thus (the reader must excuse the time-honoured practice of nonsense verses),—

'Stretched thús each bít each óther's lég and héad.'

And yet the ictus falls far more regularly (in as far as ictus and word-accent may be regarded as identical) than in Lord Derby's noble line. Not only then is accent not everything in modern poetry, but quantity is plainly something. If we can now show that accent too was something in ancient Greek poetry, then the difference between quantitative and accentual rhythm will resolve itself into one of degree, and rhythm will appear the one great unifying principle, the all in all of both modern and ancient verse. Now, as Mr. Clark remarks, 'We may infer from Aristotle (De Soph. Elenchis, c. iv.) that the accent was heard in the recitation of Homer, and from the famous story of the mistake made by the actor Hegelochus in line 279 of the Orestes of Euripides, we may infer that it was heard also in stage dialogue.'

Again, in Plato's Republic (399 a), Socrates, who is discussing with Adimantus which are the best kinds of music for educating the warrior classes in his ideal city, says, Οὐκ οἶδα τὰς ἁρμονίας· ἀλλὰ κατάλειπέ μοι ἐκείνην τὴν ἁρμονίαν, ἣ ἔν τε πολεμικῇ πράξει ὄντος ἀνδρείου καὶ ἐν πάσῃ βιαίῳ ἐργασίᾳ πρεπόντως ἂν μιμήσαιτο φθόγγους τε καὶ προσῳδίας.

This not only proves that in lyric poetry the accents had some significance, but it shows moreover that there were certain tunes, or classes of tunes, in which the rhythmical, which as rhythmicians tell us, must have been also the musical, beat, coincided more or less with the *natural enunciation* and the *accentual stress*.

On the other hand Aristoxenus, a pupil of Aristotle, tells us, Δεῖ τὴν φωνὴν ἐν τῷ μελῳδεῖν τὰς μὲν ἐπιτάσεις καὶ ἀνέσεις ἀφανεῖς ποιεῖσθαι. Now there are two ways in which the natural or accentual stress of words may be obscured, either by the musical beat (time) running counter to it, or by the musical note rising just where in the natural stress the voice would be depressed.

In modern verse some account is nearly always taken of the accent, but at the same time we often have two distinct rhythms, a musical one, and a metrical or accentual one; or indeed we may say, that every accentual or metrical rhythm is capable of being accommodated (and in the process of accommodation, more or less sacrificed) to very various musical rhythms. The musical rhythm modifies or

ACCENT AND QUANTITY. 53

disturbs the natural or accentual, both by the non-coincidence of its ictus, and by the lengthening (or τονή as the Greeks called it) of certain syllables. Thus in a popular modern Greek song the lines

Δρέψατε πάλιν ἐρασταὶ εὐδαίμονας ναρκίσσους,
Ἀπὸ τοῦ Μαΐου τοὺς τερπνοὺς καὶ εὐώδεις παραδείσους·
Καὶ τὴν παρθένον στέψατε ἥτις ὡς ἄνθος κλίνει·
Ἐγὼ δὲν κόπτω δι' ἐμέ· ἀπέθανεν ἐκείνη . . .

becomes, when sung,

Δρεψά-α-α-τε πά | λιν ἔ-ε-έ-ρασταί
Εὐδαίαι-αιμονάς | ναρκί-ι-ί-ισσους
Ἀπὸ τού-ου-ου μαί | ου τού-ους τέρπνους
Καὶ εὐώδεις πα- | καὶ εὐώδεις πα | -ραδεί-ει-εί-εισούς
Καὶ τὴν παρθέ-ε-ένον στέψα-ά-ατέ | ἥτις ὡς ἄ-α-άνθος κλίνειειέιεί
Ἐγὼ δὲν κόπτω δί ἐμά, | ἀπέθανέν ἐκεί-ει-εί-ει-νή.

For the most part, however, we may say that the musical rhythm, in English, must bear a very close relation to the accentual. Still closer, may we infer, was the relation between musical time and rhythm with ancient Greeks, inasmuch as all their quantitative measures seem to have been formed with a direct view to music, whereas much of our own verse is only accidentally accommodated to a tune by an after-thought, or *vice versâ*, the composer and the poet being usually two different persons.

The difference then between a recited and a sung verse would be found in Greek neither in the metre nor in the rhythm, but only in the tone, that is, the 'elevation,' of the voice. In other words, in recitation the accent was heard; in singing it might certainly be felt, as with us, but as far as sound goes it was swallowed up in the music. This is the view of Dr. Heinrich Schmidt (Eurhythmie, p. 13), according to whom the verse ictus = a *louder* sound, the word accent = musical elevation *of tone*. Mr. Clark, in the Essay above referred to, propounds a view exactly the opposite, supposing that the accent was heard in recitation only by means of an increase in the amount of sound, i. e. by the accented syllables being sounded louder than the rest. But if this were so, what, according to Mr. Clark's theory, became of the ictus and the rhythm? For he says, 'When the rhapsodists recited epic poems in the open air to the assembled multitudes at Olympia or Crissa, they must have chanted in monotone or nearly so, else they could not have been heard by the vast audience. So also in the theatres, the players who had to make themselves audible to thirty thousand spectators, must have chanted the dialogue in a kind of *ad libitum* recitative.' How then, one naturally asks, was the *ictus* of the verse represented? Not by more *forcible* or *louder* utterance, for that, according to Mr. Clark, was the way in which the word-accent was shown. Not by elevation in the pitch, because that is excluded by monotone. The fact is, *ictus*, which is the very essence of rhythm, has been overlooked by Mr. Clark altogether. He supposes that quantity constitutes the essence of rhythm. A more complete mistake could not be made. A number of long and short syllables may lie together in the order in which they stand in a hexameter verse, but *ictus* alone can separate them into bars, and, as by a magician's touch, clothe the dead skeleton of syllables with the life and vigour of a rhythmical succession. Mr. Perkins, in his Essay above quoted, well remarks that we can make a clock tick to any time; and we may add, a railway train often seems, by the rattling of its wheels over the regular intervals made by the joining of the rails, to beat time to a great variety of tunes, according as our fancy, or perhaps an occasional jolt, causes us to place the ictus here or there. Now this would be just the result with the hexameter, if the ictus had not been distinctly given:

the pause at the end of the line, and the quantity, would have done something, but very little, towards leading the ear towards the right ictus, and the general rhythmical effect would have been as uncertain, or nearly so, as the ticking of a clock or the jolting of a railway train. The main thing must then have been to show the *ictus*. If the reciter took care of the *ictus*, the accent would take care of itself. Certainly the accent would only be *heard* in as far as the recitative departed from the completeness of monotone. And some such slight departure did, I doubt not, occur; for to chant in perfect monotone is all but as impossible of execution, as it is wearisome to the ear. Yet, I must confess the great difficulty here is a practical one. It is very hard to realize the distinction between a high and a loud note, not indeed in theory, but in practice. It is hard to say whether in the language of ordinary life syllables are emphasized by being pronounced in a louder tone or in a higher key; the two seem always to go hand in hand. And this is really the difficulty to the modern reciter of quantitative verse: not how to combine quantity with accent, that is a very simple thing, and is a problem which we solve practically in every sentence we utter; but how to combine, and at the same time distinguish, the accent of the word, and the ictus or beat of the verse. Yet, after all, the difficulty is one of small significance. As we have before observed, the accent would be always felt, whether heard or not, and could be no more mentally ignored than it is in a modern song, where very frequently it is in direct opposition to the musical beat.

That notice was taken of the accent in writing verses will appear from the following considerations. First, we cannot ignore the accent even in modern song, where the musical beat by no means necessarily coincides with the accentual. Here, if the coincidence is too marked and constant, we get a jingling and monotonous effect. If, on the other hand, the musical beat is always at variance with the accentual, then we feel at once that the tune was never made for the words.

Precisely the same relation should we *à priori* suspect to subsist between the rhythm (= scansion = musical beat) of a Greek verse and its accentual emphasis. In other words, we should expect the accent as a rule neither wholly to coincide nor wholly to clash with the scansion, and this is precisely the case. Those lines in the ancient poets in which accent and rhythmical ictus exactly coincide, as well as those in which they are exactly opposed, are the exceptions, occasionally introduced no doubt by way of variety, but avoided as a rule.

Of lines in which the accentual and quantitative rhythm coincide, I borrow the following examples from Mr. Sophocles' 'Modern Greek Grammar,' and 'Glossary of Later and Byzantine Greek,' pp. 21 and 50 respectively.

Iliad, ii. 188:—

Ὅντινα μὲν βασιλῆα καὶ ἔξοχον ἄνδρα κιχείη.

Odyssee, ii. 121:—

Τάων οὔτις ὁμοῖα νοήματα Πηνελοπείῃ.

Ib. ii. 225:—

Μέντωρ ὅς ῥ' Ὀδυσῆος ἀμύμονος ἦεν ἑταῖρος.

Aristophanes, Ach. 682:—

Ἄνδρα Τιθωνὸν σπαράττων καὶ ταράττων καὶ κυκῶν.

Ib. Eq. 317:—

Τοῖς ἀγροίκοισιν πανούργως ὥστε φαίνεσθαι παχύ.

Ib. Vesp. 38:—

Τῆς ἀρτοπώλιδος λαθόντ' ἐκλέψαμεν τὸν ὅλμον.

Ib. Lys. 310:—

Κἂν μὴ καλούντων τοὺς μοχλοὺς χαλῶσιν αἱ γυναῖκες.

ACCENT AND QUANTITY. 57

Mr. Sophocles gives many more instances, which might no doubt be considerably multiplied.

He also adduces, among others, the following examples of a double rhythm, the one accentual, the other quantitative.

Quantitative Trochaics.

Aeschylus, Pers. 157–159:—

*Ὦ βαθυζώνων ἄνασσα Περσίδων ὑπερτάτη
Μήτηρ ἡ Ξέρξου γεραιά, χαῖρε, Δαρείου γύναι.
Θεοῦ μὲν εὐνάτειρα Περσῶν, θεοῦ δὲ καὶ μήτηρ ἔφυς,
Ἦν τι μὴ δαίμων παλαιός. . . . .

Aristophanes, Ach. 676, 712, 718; Nub. 576, 585:—

Οἱ γέροντες οἱ παλαιοὶ μεμφόμεσθα τῇ πόλει.
Τοῖς νέοισι δ' εὐρύπρωκτος καὶ λάλος χὠ Κλεινίου.
Τὸν γέροντα τῷ γέροντι, τὸν νέον δὲ τῷ νέῳ.
Ἠδικημέναι γὰρ ὑμῖν μεμφόμεσθ' ἐναντίον.
Τὴν θρυαλλίδ' εἰς ἑαυτὸν εὐθέως ξυνελκύσας.

Accentual iambic tetrameters, or στίχοι πολιτικοί, the same as all the modern Greek popular ballads.

Accentual Trochaics.

Ib. Nub. 1045; Vesp. 241, 244; Lys. 313, 365:—

Καίτοι τίνα γνώμην ἔχων ψέγεις τὰ θερμὰ λουτρά;
Σίμβλον δέ φασι χρημάτων ἔχειν ἅπαντες αὐτόν.
Ἐπ' αὐτὸν ὡς κολουμένους ὧν ἠδίκησεν· ἀλλά.
Τίς ξυλλάβοιτ' ἂν τοῦ ξύλου τῶν ἐν Σάμῳ στρατηγῶν;
Ἅπτου μόνον Στρατυλλίδος τῷ δακτύλῳ προσελθών.

Quantitatively scanned, these have the rhythm of the στίχος πολιτικός, more usually found as an accentual measure.

Rare as such exceptions are, we cannot attribute them to accident. Their comparatively frequent occurrence in Aristophanes is in itself suggestive. Is it not extremely probable that such lines were inserted by the poet, that it might be optional to the actor, as he judged best for comic effect, either to say or sing them, that is, to say them according to the accent, or to sing them according to the quantity? That accentual rhythm was perfectly well understood by the ancients, and was in fact among some nations at least much older than quantitative, is almost certain. The Saturnian measure among the Romans, the epic metre of the old German poetry, as the 'Niebelungenlied,' are essentially the same as the English popular measure, so often found in nursery rhymes, and ballads. Byron compares,

'A captain bold of Halifax, who lived in country quarters,'

with

Εἰπέ μας ὦ φιλέλληνα πῶς φέρεις τὴν σκλαβίαν
Καὶ τὴν ἀπαραγόρητον τῶν Τούρκων τυραννίαν.

We have just seen the same metre, both accentual and quantitative, in Aristophanes.

In Latin and German it occurs in a somewhat mutilated form: as indeed not unfrequently in English, e. g.

'The king was in his counting house, | counting out his money,
The queen was in her parlour, | eating bread and honey.'

In the first line, if we divide it into two κῶλα, to use the language of the rhythmicians, we get an external catalexis, which we must remedy either by pause or by τονή: in the second line we have both internal and external catalexis, which we must remedy, the first by τονή, and the second by τονὴ or pause.

Compare the Saturnian verse:—

Quód re súa diseídens áspere afleícta
Párens tímens héic vóvit vóto hóc solúto
Décumâ fácta polóucta leíbereis lubéntes.

More uncouth and truncated still is the old German epic metre:—

'Gunther und Hagen die Recken wohl gethan.
Beriethen mit Untreuen ein'n Birschen in den Tann:
Mit ihren scharfen Spiessen wollten sie jagen gehn
Bären, Schwein und Büffel; was könnte kühnres g'schehn.'

'How such lines,' observes Mr. Clark, referring to the στίχοι πολιτικοί above quoted, 'would have puzzled Aristoxenus or Dionysius!'

I think Dionysius himself gives us a pretty clear answer to the question what he would have thought of the accentual modern heroic measure, when he gives as accentual (προσῳδικούς) the following lines which scan precisely in the same way:—

Οὐ βέβηλος ὡς λέγεται τοῦ νέου Διονύσου

Κἀγὼ δ' ἐξεργασίης [reading corrupt] ὠργιασμένος ἥκω.

Hephaestion's Enchiridion completes the triplet thus:—

Ὀδεύων Πελουσιακὸν κνεφαῖος παρὰ τέλμα.

We will now once more return to the question, What was the value of the accent in quantitative rhythm? To answer that question it will be necessary to remind the reader once more that rhythm is the ἀρχιτεκτονικὴ of all verse, and quantity and accent only the subordinate means of which rhythm is the end. But rhythm would inevitably degenerate into jingle if it were not for some counteracting tendency. A verse which scans too easily runs away with the reader, and rattles off with ever-increasing speed like a railway train. Now there are two available means of checking this jingling or rattling tendency. The one is quantity, the other is accent. Both are available, whether in quantitative or in accentual rhythm. Accentual rhythm is perhaps more liable than quantitative to degenerate into jingle, because the natural accent of each word gives at once the rhythmical ictus; the verse consequently tends to scan itself. This tendency may be remedied partly by the inherent quantity of certain long syllables upon which no accent falls; partly by introducing an occasional variation between that rhythmical ictus which is given by the general or pervading accentual scansion, and the actual stress on particular words; so that the word-accent shall only generally, and not in every case, represent the rhythmical beat. Both means are needed, because, firstly, in accentual rhythm, quantity is of so little account, that its retarding tendency is not sufficient of itself to prevent a verse from becoming jingling and monotonous; and secondly, the variation in accent must be restrained within narrow limits, or it would spoil the music of the rhythm.

Compare the somewhat monotonous and jingling rhythm of the ordinary modern Greek στίχος πολιτικός—

Καλὰ τὸ ἔχουν τὰ βουνὰ, καλόμοιρ' εἶν' οἱ κάμποι,
Ποῦ Χάρον δὲν παντέχουνε, Χάρον δὲν καρτερούνε·
Τὸ καλοκαίρι πρόβατα, καὶ τὸν χειμῶνα χιόνια.
Τρεῖς ἀνδρωμένοι βούλονται τὸν ᾅδη νὰ τσακίσουν,
Ὁ ἕνας λέγει, τὸν Μάϊ νὰ βγῇ, ἄλλος τὸ καλοκαίρι,
Κ' ὁ τρίτος τὸ χινόπωρο, ποῦ πέφτουνε τὰ φύλλα.
Κόρη ξανθὴ τοὺς μίλησεν αὐτοῦ 's τὸν κάτω κόσμο·
' Πάρτε με, ἀνδρωμένοι μου, κ' ἐμὲ 's τὸν πάνω κόσμο.'
' Κόρη, βροντοῦν τὰ ροῦχά σου, φυσοῦν καὶ τὰ μαλλιά σου,
Κτυπάει καὶ τὸ καλίγι σου, καὶ μᾶς νογάει ὁ Χάρος.'
''Εγὼ τὰ ροῦχα βγάνω τα, καὶ τὰ μαλλιὰ τὰ κόβω,
Καὶ τὰ καλιγοπάπουτσα 's τὴν σκάλα τ' ἀπιθόνω.
Πάρτε με, ἀνδρωμένοι μου, κ' ἐμὲ 's τὸν πάνω κόσμον,
Νὰ πάω, νὰ ἰδῶ τῂ μάννα μου, πῶς θλίβεται γιὰ μένα,
Νὰ πάω, νὰ ἰδῶ τ' ἀδέρφια μου, πῶς κλαίουν γιὰ ἐμένα.'
' Κόρη, σένα τ' ἀδέρφια σου εἰς τὸν χορὸ χορεύουν,
Κόρη, σένα ἡ μάννα σου 's τὴν ρούγα κουβεντιάζει.'—

with the lines quoted above:—

Δρέψατε πάλιν ἐρασταὶ εὐδαίμονας ναρκίσσους
Ἰπὸ τοῦ Μαίου τοὺς τερπνοὺς καὶ εὐώδεις παραδείσους·

ACCENT AND QUANTITY.

Καὶ τὴν παρθένον στέψατε, ἥτις ὡς ἄνθος κλίνει·
Ἐγὼ δὲν κόπτω δι' ἐμὲ· ἀπέθανεν ἐκείνη.
Δὲν κόπτει ὁ ἀνέραστος μυρσίνης κλάδον πλέον·
Χλευάζει τὴν ὀδύνην του τὸ ἄνθος τὸ ὡραῖον.
Δύναται μόνον πένθιμα, κυπάρισσον, νὰ δρέψῃ
Βεβαρημένης κεφαλῆς τὸ μέτωπον νὰ στέψῃ.
Κ' ἐγὼ ἠγάπησα ποτέ, κ' ἐγὼ ἀντηγαπήθην·
Ἀλλὰ δὲν ἐλησμόνησα πλὴν φεῦ! ἐλησμονήθην.
Δὲν εἶναι ὁ βίος Μάϊος αἰώνιος· δὲν εἶναι·
Μαραίνονται αἱ ἀνθηραὶ τοῦ ἔρωτος μυρσίναι·
Καὶ φεύγει ἡ νεότης μας, ὡς ἀστραπὴ ταχεῖα,
Ὡς ὅρκοι σταθερότητος εἰς στήθη γυναικεῖα.

Here it will be observed δρέψατε stands as regards the metre for δρεψάτε, ἐρασταὶ for ἔρασται, ἥτις for ἠτίς, δύναται for δυνάται, ἀνθηραὶ for ἄνθηραι, ἀστραπὴ for ἄστραπη, and so on: the word-accent sometimes clashing with the ictus, as in δρέψατε, δύναται, sometimes standing in the place of the fainter ictus, as in ἀστραπὴ, βεβαρημένης, κεφαλῆς. The quantity of certain syllables has also a retarding influence, as in ἀντηγαπήθην, which stands *irrationaliter* for ἀντηγαπήθην. I consider the above one of the most perfect examples I have met in any language, of melody without monotony, and rhythm relieved from jingle.

In quantitative verse the same principles may be seen at work, but as accent is here the secondary element, and one rather felt than heard, the influence of quantity as a retarding force comes more prominently forward. The hexameter, according to its original rhythmical intention, consisted of dactyls, as

Ἀνδρά μοι ἔννεπε Μοῦσα πολύτροπον ὅς μάλα πολλά,

with one spondee at the end to indicate, as it were, that the rhythm had run itself out of breath, and must pause, before beginning again. Here the long syllables, with the exception of the final *syllaba anceps*, all receive the ictus. Spondees were then substituted for dactyls, in the hexameter verse :—

> 'Tardior ut paullo graviorque rediret ad aures.'

It is true that, metrically, the long syllable is regarded as equal to two short syllables, but the rhythmical effect is different, because, now, long syllables occur without the ictus. No one doubts that the spondaic hexameter is slower and more majestic than the dactylic. A stronger measure was adopted to restrain the impetuosity of the iambic tragic verse, in accordance with the principle that Rest is the chief characteristic of Greek tragedy. Here in alternate feet long syllables were substituted for short at the discretion of the poet. The ear tells us at once why the long syllables were only allowed in the first half of each μέτρον: that is, before the second, and not before the fourth syllable. These second syllables received the stronger ictus; therefore the effect of the long syllable immediately preceding was partially neutralized: had a long syllable stood before the weaker ictus, it would have overpowered it, and spoilt the rhythm.

So much for the influence of quantity considered as a check to the rapidity of rhythm.

We shall now proceed to show that accent had also a real though a secondary importance in this respect. The verses of Virgil are acknowledged to run more smoothly than those of Lucretius. Why? Mainly, without a doubt, because Virgil's scan accentually as well as quantitatively, not indeed completely, or they would be mere jingle, but comparatively.

Compare, for instance—

> 'Títyre, tú patulae recubans sub tégmine fági
> Silvestrem, tenui Musam meditáris avéna,'

with

'Quórum Agrigentínus cum primis Empédocles ést.'

The fact is, Virgil seems to have exquisitely struck the mean between lines that scan themselves and lines that can hardly be scanned. None read like mere prose, none are mere jingle.

Lucretius mostly fell into one of the two opposite extremes. Either his lines read accentually, are mere prose, or they scan themselves, which, though with him a rarer, is a yet greater defect. E.g.—

'Hic est vasta Charybdis et hic Aetnaea minantur.'

Such lines are great favourites with schoolboys, and are proportionately rare in Virgil.

If we compare the Latin hexameter with the Greek, we shall find the main difference to consist in this: that in Latin, accent and ictus nearly always coincide at the end of the verse, the contrary being only possible when the last word is a monosyllable, as in

'Empédocles ést;   odóra cánum vís:'

inasmuch as the last syllable but one in Latin, if long, invariably receives the stress. In Greek, on the other hand, such endings as

ἄλγε' ἔθηκε,   Δαναοῖσιν ἀρηγών

are common.

Greek verse has thus the advantage of very great variety as compared with Latin. At the same time, the relation of accent and ictus is so nicely observed, that there is hardly in all Homer a line which, accentually read, sounds like mere prose.

The same holds good of iambic verse, while in the choric measures there is nearly always an accentual rhythm, which, though it does not exactly coincide with the quantitative, is generally sufficient to indicate it: for example—

> Ἰὼ γενεαὶ βροτῶν,
> ὡς ὑμᾶς ἴσα καὶ τὸ μηδὲν ζώσας ἐναριθμῶ.
> τίς γάρ, τίς ἀνὴρ πλέον
> τᾶς εὐδαιμονίας φέρει
> ἢ τοσοῦτον ὅσον δοκεῖν
> καὶ δόξαντ' ἀποκλῖναι;
> Τὸ σόν τοι παράδειγμ' ἔχων,
> τὸν σὸν δαίμονα, τὸν σόν, ὦ τλάμων Οἰδιπόδα, βροτῶν
> οὐδὲν μακαρίζω.

Or again—

> Τροχοδινεῖται δ' ὄμμαθ' ἑλίγδην,
> ἔξω δὲ δρόμου φέρομαι λύσσης
> πνεύματι μάργῳ γλώσσης ἀκρατής.

Here the last line gives the clue to the quantitative scansion, but a regular accentual rhythm runs through the first two.

In the iambic trimeter the Greeks seem specially to have avoided the regular coincidence of ictus and accent at the end of a line. The immense majority of verses, whether in Aeschylus, Euripides, Sophocles, or Aristophanes, have no accent on the last syllable, and at least thirty out of every fifty will be found to have the accent on the last syllable but one. The later imitators observed this, and it finally became a rule that the end of every iambic verse should be accented on the penultimate. The same desire to check the too rapid run of the iambic trimeter was the origin of the choliambic verse. All the choliambics of Babrius are accented on the last syllable but one. Thus, in the desire to avoid jingle, the later poets fell into the opposite extreme of harsh monotony, which the fine taste of the great originals enabled them to avoid. There is, then, a law in the very lawlessness of the Ancients—'Ars est celare artem.'

ACCENT AND QUANTITY.

What has been called the clashing of the accentual with the quantitative beat constitutes the real beauty of quantitative measure.

It is this τύπος ἀντίτυπος which makes the charm and melody of the old heroic verse. The accent and quantity of these two words as well as the thought expressed in them seem to me exactly to embody the idea of beauty in quantitative versification, which is, as beauty always is, the harmony of contrasts. Where both coincide, as very rarely in Epic poetry,—

'Indignor quandoque bonus dormitat Homerus,'—

then the other part of the line (in which, happily for my illustration, this coincidence takes place) is realized:—

καὶ πῆμ' ἐπὶ πήματι κεῖται.

The rhythm of Greek prose was, no doubt, wholly accentual, and is to my mind completely destroyed if read according to the Latin accent, as is done in our schools and universities. I will give as an example the concluding words of Aeschines' oration against Ctesiphon:—

Ἐγὼ μὲν οὖν ὦ γῆ καὶ ἥλιε καὶ ἀρετὴ καὶ σύνεσις καὶ παιδεία, ᾗ διαγινώσκομεν τὰ καλὰ καὶ τὰ αἰσχρά, βεβοήθηκα καὶ εἴρηκα. Καὶ εἰ μὲν καλῶς καὶ ἀξίως τοῦ ἀδικήματος κατηγόρηκα, εἶπον ὡς ἐβουλόμην εἰ δὲ ἐνδεεστέρως, ὡς ἐδυνάμην. Ὑμεῖς δὲ καὶ ἐκ τῶν εἰρημένων λόγων καὶ ἐκ τῶν παραλελειμμένων αὐτοὶ τὰ δίκαια καὶ τὰ συμφέροντα ὑπὲρ τῆς πόλεως ψηφίσασθε.

Compare the following words from the conclusion of a modern Greek funeral oration on Lord Byron:—

Σὺ δέ, ὑπερήφανον ΣΟΥΛΙ, ἔρημον καὶ ἐγκαταλελειμμένον, ἐνῷ φρίσσεις σήμερον ἀπὸ τοὺς ἤχους τοῦ πολέμου, τοὺς θορυβοῦντας τὸ ἔδαφός σου, κηδεύομεν ἡμεῖς ἡσύχως τέκνον σου προσφιλές, τοῦ ὁποίου οἱ ὀφθαλμοί, διὰ παντὸς κλεισθέντες, δὲν θὰ σὲ ἴδωσιν ἐλεύθερον.

In conclusion, with regard to the practical question, how we are to pronounce Greek, I can only state, from my personal experience and that of others similarly circumstanced, my unalterable conviction, that the man who has once learned to read Greek fluently, with accent and intonation as the Greeks read it, will never be able to tolerate either Homer or Xenophon or Sophocles read with the Latin accent and the miscalled Erasmian pronunciation.

Any one who has followed the arguments and evidence adduced in the preceding chapter, must, I am sure, be convinced that the way in which the ancient Greeks pronounced their language was at least far more like the present Greek pronunciation, handed down as it has been by an unbroken line of tradition, than the wholly arbitrary system which the followers of Erasmus have invented: while few have ever questioned, I may say among continental scholars no one has ever doubted, the propriety of reading Greek according to the accent.

If, moreover, the Greek accent alone preserves the true rhythm of the noble orations of Demosthenes; if a practical familiar sense of it is absolutely necessary, as I have tried to show it is, in order to distinguish a bad verse from a good one, is it not time we abandoned, once and for ever, a barbarous method, whose only justification is that it enables Englishmen to speak Greek so that, in the words of Fuller, they can understand one another, which nobody else can? I subjoin a short sentence, with an interlinear English transcription embodying the chief peculiarities of modern Greek pronunciation:—

'Ο οὐρανὸς καὶ ἡ γῆ οὐκ ἐπλάσθησαν   εὐθύς,   ἀλλὰ ἀνεπ-
O ooranos tkĕh ee yee ook eplástheessan ephtheéss allá anep-

τύχθησαν   ὀλίγον   κατ' ὀλίγον·   οὐδ', οἱ ἄνθρωποι οἱ υἱοὶ
teékhtheessan oleéghon kat' oleéghon oodh, ee ánthropee ee ee-eé

ACCENT AND QUANTITY. 67

τοῦ Θεοῦ	ηὑρέθησαν	ἐξαίφνης	τέλειοι	ὡς	καὶ	νῦν,	οὐδ᾽
too theoó eebhrétheessan exéphneess télee-ee oas tkĕh neen oodh'
ἐκ τοῦ βάθους τοῦ σκότους καὶ χαοτικῆς συγχύσεως
ek too bháhthooss too skoa-tooss tkĕh khaoteekeess seengkheéssĕoss
ἀγγέλων σάλπιγξιν προεκλήθησαν, οὐδὲ τὸν πόλεμον φύσει
angélloan sálpeengxeen proekleétheessan oodhè ton-bólemon féessee
ἀγαπῶσι, ἀλλὰ περὶ τῆς ἑαυτῶν σωτηρίας φρον-
ah-gh-ah-poássee ahláh peri-tees eh-ahphtoan soateereéahss phron-
τίζοντες, φεύγουσι τὴν ὁπλίαν, καὶ ἐμπίπτουσιν
deézondess phébhghoossee teen ah-oa-pleé-ahn tkĕh embeéptoosseen
ἔρισι καὶ μάχαις, καὶ τὴν αὐδὴν τοῦ Ἄρεος
érreessee tkĕh máhkhebss tkĕh teen ah-bhdheén too 'Ahrĕos
φθέγγεσθαι μανθάνουσι.
phthénggestheh mahntháhnoossi.

N.B.—The circumflex accent sounds as the acute, and there is no reason to think that this was ever otherwise; the circumflex being simply a way of recording the fact that an oxytone syllable had swallowed up a barytone by means of contraction: the acute accent, therefore, is plainly the predominating one, while the grave would be felt just in proportion as the uncontracted form was present to the mind. When ἀγαπά-ει becomes ἀγαπᾷ, there is no reason to think that the ' is heard any more than the *iōta subscriptum*, which is swallowed up by the α, just as the grave accent is by the acute. As to the *written* grave accent, it indicates that the syllable on which it stands receives a slight stress as compared with the unaccented syllables, but one which is almost lost by comparison with the accent of the word which follows it; so that a word accented on the last syllable reads almost as if it were part of the next.

CHAPTER IV.

On the Origin and Development of Modern Greek Accidence.

IF the question were asked, what is the origin of the Greek of the present day? is it the offshoot of Byzantine literature, the creation of Church fathers, or of philosophers, sophists, and rhetoricians, or is its source to be looked for in the common dialect of the Ptolemaic era, in the idioms of Dorians, Aeolians, and Boeotians, or the vulgarisms of the Athenian market-place? the true answer, perhaps, would be, it had its beginning in none of these and in all of them: in none of them alone, and in all of them together.

In speaking of the history of a language we should bear in mind the distinction between its outer and inner part, the form and the matter, the skeleton of grammar, and the life which makes that skeleton a living body with a living soul. These two parts of language should never be confounded, and yet it is sometimes hard to keep them separate. For there is an essential, as well as an actual connection between them, which may be set forth as follows.

The mere shapes and changes of words in a language may be called its grammar, while the thought of which these shapes and changes are the expression may be spoken of as the metaphysic of the age to which it belongs. But between this outer part—the grammar, and this inner part—the thought, comes a third something, which is neither altogether outward nor altogether inward, and which, for want of a better name, we may call the logic of a language, or the way in which the thought finds utterance in words.

Now, just as the metaphysic of one age will tend to become the logic of the next, so logic will in its turn become petrified into grammar, as we shall soon see by examples in the language before us. Hence the difficulty of drawing a rigid line of demarcation between the mere vehicle of thought and the thought itself. Grammar and thought, linked as they are in the nature of the case by logic, which is the way in which the one finds utterance in the other, merge together by scarcely felt degrees, like the waves of the stream of time which bears them along, so that it is often hard to say whether we are treading in the domain of philosophy or of grammar, or lingering on the border-land between the two.

The combination of causes in producing phenomena is however no excuse for confusing them, when those phenomena are to be explained; and when we are attempting to write the history of a language, we must beware of attributing every change and development to one source. We should begin by inquiring whether there be any part of language which is quite independent of the progress of human thought. If there be, we may then proceed to inquire what are the causes which may have affected its development. Then we can go on to consider the influence of intellectual progress on such part of language as must be considered liable to be affected by it.

Nor can we be long in admitting that there is that in language which may be changed independently of the advance of thought, or remain unchanged in spite of it; and this is the mere form which words or inflections assume, which is a very different thing, it must be remembered, from changes in their usage and meaning; or, again, from their disuse or introduction. To make this clear by an example. It is plainly, as regards the history of thought, a matter of indifference whether the word οἶνος be written with or without a digamma, whether we write ἐντὶ as in Doric, ἐστὶ as in Attic, or εἶνε as in modern Greek, whether ἑωυτοῦ as in Herodotus, ἑαυτοῦ or αὑτοῦ. It is very different when the Homeric demonstrative ὁ, ἡ, τό becomes the simple article, or when the infinitive mood in later Greek is supplanted by the subjunctive with ἵνα.

In accordance with the above remarks it is proposed in the following pages, first, to consider the mere forms of words and inflections, or the purely outward part of the Greek language; then the structure, in which the movement of thought already begins to play a part; finally, the use and formation of words, in which the inner life of the language attains its greatest significance.

First, then, as to mere grammatical forms; or,

I. The Accidence of Modern Greek.

It must not be supposed that every form discussed under this head is in common use in the language of literature and of educated men. The cultivated language for the most part preserves the grammatical forms of the age of Thucydides, avoiding, as a rule, all the extremities of the later Attic dialect, as, for instance, θάλαττα for θάλασσα, or χερρόνησος for χερσόνησος. In the language of the common people, however, the following peculiarities may be briefly noticed.

OF MODERN GREEK ACCIDENCE. 71

a. δόξα, and words like it, make in the genitive τῆς δόξας, in the plural ᾑ δόξαις, acc. ταῖς δόξαις = τὰς δόξας.

b. A host of nouns belonging to different declensions are made to follow one. Thus ταμίας, Ἅλυς, Μάρτις, or Μάρτης, contracted from Μάρτιος, Ἄρης, Πάρις, κεφαλᾶς, are, in the singular number, all declined alike, namely, by cutting off the sign of the nominative -ς, in the genitive and vocative, and changing it to ν for the accusative.

This ν is dropped in pronunciation where the phonetic laws of the language admit it.

c. The plural of many words, especially of foreign origin, is formed by adding -δες to the stem, as πασάδες from πασᾶς, pashas; μαϊμούδες from ἡ μαϊμοῦ, monkeys; μαννάδες, from ἡ μάννα, mothers.

These plurals are always paroxytone, whatever the accent of the word in the singular.

d. Many feminines, whose root vowel is ω or ου, take ς in the genitive singular, as ἡ μαϊμοῦ, τῆς μαϊμοῦς, ἡ Κῶ, τῆς Κῶς (exactly the reverse of the classical form, which in this case is ἡ Κῶς, τῆς Κῶ).

e. There are a few irregular nouns of a compound declension, especially verbals, in ιμον, as τὸ γράψιμον, genitive τοῦ γραψίματος, plural τὰ γραψίματα.

f. Metaplastic nouns or secondary formations are common, as ἡ αἶγα, ὁ πατέρας, ὁ βασιλέας.

g. Of the pronouns, ἐμὲ often appears as ἐμένα, and σε as ἐσὲ and ἐσένα, ἡμεῖς becomes often ἐμεῖς, and in the accusative both ἐμᾶς and μᾶς. The latter, used as an enclitic, supplies the place both of ἡμᾶς and ἡμῶν.

ὑμεῖς becomes σεῖς and ἐσεῖς, acc. and enclitic possessive σᾶς, σας. The article, as enclitic and proclitic, is used for the personal pronoun in oblique cases.

In the verbs:

h. λέγουσι becomes λέγουν or λέγουνε. For ἔλεγον we have

ἔλεγα; for ἔλεξας, ἔλεξες; for ἐλέξατε, ἐλέξετε. In the passive, instead of λέγῃ or λέγει, we find λέγεσαι, for λεγόμεθα, λεγόμεστε, λεγόμασταν, and various other forms down to the tragic λεγόμεσθα.

For ἐλέχθην we get ἐλέχθηκα. In the imperative aorist act. λέξε for λέξον, and do. passive λέξου for λέχθητι.

i. In the present tense of contracted verbs in άω, ῶ, the third person is often uncontracted, as ἀγαπάει for ἀγαπᾷ. Ἀγαπῶσι appears sometimes as ἀγαποῦν or -οῦνε, sometimes as ἀγαπᾶνε. Ἀγαποῦμεν is written for ἀγαπῶμεν, whereas νοέει, νοεῖ, and the like generally become νοάει, &c.; ἐτίμων is ἐτιμοῦσα, -ες, -ε; -όο becomes -όνω, on the analogy of δύνω for δύω, ἐντύνω for ἐντύω; so δέω becomes δένω. In ancient Greek we may regard αἴνω (pronounced ένω) as a strengthening of ἔω, and ἄνω as a strengthening of ἀω.

j. The verb εἰμί presents all the appearance of a verb in the middle voice, being conjugated thus: εἶμαι, εἶσαι, εἶνε, εἴμεθα, εἶσθε, εἶνε; impf. ἤμουν, ἦσο, ἦτο, ἤμεθα, ἦσθε, ἦτον; inf. εἶσθαι; imper. ἔσο.

k. The present participle active often appears as an indeclinable metaplastic in ας : ὄντας, λέγοντας, &c. The feminine λέγουσα is however by no means disused. The only other participles in use among the uneducated are the present passive and perfect passive, the latter minus the reduplication, as γραμμένος, θλιμμένος, θραμμένος. The present participle sometimes appears as though formed from the conjugation in -μι, e.g. ἐρχάμενος, λεγάμενος. The termination -μι, however, is never found in the common language of the people.

Such are the main features of modern Greek accidence. Let us attempt to account for them and to trace their development. We will begin by inquiring what causes remain to us, when we have eliminated those which belong to the intellectual movements of the Greek mind, and, of course, could explain nothing so merely external as the bare accidence of a language.

First amongst the influences which would remain to be considered is the levelling tendency common to all languages, or, in other words, the ever-increasing desire to do away with irregularities in grammar.

It may be said that all language is originally regular in intention, but in the first formation of words, the stubbornness of matter, that is, the difficulty of pronouncing certain combinations of sounds, causes irregularities in the result. These irregularities are then transmitted from race to race, and the reason of them being forgotten, their existence becomes an inconvenience, and a levelling tendency sets in[1].

So in English we now say, *he climbed, he helped,* for *he clomb, he holp,* and in Spanish the participle *apreso* has almost given way to *aprendido.* Here then at once we see the explanation of such forms as τοῦ Ἄρη, τοῦ Ἅλυ, &c. The first instance of the latter form, so far as I am aware, is to be found in an anonymous writer of the tenth century, known as Theophanes Continuatus.

In Constantine Porphyrogenitus, also an author of the tenth century (905—959), we get μονογενῆ as the vocative of μονογενής. Porphyrogenitus, as he tells us, himself, used frequently the current forms of the vulgar Greek of his day, excepting in his Life of St. Basil, which is written in an artificial language in imitation of classical writers. His numerous modernisms will be noticed in their place. The very same tendency made the ancient Greeks say τὴν ἔριν instead of τὴν ἔριδα, τὸν γέλων for τὸν γέλωτα, and the like.

[1] Accordingly Sanscrit is more irregular than Greek, and Greek than Latin; that is, the older a language is, the less regular is its grammar.

We have also in Homer ἔρος, ἔρον for ἔρως, ἔρωτα. Another similar influence is the tendency to metaplasms or secondary formations. From one point of view this may be regarded as one of the forms of the tendency to simplification above noticed, for it is plain if we turn βασιλεύς, γέρων, Ἄραψ, ἀνήρ, into βασιλέας, γέροντας, Ἄραβας, ἄνδρας, and decline them all like ταμίας, we have got one scheme of declension instead of five. But still it remains to be explained how such a form as ἄνδρας could arise from ἀνήρ, or βασιλέας from βασιλεύς. If we turn to the Septuagint we shall find our answer. There such forms as τὸν βασιλέαν, τὴν αἴγαν are of frequent occurrence, and it is plain that such forms postulate the nominatives ὁ βασιλέας, ἡ αἴγα. Yet such forms are nowhere found till we enter the confines of modern Greek (if we except a few names of animals and birds occurring in Aristotle's Natural History, as, for instance, ἀσκαλώπας from ἀσκαλώψ). These metaplastic accusatives may have first existed alone, and the nominatives and other cases may have been formed from them. Yet the fact that the original form of γέρων, κ.τ.λ. was γέροντς, may explain why γέροντας, which is only γέροντς made pronounceable, is the vulgar equivalent of the classical γέρων. For were γέροντας simply metaplastic, we should expect always to find only γέροντα as the genitive, but γέροντος, ἀνδρός, πατρός, &c. are the more usual forms even in the vernacular. In all likelihood the ν was added to the old accusative merely from euphonic reasons to avoid the hiatus. It may be that it was almost silent, or seemed so to a Greek ear, when followed by a consonant, even when it formed an essential part of the word. This is the case in the present day, and the explanation of it is to be found in the peculiarity of Greek pronunciation. All consonants are pronounced by the Greeks with the utmost force and distinctness of which they admit; and ν, being incapable of emphatic utterance, is by comparison scarcely heard except when followed either by a vowel or some consonant, the pronunciation of which it affects and thereby preserves its own existence. Thus in τὴν Αἴγυπτο(ν) the ν of τὴν is never lost, whereas in τὴ(ν) Σάμο(ν) it is completely evanescent; while in τὴν πόλιν (pronounced τημ-bólin) it is preserved.

Now where the ν is so evanescent a letter, its presence is naturally imagined wherever it would facilitate pronunciation, and it would soon be liable to be written, though not sounded, even where there were no such reason for its introduction. There may however have been a special reason for accusatives like αἶγαν and βασιλέαν. Comparative philology teaches us that a ν has been lost in these accusatives, as also in the pronouns σέ and ἐμέ. What wonder then if this same ν should have lived on in the mouth of the common people, and appeared in the Septuagint, the language of which is so evidently, as far as it departs from the classical standard (a few Hebraisms of course excepted), the vulgar Greek of the period. This consideration suggests a further explanation of the grammatical phenomena of later and modern Greek. This is nothing else than the simple and well-known fact that archaisms are constantly perpetuated in the language of the vulgar which have long since been lost to literature. Our own dialects are sufficient proof of this, to go no further. Witness *I can-na, he's no recht, kie, we do'n,* for *I cannot, he's not right, cows, we do*—where we have sounds or grammatical forms preserved to us which cultivated English ignores. Now to speak first of the language of the Septuagint, no mistake could be greater than to imagine that it was an artificial dialect, the results of an indiscriminate reading-up of the language. According to this theory, as recently enunciated by the Grinfield lecturer on the Septuagint at Oxford (Michaelmas Term, 1868), the Greek of the Septuagint is a farrago of words culled at random from Epic poetry, Attic Prose, and every conceivable dialect, and with a grammar, we are left to suppose, invented by the writers themselves. With the utmost respect for the learned lecturer, I would submit that such a theory is improbable in itself, and does not explain the phenomena of the Septuagint. First, it is inconceivable that there should not have been found, even at the time when the earliest parts of the translation were made, Jews at Alexandria perfectly familiar with Greek as a spoken language. Again, if the translators had not been familiar with the language, it is impossible that they could have escaped grammatical slips such as using an imperfect for an aorist. Finally, the peculiar forms and usages which are found are easily explained by a reference to modern Greek and other unclassical Greek writers. For example, πιάζω is not peculiar to Doric, but occurs in the Revelation of St. John, and is common in modern Greek. Ἐδολιοῦσαν is an imperfect from δολιόω (3rd person plural), and is explained by the consonantal form ἐλέγοσαν, a Septuagint form, &c., and further illustrated by the modern Greek forms ἐδολιοῦσα, ἐτιμοῦσα, of which the 3rd person plural is respectively ἐδολιοῦσαν and ἐτιμοῦσαν. We may say if we like that such a form as ἐδολιοῦσαν or ἐλέγοσαν for ἔλεγον follows the conjugation in μι, but we must not forget that there was originally no other conjugation, and that the σ in the 3rd person of ἐδολιοῦσαν is, etymologically speaking, just as much in its right place as in ἐδίδοσαν, ἴστασαν, ἐτίθεσαν. What the σ does in this position is indeed a mystery, as it has no place in Sanscrit, and as far as I know its presence has not been explained. But if it was found, as it seems to have been, convenient to insert it for phonetic reasons here, we can see that it would be especially so if the usage of the language at any period required the imperfect to end in α instead of ον. Such a form as ἐδολιοῦα would plainly clamour for a sigma. It is true that σ is in Greek more often left out than inserted; but the tendency to do the one, implies, as a general rule, the tendency to do the other. It is a moot point whether ς and ν in such cases as εὐθύ-ς, οὕτω-ς, ἀλὶς, ἀλὲν are ephelcystic or etymologic, i.e. added when found, or omitted when absent. With ἀλὶς might be compared in modern Greek τίποτες. In such cases the force of analogy must be taken into account. Now that α was, for the termination of the imperfect, at least as old as ον, is just as likely as not. Originally, as we see from Sanscrit, the termination of the 1st aorist and of the 2nd aorist and imperfect were the same. In Homer we have ἦα, ἴον, and ἦα; in Ionic both ἔην and ἔα for ἦν, 'I was.' In order to account for the diphthong ου, however, we should have to suppose either that ν was changed to α after the contraction ἐδολίουν from ἐδολίοον had taken place, in which case the accent in such a word as ἐδολιοῦσα would be a mystery, or else, as appears to me to have been the fact, there was a paragogic vowel slipped in between the ο and the α. This seems to have been so in the case of ἦα for ἔα, ἔην, and ἦεν for ἔεν, and ἔην, which would appear to present us with a pair of paragogic ἰ's (ἰ-ε-ε-εν). However that may be, we have the termination -σα for the imperfect of contracted verbs in modern Greek, and of contracted verbs only. In the Septuagint we have the termination -σαν in the 3rd person plural of many verbs, but as far as I know no trace of the σ in any other person. Yet the σ has just as much right (pace grammaticorum) to exist in any other person as in the 3rd, and it is my belief that in many parts of Greece where in the first person α was the favourite termination (εἶδα for εἶδον, εἶπα for εἶπον, which we have in the Septuagint and New Testament), ἐδολιοῦσα, ἐμισοῦσα, &c. would inevitably arise.

At any rate, it is important to remember that all the Greek that was spoken from Homer's day to the era of the Ptolemies is not to be found in books, still less in Grammars, and, above all, that vulgar dialects both of ancient and modern times should be expected to contain far more archaisms than innovations.

Let us see whether this principle will carry us further in the explanation of modern Greek forms. First then as to the nominative δόξαις for δόξα. How are we to account for the ι? Schleicher, in his 'Comparative Grammar,' following as I believe in the steps of Bopp, postulates δοξα-ι-ας or some such form as the original plural of δόξα. It is but right to state that Professor Max Müller differs from this view, but at any rate it is remarkable that the modern Greek form supplies exactly one of the stages of transition that the theory of Bopp and Schleicher demands. As to the accusative ταῖς δόξαις, that is the Aeolic form, and as such an acknowledged archaism. Ταῖς δόξαις is ascertained to be a representative of τὰνς δόξανς, the modification of the vowel indicating the loss of the ν.

Turning next to the pronouns, we have already observed that ἐμένα and ἐσένα for ἐμέ and σέ preserve the original ν (in Sanscrit m, mām, and tvām) of the accusative. 'Εμεῖς is referred to by Plato (Crat. 418 c) as an older form for ἡμεῖς. As to the enclitic and proclitic use of the article, it is (except for the accent in the latter case) the same as the Homeric usage, e.g. Τὸν ἐσκότωσε, 'he killed him;' ἀπεσύλησέ τους, 'he spoiled them.' Passing to the verbs, we find in λέγουν or λέγουνε the traces of the old form λέγοντι (ἔχοντι is quoted, I believe, by Hesychius as a Cretan form). In the passive the forms λέγεσαι, 2nd person present, λεγόμαστε or λεγόμεσθα as well as λεγόμεθεν, are so plainly archaic forms that they need no explanation. In St. Paul's Epistle to the Romans we have already καυχᾶσαι, 'thou boastest.' In the imperative aorist active λέξε for λέξον is Homeric. As to the imp. aorist passive λέξου, I cannot but agree with Dr. Mullach that it is the classical middle 1 aor. imper. of verbs in μι used as a passive, there being no middle voice in modern Greek, as there was none in the κοινὴ διάλεκτος. Few who compare such forms as στάσο with the corresponding modern στάσου, δέξου will be able to doubt this.

The verb εἶμαι (εἰμί), so far as it presents us really with a middle form, has the precedent of the Homeric ἧσο, which is precisely the modern Greek imperative, not to speak of the future ἔσομαι. But nearer examination shows us that εἶμαι is not conjugated throughout as a middle. The third person singular and plural εἶναι or εἶνε, the latter being more correct in writing, while in pronunciation the two forms are the same, is plainly not for εἶται and εἶνται. Now the formation of this word we are able to trace through its various stages. The oldest shape in which it appears is ἐντί, which in the Doric dialect was the same for both numbers. This ἐντί appears already in classical Greek as ἔνι in such phrases as οὐκ ἔνι, ἔνοι for ἐστὶν οἱ. It is not unlikely that it was the vulgar word in regular use for ἐντὶ or ἐστί, though known to literature only in such short phrases as the above. In the Acts of the Council of Constantinople (536 A.D.), we find ἔνι used simply for ἐστί, 'Τίς ἔνι Νεστόριος.' In Ptochoprodromus, the first Romaic writer, we get ἔνε, and soon afterwards the present form εἶναι or εἶνε.

One other principle which seems to have been at work in the development of modern from ancient Greek is the principle of extended analogy. From this point of view modern Greek may be called the logical result of ancient Greek. In ancient Greek the dual number was disappearing; in modern Greek, as already in the κοινὴ διάλεκτος, it is gone. The middle voice as a separate formation was on the wane. In the New Testament we have ἀπεκρίθη for ἀπεκρίνατο, much earlier ἐδέχθη for ἐδέξατο; in modern Greek the only relic of the ancient middle appears in the passive imperative aorist. In later Greek we have many instances of a tendency to dispense with a separate form for the perfect, using the aorist instead. In modern Greek the perfect has disappeared, leaving perhaps a trace of its former existence in such an aorist as εὑρῆκα for εὕρηκα. Already in the Septuagint we get εὕρηκαν and ἑωρακαν, for εὑρήκασι and ἑωράκασι. Verbs in μι have entirely disappeared in modern Greek, leaving behind them only such remnants as the participles λεγάμενος, ἐρχάμενος above noticed. The termination ηκα in ἐλέχθηκα, ἐγράφηκα, &c., seems but a following out of the analogy of ἔδωκα for ἔδων, ἔθηκα for ἔθην, and so forth. Mr. Walker, High Master of the Manchester Grammar School, has called my attention to the fact that the termination κα for perfects is almost unknown to Homer.

Under the head of extensions of analogy we may place the double or mixed declensions, as τὸ γράψιμον, τὰ γραψίματα, with which we may compare τὸ ὄνειρον, τὰ ὀνείρατα, &c. It is worthy of notice that the plural τὰ ὀνείρατα is the only one known to the common people (in Athens at any rate), and I have been corrected myself by my landlord in that city, a man who barely knew how to read, for saying τὰ ὄνειρα.

Phrynichus, the grammarian, notices the increasing use of this termination -ιμον, and complains particularly of the employment of τὸ γελάσιμον for τὸ γελοῖον. One cannot but be glad that the forms prevailed in spite of Phrynichus, for they are a real gain to the Greek language. They constitute a class of verbal substantives with a shade of meaning not accurately expressed by any other word. Certainly there is no adequate ancient Greek translation of ἀκούω σμίξιμον σπαθιῶν, 'I hear the clash of mingled swords.' The force of the termination -ιμον is that it places the word to which it is added midway between concrete and abstract; e. g. κόψις would mean cutting, κόμμα a cut; but τὸ κόψιμον a number of cuttings or stabbings, and is used to describe, as no other word could, an internal pain; German *Leibschnei-*

den. In the plural, as well as in the oblique cases of the singular, it is rather the concrete side of the meaning which comes into prominence. Hence we have the endings appropriate to a concrete meaning—γραψίματος, γραψίματα. The same explanation no doubt holds good with regard to ὄνειρον, which may mean either dreaming in the abstract, or a dream; while ὀνείρατα means always *particular dreams*.

It remains that we should notice the influence of dialects in the forms of modern Greek. The κοινὴ διάλεκτος was probably so called quite as much from the fact that it was no dialect in particular but a mixture of all, as that it was generally understood. Pindar's language was called by grammarians κοινή, because they regarded it as a mixture of more than one dialect.

Now the fact that the Greek of the Septuagint presents us with forms belonging to different dialects is one reason for the false notion above referred to, that the translators took their words at random from the several dialects, much as an indiscriminating schoolboy might do in our own day. We are apt to forget that the Greek language was just as familiar to the Hebrews who wrote the Septuagint, as their own tongue. Just as they adopted the language of 'stammering lips' in Babylon, so they spoke Greek under the Ptolemies; and, in all likelihood, both spoke and wrote that language with greater ease than their sacred tongue. The only natural explanation of the appearance of Doric forms like πιάζω and rare Homeric words like ἀγέρωχος in the Septuagint, is that they were current in the vernacular of the period. Πιάζω is to this day the modern Greek for 'to catch,' and in this sense it is that it is used in the Bible (cf. Latin *opprimere*), while ἀγέρωχος is actually found in the Romaic popular ballads collected by Passow. We are continually reminded of the existence throughout the history of the Greek language (at any rate beginning with the time of

Aristophanes), of a common spoken dialect quite distinct from the cultivated language of literature, but seldom coming to the surface. As often as it strove to raise its head, some tyrant grammarian, a Phrynichus, a Dionysius, or a Choeroboscus beat it down, till at last a poor monk, nicknamed Ptochoprodromus, in the eleventh century, by his example liberated Greek for ever from the shackles of the grammarians, and showed that a language has neither power nor beauty except it be free.

Meanwhile, of course, the language of literature, of the schools, and of the law-courts was comparatively stationary, while that of the people was continually developing and changing, as must ever be the case with a living spoken language. No doubt one of the first changes that came over the popular dialects was that they became mixed and merged in one. Probably it was only a very old Megarian who, even in the days of Aristophanes, would be heard in the Athenian market-place expressing himself thus,—

ἄμβατε ποττὰν μάδδαν αἴ χ' εὑρητέ πα.

Constant intercourse with men from other parts would soon soften down dialectic distinctions, especially when all political divisions were lost in the Macedonian monarchy. Doubtless the Attic dialect, as that of the most cultivated portion of the nation, would give the leading tone to the κοινὴ διάλεκτος, but at the same time we should quite expect isolated provincialisms to survive. This is actually the case not only in the language of the Septuagint, but also in the modern language of Greece. The modern Greek, when speaking in the vernacular of his country, says μικρὴ with the Ionians of old, δόξας with the Dorians, ταῖς τιμαῖς for τὰς τιμὰς with the Aeolians, ἴσο and φεῦξε for ἴσθι and φεῦξον with the Epic poets. Yet we may be well assured that the shepherd or vine-dresser who speaks in this way is as ignorant of the language of Dorians, Ionians, or Epic poets, as a South-Sea islander. As peculiarly characteristic of the Boeotian variety of Doric Greek we may notice the preference of ου for υ. So too in modern Greek we have κουτάλιον for κυτάλιον from κυτάλη, τρούπα for τρύπα. Sometimes this ου represents an η, as σουσάμι for σησάμιον, σουπιαῖς for σηπίαι; compare κρουνὸς and κρήνη.

With reference to such forms as νοάω for νοέω, we may remind the reader, that, as we have seen above in the chapter on pronunciation, άω and έω were originally one. So too ἔλεξες for ἔλεξας is only another instance of the equivalent value of short α and ε. This again we see in βέλτερος, βελτίων, from βελτός, which means that which may be put, placed, or thrown; βελτὸς standing for βαλτός, the regular verbal adjective of βάλλω: (for the change of α and ε under similar circumstances compare παλτὰ and πέλτης;) for the etymology of βέλτερος &c. compare φέρτατος, φέρτερος, from φερτός, i. e. what is bearable; hence in the comparative degree more bearable or preferable. The forms βαλτὸς and φερτὸς are common verbal adjectives in modern Greek.

The paragogic ε in such words as ἐλλογέω, &c., had a tendency to become ι; so διατάζω, the modern Greek and most ancient form, as I believe, of διατάσσω, must have passed through the following stages: διαταγέω = (I am a διαταγός,) διατάγιω, διατάγjω, διατάζω, διατάσσω. Ταγέω is found in Aesch. Persae, 764.

The disappearance of the dative case from the common vernacular of Greece belongs rather to the head of Accidence than Syntax, as I believe it is mainly attributable to pronunciation. We have seen already, that in the vulgar dialect both ω and οι tend to become ου. This will account for the fact that τῷ εἶπε becomes in modern Greek τοῦ εἶπε, and μοὶ εἶπε, μοῦ εἶπε. Add to this the fact that the Greek idiom, especially the later Greek idiom, often places the genitive as a kind of *gen. commodi*, in which position it really stands for the dative, as Ἐθεράπευσεν αὐτοῦ τὴν θυγατέρα, a mode of expression which meets us in almost every page of the New Testament,—and the wonder will rather be how the dative should so long have maintained its rights, than that it should have finally disappeared.

CHAPTER V.

The Origin and Development of Modern Greek Syntax.

HAVING now, as far as our time and space allow, disposed of the mere grammatical forms of the modern Greek language, let us go on to examine

THE SYNTAX OF MODERN GREEK.

Here we have left the region of archaisms and dialectic forms, and enter the territory of the history of the human mind. To the mere philologer the former part of the inquiry may seem the more interesting; for the philosopher the succeeding portion will present the greater attraction. That we may obtain in the outset a general view of the difference in structure and expression, we will compare part of the eighth chapter of Plutarch's Life of Cæsar, as translated by Mr. Rangabes, with the original as written by Plutarch.

Ἡ γνώμη λοιπὸν αὕτη ἐφάνη φιλάνθρωπος, καὶ ἰσχυρὸς ὁ λόγος ὅστις ἐρρέθη περὶ αὐτῆς. Δι' ὃ

Οὕτω δὲ τῆς γνώμης φιλανθρώπου φανείσης καὶ τοῦ λόγου δυνατῶς ἐπ' αὐτῇ ῥηθέντος οὐ ου μόνον οι μετ᾽ αυτὸν ἐγερθέντες παρεδέχοντο τὴν πρότασιν αὐτοῦ, ἀλλὰ καὶ πολλοὶ τῶν προομιλησάντων, ἀρνούμενοι τὰς ἰδίας των γνώμας, παρεδέχοντο τὴν ἐδικήν του, ἕως ὅτου ἦλθεν ἡ σειρὰ τοῦ Κάτωνος καὶ τοῦ Κάτλου. Οὗτοι δ᾽ ἠναντιώθησαν μεθ᾽ ὁρμῆς, καὶ ὡς ὁ Κάτων μετὰ τοῦ λόγου ἔρριψε καὶ ὑπόνοιαν κατ᾽ αὐτοῦ, καὶ ἐξανέστη κατ᾽ αὐτοῦ βιαίως, οἱ μὲν ἄνδρες παρεδόθησαν ὅπως θανατωθῶσι· κατὰ δὲ τοῦ Καίσαρος, ἐν ᾧ ἐξήρχετο τῆς βουλῆς, πολλοὶ τῶν νέων τῶν φρουρούντων τὸν Κικέρωνα τότε, ὁρμήσαντες, ἔστρεψαν γυμνὰ τὰ ξίφη κατ᾽ αὐτοῦ. Ἀλλὰ λέγεται ὅτι ὁ Κουρίων, περικαλύψας τότε αὐτὸν διὰ τῆς τηβέννου του, τὸν ἐξήγαγε· καὶ ὁ Κικέρων, ὅταν οἱ νέοι προσέβλεψαν εἰς αὐτὸν, ὅτι ἔνευσεν ἀποφατικῶς, φοβηθεὶς τὸν δῆμον, ἢ τὸν φόνον ὅλως ἄδικον καὶ παράνομον θεωρῶν. Τοῦτο ὅμως δὲν ἠξεύρω πῶς ὁ Κικέρων, ἂν εἶναι ἀληθές, δὲν τὸ ἔγραψεν εἰς τὸν περὶ τῆς ὑπατείας λόγον του· κατηγορεῖτο δ᾽ ὕστερον ὅτι δὲν ὠφελήθη τότε ἐκ τῆς εὐκαιρίας ἥτις ἀρίστη παρουσιάζετο εἰς αὐτὸν κατὰ τοῦ Καίσαρος, ἀλλ᾽ ἐδειλίασεν ἐνώπιον τοῦ δήμου, ὅστις ὑπερτάτως ηὔνόει τὸν Καίσαρα.

μόνον οἱ μετὰ τοῦτον ἀνιστάμενοι προσετίθεντο, πολλοὶ δὲ καὶ τῶν πρὸ αὐτοῦ τὰς εἰρημένας γνώμας ἀπειπάμενοι πρὸς τὴν ἐκείνου μετέστησαν, ἕως ἐπὶ Κάτωνα τὸ πρᾶγμα καὶ Κάτλον περιῆλθε. Τούτων δὲ νεανικῶς ἐναντιωθέντων, Κάτωνος δὲ καὶ τὴν ὑπόνοιαν ἅμα τῷ λόγῳ συνεπερείσαντος αὐτῷ καὶ συγκατεξαναστάντος ἐρρωμένως, οἱ μὲν ἄνδρες ἀποθανούμενοι παρεδόθησαν, Καίσαρι δὲ τῆς βουλῆς ἐξιόντι πολλοὶ τῶν Κικέρωνα φρουρούντων τότε νέων γυμνὰ τὰ ξίφη συνδραμόντες ἐπέσχον. Ἀλλὰ Κουρίων τε λέγεται τῇ τηβέννῳ περιβαλὼν ὑπεξαγαγεῖν, αὐτός τε ὁ Κικέρων, ὡς οἱ νεανίσκοι προσέβλεψαν, ἀνανεῦσαι, φοβηθεὶς τὸν δῆμον, ἢ τὸν φόνον ὅλως ἄδικον καὶ παράνομον ἡγούμενος. Τοῦτο μὲν οὖν οὐκ οἶδα ὅπως ὁ Κικέρων, εἴπερ ἦν ἀληθές, ἐν τῷ περὶ τῆς ὑπατείας οὐκ ἔγραψεν· αἰτίαν δὲ εἶχεν ὕστερον ὡς ἄριστα τῷ καιρῷ τότε παρασχόντι κατὰ τοῦ Καίσαρος μὴ χρησάμενος, ἀλλ᾽ ἀποδειλιάσας τὸν δῆμον ὑπερφυῶς περιεχόμενον τοῦ Καίσαρος.

Here the words are all ancient Greek; but there is a strange departure from the old simplicity of expression, combined with a sort of effort to say a great deal, and a certain indescribable insincerity of language which is in itself a history. The mere words, the outer shell, are still the same as Plutarch himself, or even Thucydides, might in certain connections have employed; but a change has passed over the spirit of the whole. It is as though a new soul had taken up its abode in an old body, or as if, to take a simile from an ancient story of Sacred Writ, the rough, out-spoken, stalwart elder brother were being counterfeited and supplanted by a wily younger one. 'The hands are the hands of Esau, but the voice is the voice of Jacob.'

We will now proceed to consider the syntax of modern Greek somewhat more particularly, and that we may follow a definite order we will begin with that part of syntax which seems most nearly to enter into the accidence of the language.

The compound tenses of the verbs may fairly claim our first attention. In modern Greek the future is formed in three ways. By the particle θὰ with the subjunctive; by the verb θέλω used personally, and followed by the infinitive; and, thirdly, by the same verb used impersonally, followed by the subjunctive. Thus γράψω becomes θὰ γράψω, θέλω γράψει(ν) for γράψαι(?) or θέλει ('νὰ) γράψω. Θὰ γράψω is usually regarded as a contraction for θέλει νὰ = θὲ νὰ = θὰ γράψω; but such a contraction would be quite without analogy, and I am much disposed to look upon θὰ as a mere particle, to speculate on the etymology of which would be hazardous, though it may be either a part or a fragment of τάχα, a possible dialectic form of which would be θα-κα; cp. κιθών and χιτών, ἐνθεῦτεν, ἐντεῦθεν. I cannot but think we have this very particle θὲ or θὰ in the optative interjection εἴθε and αἴθε: εἴθε ἔλθοι is in modern Greek εἴθε νὰ ἔλθῃ, which might be also written εἰ θὲ νὰ ἔλθῃ. That θὰ is equivalent in force to ἴσως, τάχα, κε, πως, ἄν, &c., is evident from the fact that, in modern Greek, τάχ' ἔλθῃ and ἴσως ἔλθῃ may be used without θά. In ancient Greek εἴ-θε ἔλθοι is plainly equivalent to εἴπως ἔλθοι. I am the more inclined to regard θὰ as a simple particle because its use with the subjunctive corresponds to the use of κε in Homer, with the same mood, while its employment with the imperfect, as θὰ ἐπεθύμουν (vulg. θὰ ἐπεθυμοῦσα), answers precisely to the classical ἐπεθύμουν ἄν; only that this usage is more exact in modern Greek, it being impossible to say θὰ ἐπεθύμησα in the same sense. This would mean, not, 'I should have wished,' but, 'I probably did wish.' It is worth consideration whether ἄν with the aorist indicative in ancient Greek has not sometimes the same meaning. However that may be, with θὰ, if it be a simple particle, we have nothing at present to do. Θὰ πολεμήσω is just as much in the spirit of ancient Greek as κε πολεμήσω.

But with θέλω γράψει and θέλει γράψω the case is different. Θέλω γράψει explains itself. But what induced the Greeks to grow discontented with their simple future γράψω? It seems to have been nothing else than a certain wastefulness of speech always observable in the Greek language, as in such phrases as ἔτυχεν ὤν, μέλλει ποιεῖν (which latter is after all but another kind of compound future); but this tendency to waste words always increases in proportion as solidity of character and depth of thought begin to wane. Inanity always vents itself in expletives: and it is no wonder that we cannot write Cicero's Latin without swearing Cicero's oaths. Now every needlessly forcible expression is only another kind of expletive; it fills up a proportionate void in the mind of the speaker and the hearer, and may be compared to a still more feeble resource of modern times, the printer's trick of italicising. The Nemesis of waste is want;

and so we find in the present case. θέλω γράψει having come to mean, 'I shall write;' the need arises of a separate phrase for 'I will write.' This accordingly is expressed by the still more explicit mode of speech θέλω ἴνα γράψω, θέλω 'νὰ γράψω. This use of ἴνα begins in the New Testament, where it is extremely common. But this leads again to a further need; if ἴνα γράψω in this and other cases is to be equivalent to γράψαι, what are we to do if we want to say ἴνα γράψω in good earnest? We must have recourse to a further periphrasis, and say διὰ 'νὰ (δι' ἴνα) γράψω. This process is like the career of a perpetually insolvent debtor borrowing money at compound interest. The same principle may be seen at work in a vast number of words and expressions. To notice a few. The preposition διὰ, *through*, becomes διαμέσου, ἀνὰ grows into ἀνάμεσον, μετὰ is felt to be too weak to express the relation *with*, and accordingly ὁμαδῆ ('μαζῆ) is pressed into the ranks of the prepositions. Τίς becomes ποῖος; τὶς, κᾶτις, κἀνεὶς, or κᾶμποσος = respectively *some one*, *any one*, and *some*. Τώρα (τῇ ὥρᾳ) supplants the simple νῦν; πᾶς and ἕκαστος become καθεὶς, first, as most frequently in the New Testament, used only in the accusative καθ' ἕνα, but soon regarded and declined as one word, as already in the epistles of St. Paul: ὅς and ὅστις become ὁ ὁποῖος (cp. *il quale*, *el cual*, *le quel*, in Italian, Spanish, French, as also ποῖος with *quel*, &c.). For the old ποῖος the Greeks often say ποῖός τις, and the common people τί λογῆς; (the τί being used indeclinably, like *wasfür* in German). Τί λογῆς must have meant originally, 'of what vintage or gathering?'

Examples of this kind might be multiplied without end; but the limits of our space warn us not to linger too long on any one subject, however full of interest. We would rather point the way and draw the outlines which we think, with Aristotle, 'any one may fill up for himself.'

The third or impersonal form of the future, θέλει γράψω, we

prefer to consider a little later on when we come to examine the influence of Greek systems of thought upon the development of the language. We will say now a very few words on the compound perfects. Of these there are two, ἔχω (γε) γραμμένον, which is simply a more explicit way of saying γέγραφα, and will be quite familiar to the classical scholar, and ἔχω γράψει from ἔχω γράψαι, which is difficult to explain, rather from the want of illustration and analogy in ancient Greek or other languages, than from any inherent unreasonableness in the thing itself: yet we may compare the use of the German infinitive for the participle in phrases like *ich habe ihn sprechen wollen*, &c. Perhaps the idea present to the minds of those who first used it may have been, that as τὸ γράφειν, and even if the case required it τὸ γράψαι, might mean 'the writing,' so ἔχω γράψαι might be used for 'I have a writing,' of anything as a deed done, γεγραμμένον μοί ἐστι. At any rate, he who is not scandalized at ἑκὼν εἶναι need not be offended at ἔχω γράψαι.

It might be worth some one's while to see whether in certain cases οὐκ ἔχω γράψαι, οὐκ ἔχω εἰπεῖν, οὐκ ἔχει ἀποδεῖξαι, and the like, may not admit of a perfect sense, as used by Herodotus and other classical authors. With reference to both the future and perfect tenses in modern Greek, it is to be observed that being duplicate, according as the infinitive aorist or imperfect is employed, they give a greater precision of meaning than the simple forms γράψω or γέγραφα are capable of expressing. Γράψω in ancient Greek might mean either 'I will write' (e. g. a letter), or, 'I will be an author.' In the one case it would be in modern Greek, θὰ γράψω, θέλω γράψει, or θέλει γράψω; in the other, θὰ γράφω, θέλω γράφει, or θέλει γράφω.

CHAPTER VI.

The Origin and Development of Modern Greek Phraseology.

LEAVING for the present the subject of syntax, let us notice some changes in the meaning of words.

In the language of Greece as it is in our own day, we shall be surprised and interested to find the eminently Greek tendency to euphemism carried out to a still further extent than in ancient Greek. Αὐθέντης means no longer 'murderer' but 'master.' Possibly during the period of Turkish supremacy the Greeks thought it came to much the same thing. This I have put under the head of euphemisms, though it appears to be a kind of inversion of the euphemistic tendency, inasmuch as a bad meaning has given place to a better one. But in all probability it is a real euphemism. Αὐθέντης in the sense of murderer probably stands as a separate idiom from αὐθέντης, master. Αὐθέντης, meaning according to its derivation 'the very doer,' was employed to denote the doer of a particular crime. This etymological sense 'real doer' was most likely never lost among the common people, and when, as especially under the Turkish dominion, δεσπότης was felt to be an odious term, αὐθέντης would be applied to the master, half to soften down the bitterness of the relation in the mind of the slave, half flatteringly and fawningly towards the master, as though the meaning were 'he is the real doer of all that is done, we are nothing but the tools.' A more palpable instance of euphemism may be found in such words as σκοτόνω, 'I darken,' for kill, ψοφάει of an animal dying; compare the French *crever*, and the German *crepiren*. The meaning is literally of course 'to make a noise.' Death is still called Χάρων in the popular dialect, Χάρος or Χάρωντας, etymologically(?) 'the joyful God.' Βασιλεύει ὁ ἥλιος means 'the sun sets.' Such euphemisms are quite in the spirit of the Greek language in all ages. Who does not remember at the sound of σκοτόνω the grand Homeric periphrasis for death, σκότος ὄσσε κάλυψεν? and who that gazes on the setting sun, as the Greek shepherd has so often done, from some commanding height, but feels the majesty of the great Ruler of the skies more sensibly as he lights up with his last golden rays, ocean, islands, clouds and mountain tops, and owns the fitness of the words put by Campbell into the mouth of the 'Last Man' who sees the sun set never to rise again:—

> 'Yet mourn I not thy parted sway,
> Thou dim discrowned king of day'?

If there is a difference between the euphemisms of ancient and modern Greece, it is perhaps that the modern ones are more stereotyped and fixed; that the language of poetry has become the language of life.

Thus much of the euphemisms in the Greek of our own day. There is however many a word which bears the impress of a deeper and harder kind of thought than that which is content with softening stubborn facts into gentle metaphors.

The biography of a new word and expression would often be a page from the history of philosophy.

The whole language in its vocabulary, as well as in its structure, appears to have undergone a change from truth to fiction, from Nature to Art. If it be asked, When did this change begin? the answer is, With the beginning of speculative thought; an answer perhaps none the less true because it is indefinite.

What has philosophy done for language generally, and what for Greek in particular? might prove no uninstructive enquiry. The most comprehensive reply to the question would seem to be, that it gave terms for thoughts as well as for things. The main feature of a language before the beginning of speculative thought, is a kind of honest simplicity. Men call a spade a spade, not an agricultural implement.

Before philosophy, human research is a mere registration of given phenomena. It asks only what is there? Philosophy asks, why is it there? then, how is it there? and lastly, is it there at all?

When new questions are asked, new answers must be given; and new answers require new words, or at least words with new meanings.

Even the Ionic philosophers have handed down a host of words to the colloquial language of to-day. Such are φύσις, ἀρχή, στοιχεῖον, ἐξάτμισις, ἀναθυμίασις, ἀνάλυσις, κόσμος, ἄπειρος, πύκνωσις, ἀραίωσις. Could any of these words write its own biography, what a strange history that would be! Had any of them been gifted with the tongue of a prophet, how it would have amazed the sages of old!

The unlettered Athenian in the Café de la Belle Grèce, as he melts a lump of sugar in a cup of coffee, little dreams that the name by which he calls the process (ἀνάλυσις) meant, in the mouths of the old Ionic philosophers, the dissolution of the elements of created things in decay or death; and scarcely could Heraclitus, with all his admiration of antipathies, have divined that κόσμος, the divine order of nature, and ἄπειρον, the formless void, should ever be wedded together in one expression, κόσμος ἄπειρος, and mean a 'countless multitude,' perhaps a disorderly rabble. Could Anaxagoras have foreboded that κόσμος, which expressed to him divine beauty and perfection of arrangement—πάντα χρήματα ἦν ὁμοῦ, εἶτα νοῦς ἐλθὼν αὐτὰ διεκόσμησε—should in a very few hundred years become the subject of the Christian lament, 'the whole world lieth in wickedness'? Who could foresee that τὸ ἄλογον, which would mean in the mouth of Heraclitus so much of matter as was untouched by the heavenly fire of reason, should come to signify in our own day a horse; or that στοιχεῖον, an element, should presently become a ghost, the δαίμων of the ancient Greeks, haunting murmuring rills or whispering groves, and terrifying the simple shepherd as he tends his flocks upon the lonely mountain side? Scarcely could Democritus and Leucippus have guessed, that of their philosophical terms σχῆμα, θέσις, and τάξις, the first should mean in the present day, 'a monk's habit,' the second, 'a place in a coach,' and the third, 'a class' in a steam-packet or a railway train, any more than Pythagoras could have foreseen that his doctrine of the Pilgrimage of Souls should have taken such firm root in popular superstition and popular poetry, that those lines of Xenophanes,

> Καὶ ποτέ μιν στυφελιζομένου σκύλακος παριόντα
> Φασὶν ἐποικτείραι καὶ τόδε φάσθαι ἔπος·
> Παῦσαι, μηδὲ ῥάπιζ', ἐπειὴ φίλου ἀνέρος ἐστὶ
> Ψυχὴ τὴν ἔγνων φθεγξυμένης ἀίων·

should have found their echo in such words as these, uttered by the hero Tsamados in the person of a bird of the air:—

> Ἐγὼ πουλὶ σοῦ φαίνομαι ἀλλὰ πουλὶ δὲν εἶμαι·
> Εἰς τὸ νησὶ ποῦ ἀγνάντια εἶναι τῶν Ναβαρίνων,

Ἐκεῖ τὴν ὑστερην πνοὴν ἄφησα πολεμῶντας.
Ὁ Τσαμαδὸς εἶμαι ἐγὼ καὶ ἦλθα εἰς τὸν κόσμον.
Σ τοὺς οὐρανοὺς ποῦ κάθομαι καθάρια σᾶς 'ξανοίγω·
Μὰ νὰ σᾶς 'δῶ ἀπὸ κοντὰ εἶναι ἡ 'πιθυμιά μου.

To take another instance, how has the common language of modern Greece reversed the judgment of the Eleatics, when τὸ ὄν no longer means the most abstract but the most concrete Being, as ὁ ἄνθρωπος οὗτος εἶναι τὸ δυστυχέστατον ὄν τοῦ κόσμου!

Even the Sophists have a claim, and not the least, to our attention. If these thinkers, or as some would perhaps be inclined to call them, talkers, have little right to the name of philosophers, it should still be remembered that they more than any philosopher, not excepting Plato, who owed more to them than he was aware, left their mark upon the Greek language, a mark which has never since been effaced. Before their time men were in the habit of saying what they thought; since they have rather inclined to think what they should say, a tendency from which even genius cannot now wholly shake itself free. Before the Sophists, thought was everything and expression as an end nothing; hence while it was often laborious, it was always unstudied. Since their age, expression has been too often either everything or more than half the whole. Antithesis, emphasis, precision of language, nice distinctions, well-balanced sentences and smoothly-rounded periods, these are the work of the Sophist and the delight of the Rhetorician. We can mark this leaven working already in the speeches reported by Thucydides, not so much as they were but rather as they ought to have been spoken: we can trace it in the orations of Demosthenes, it is the paramount feature in Isocrates and the later orators of Greece, and reaches a kind of climax in the discourses of Chrysostom. What a gulf is fixed between a Chrysostom and a Nestor! And if we listen to any sermon or public address in Athens at this day, our ears are struck by the same balancing of epithets, the same rounding of sentences, which constituted in so great measure the art and the power of the early Rhetoricians. Here is a brief extract from a funeral oration on Lord Byron:—

Τί ἀνέλπιστον συμβεβηκός! Τί ἀξιοθρήνητον δυστύχημα! ὀλίγος καιρὸς εἶναι, ἀφ' οὗ ὁ λαὸς τοῦ πολυπαθοῦς Ἑλλάδος ὅλος χαρὰ καὶ ἀγαλλίασις ἐδέχθη εἰς τοὺς κόλπους του τὸν ἐπίσημον τοῦτον ἄνδρα, καὶ σήμερον ὅλος θλῖψις καὶ κατήφεια καταβρέχει τὸ νεκρικόν του κρεββάτι μὲ πικρότατα δάκρυα, καὶ ὀδύρεται ἀπαρηγόρητα. ὁ γλυκύτατος χαιρετισμὸς ΧΡΙΣΤΟΣ ΑΝΕΣΤΗ ἤγεινεν ἄχαρις τὴν ἡμέραν τοῦ Πάσχα εἰς τὰ χείλη τῶν Ἑλλήνων χριστιανῶν,......Δεκτὰ βέβαια, ἀγαπητοί μου Ἕλληνες, πολὺ δεκτὰ εἶναι εἰς τὴν σκιάν του τὰ δάκρυά μας διότι εἶναι δάκρυα τῶν κληρονόμων τῆς ἀγάπης του· ἀλλὰ πολὺ δεκτότερα θέλει ἦναι τὰ ἔργα μας διὰ τὴν πατρίδα· αὐτὴν καὶ μόνην τὴν εὐγνωμοσύνην ζητεῖ ἀπὸ ἡμᾶς εἰς τὰς εὐεργεσίας του, αὐτὴν τὴν ἀμοιβὴν εἰς τὴν πρὸς ἡμᾶς ἀγάπην του, αὐτὴν τὴν ἐλάφρωσιν εἰς τὰς ταλαιπωρίας του, αὐτὴν τὴν πληρωμὴν διὰ τὸν χαμὸν τῆς πολυτίμου ζωῆς του.

For the purpose of Sophists and Rhetoricians, which was 'not to convince but to persuade,' new words were needed. Such words, for example, as τῷ ὄντι—*indeed*, literally *in being, in the world of real existence* (no bad comment on the consistency of a school whose leading axiom was that there was no such thing as Truth)—τοὐλάχιστον, κατ' ἀλήθειαν, δηλαδή, ἤγουν, are the true children of the Sophists and have survived to this day; in fact, without them it would be impossible to carry on a connected conversation, or pen an article for a newspaper. On the other hand, the simpler and less explicit particles, such as μήν, γε, οὖν, τοί, γάρ, have in modern Greek either received a restricted sense, and thus been made as explicit as was required, or have been supplanted by others. So γὰρ and οὖν, which are very expressive but not at all explicit, have been entirely displaced by διότι and λοιπόν, which are very explicit but not at all expressive. As the first stage of the displacement of γὰρ by διότι and οὖν by λοιπόν, we may observe the frequent use of ὅτι for γὰρ in the New Testament, which is I believe much more frequent than is the case in the Septuagint, and the constant occurrence of λοιπὸν for οὖν in Polybius, wherever rather an emphatic οὖν is required.

To Socrates may perhaps be traced, or at any rate with his teaching may be closely connected, the modern meaning of such words as καθόλου, διόλου, ὅλως (often emphatically joined for the sake of greater force—ὅλως καθόλου, ὅλως διόλου), ἀρετή, εἰρώνεια, ἠθικός, ἐπιστήμη, διορισμός.

The Cyrenaics appear to have invented the word μερικός, *particular* (as in the phrase μερικαὶ ἡδοναί), which in modern Greek survives in the sense of *certain, some*, having degenerated from a philosophical term to a mere part of grammar. So true is the remark above quoted that the metaphysics of one age will become the logic and finally the grammar of succeeding generations. A like fate has befallen some terms of the Platonic philosophy; as εἰδικὸς from εἶδος, *specific*, which is now nothing more than part of the possessive pronoun ὁ εἰδικός μου, τὸ εἰδικόν της, &c., *mine, hers*, and so on. A curious and interesting instance of a somewhat complicated metaphysical significance in certain grammatical forms is presented by the history of the pronoun αὐτός. This word expressed originally what may be called the feeling of subjectivity rather than the idea: for the subject as an idea had as yet no existence. Nevertheless the subject appeared in the world very often in an objective light, and in Homer this is expressed by putting together the objective particle ἑ with the subjective αὐτὸς in the oblique cases, as ἑ αὐτόν, οἱ αὐτῷ, ἕο αὑτοῦ, but it had never yet occurred to the Greeks actually to join the two together as subject-object. This by a kind of anticipation of philosophy occurs first in the more thoughtful age of Attic and Ionic literature, where we get ἑαυτόν. But both in the Homeric and Attic age there was as yet nothing but a kind of unconscious registration of metaphysical facts. The subject never till the time of the Sophists, and probably not until long afterwards, got so clear of itself that it could be spoken of as an objective reality, as a thing. Yet such must have been the case to a great extent before the modern Greek substitute for ἑαυτόν, ἐμαυτόν, &c. could arise; before men could say τὸν ἑαυτόν μου, τὸν ἑαυτόν του, &c. There may come a time perhaps when this tendency to objectivity in the subject may go farther still, and men will find no difficulty in contemplating the subject as an object, not only in its objective relations (as in the oblique cases), but even in its most subjective state, as the nominative. In this respect, the English language is ahead of the Greek, for we can say 'himself' in the nominative, though we almost require a 'he' to help it out; whereas ὁ ἑαυτός του in Greek would be a barbarism;—ὁ ἴδιος being used in such cases instead of the classical αὐτός.

In passing from Socrates and the Cyrenaics to Plato, we must not forget the Cynics, who have left their stamp on the language in such words as αὐτάρκης, αὐτάρκεια.

If the Sophists gave a new direction to language, to Plato belongs the credit of having not inconsiderably increased its power of utterance. In truth the Sophists and Plato together seem in great measure to have conquered the difficulties of expression, and by so doing to have given to Greek one of the characteristics of a modern language. As a mere matter of style Plato comes nearer to a modern Greek writer than Polybius, or any Hellenistic or ecclesiastical writer. We seldom reflect what labour and art were once employed in beating out those convenient expressions, those ways of turning a sentence, which make the flow of a modern language so easy and its sense so clear and precise. Here indeed other men have laboured and we have entered into their labours.

Besides words to which the Platonic philosophy gave a new sense, as δημιουργός, 'creator,' with all its derivatives, one is struck by the fact that many of his commonest phrases and words have established themselves in the colloquial language of the present day.

Πρὸς τούτοις, ὅπως δήποτε, ἴσως, φαίνεται, παντάπασιν, ἆρά γε, μάλιστα, τοίγαρ, common and necessary helps to conversation in modern Greek, are the very hinges of the Platonic dialogues, and when one hears a common peasant say μάλιστα for *yes*, or πῶς δὲν εἶδα = πῶς οὐκ εἶδον; in emphatic affirmation, one cannot but be struck by such modernisms of Plato, or if the reader will, such Platonisms in modern Greek.

But while modern Greek is indebted largely to Plato for its form, to Aristotle it owes much of its vocabulary. If we would understand how such words as ὕλη, ὑποκείμενον, παράδειγμα, ὑπάρχειν, πρότασις, ὄρεξις, οὐσιώδης, ἐνδέχεται, χορηγεῖν came to have their present meaning, it is almost necessary to go to Aristotle for the explanation. And yet how Aristotle himself would wonder at their modern employment. Γραφικὴ ὕλη, 'writing materials;' οὐσιώδης διαφορὰ ὑπάρχει, 'an essential difference exists;' σοὶ εὔχομαι καλὴν ὄρεξιν, 'I wish you a good appetite;' ἄμεσος πρότασις, 'an immediate proposal;' ὑποκείμενον ἀπαραδειγματίστου ἐνεργείας, 'a subject of unexampled activity.' He would either think that every fool was his disciple, or that all his disciples were fools.

The Stoics were not much of independent speculators, but perhaps there is one idiom in modern Greek which may be an echo of Stoic resignation, namely the third form of the compound future already noticed, θέλει ν' ἀποθάνω for ἀποθανοῦμαι, as though it were, 'It wills that I should die,' that is, it is the will of that great unknown impersonal necessity, whom we sometimes worship with the name of God.

As regards the philosophers, the history of innovations may almost be said to close with Aristotle and the Stoics.

Succeeding schools having lost the grain, continued to thrash out the straw of Aristotle or of Plato, until words had little meaning left, and men had little hope of anything better.

Yet in spite of the deadness of philosophers, and the active opposition of grammarians and pedants, the Greek language did not stand still. The conquests of Alexander and the consolidation of Greece gave rise to what was called the κοινὴ διάλεκτος.

CHAPTER VII.

The Historical Development of Modern from Ancient Greek.

HITHERTO we have sketched the outlines of what may be called the basis of modern Greek, of which the principal elements seem to have been first as regards its accidence, archaisms, preserved in the vulgar dialect from generation to generation, a tendency to simplification or regularity both in declension and conjugation, and the mixture of dialects previously distinct; secondly, as regards its syntax, and the use and meaning of words, a change in the mode of thought and expression.

Having now considered the origin of modern Greek, let us proceed briefly to trace its development, beginning with the so-called Hellenistic Greek.

To the first or Macedonian age of the κοινὴ διάλεκτος belongs the Greek of the Septuagint, though there is every reason to believe that this translation was made at various times, and by persons very variously qualified to fulfil their task. And here I may be allowed to remark, how very important is a knowledge of modern Greek for the study of the Septuagint; and I need not add of the New Testament also. So much the more in the latter case as we have there to deal with the meaning of an original instead of only with a translation. It is a mistake to think that classical Greek + Hebrew will give us the Greek of the Septuagint.

It is very easy to explain everything as a Hebraism, and the less our knowledge of Hebrew the more readily does the explanation suggest itself. Now there are Hebraisms in the Septuagint, and, though in a less degree, in the New Testament; but all unusual phrases are not Hebraisms. Polybius, certainly a contemporary of many of the translators of the Septuagint, may have many Latinisms in his writings, but all his peculiarities are not Latinisms. Whatever light may be thrown on the Septuagint and on Polybius by Hebrew and by Latin, infinitely more may be gained both for the one and the other from a study of modern Greek. And what perhaps sounds still stranger, the Greek of the present day affords a better commentary on the language of Polybius, of the Septuagint, and of the New Testament, than either the writings of contemporary historians, rhetoricians, grammarians, and philosophers, who for the most part wrote a purely artificial Greek—or than from the many thousand ponderous tomes which encumber the threshold of verbal criticism.

To speak first of the Septuagint. We have already shown how the grammatical peculiarities of its authors are the first appearance of the same forms which are familiar to us in modern Greek. But more than this, the phraseology of the Septuagint is modern to an extent which is quite marvellous, when compared with that of contemporary writers, and only explicable by the assumption that the writers are using the common vernacular, which had already become in its spirit and essence much what modern Greek now is. For example, Ἔξελθε ἐκ τῆς γῆς σου, καὶ ἐκ τῆς συγγενείας σου...πάντες ἐξέκλιναν, ἅμα ἠχρειώθησαν,... τάφος ἀνεωγμένος ὁ λάρυγξ αὐτῶν, sound just like modern Greek familiar phrases. Let us mention a few well-known words, common to the Septuagint and modern Greek. Ἐπισκέπτομαι, 'I visit;' ἀποκρίνομαι (passive), 'I answer;' ἐπιστρέφω, 'I return;' ἡγούμενος, 'a leader' (in modern Greek the superior of a monastery); προσκυνῶ, 'to worship' or 'salute;' ἑτοιμάζω, 'make ready;' ἐνώπιον, 'in the presence of;' προσκόπτω and πρόσκομμα, πειράζω, 'to tempt;' ἀκολουθῶ in preference to ἕπομαι; κοιμῶμαι in preference to εὕδω; ὅλος for πᾶς; ἕως ἑνός, 'as many as one;' κατοικῶ, for 'to dwell;' καθέζομαι and καθίζω, for 'to sit;' τὰ ἱμάτια, for 'the clothes;' ὑπάγω for εἶμι. Besides words of this kind, there are others, the present usage of which dates from the Septuagint, words to which Jewish ideas have given a new and higher meaning.

Οὐρανὸς is no longer the mere blue sky, or a mythical name for one of many deities, but the habitation of the Ancient of Days. Ἁμαρτία no longer a mistake, but the fundamental error of mankind, estrangement from God, and the breaking of his perfect law. Πίστις becomes the trusting obedience of faithful Abraham, and of all the saints. Δόξα is the glory, or sometimes the honour of the Almighty. Ὁ Κύριος is no longer the man in authority, but the name of the Lord of lords, and the King of kings.

Before going on to the New Testament the order of time demands a few words for Polybius. It cannot be said that the general run of his sentences is so modern as the Septuagint or the New Testament. Many of the novelties of this author are equally found in the New Testament. For example, he uses πλὴν for ἀλλά, ὅταν and ἂν for ὅτε and εἰ. Other modern usages are ἀκμὴν for ἔτι, as already Theocritus, iv. 60. Cf. Anthologia, P. vii. 141. Ἴδιον frequently for ἑαυτοῦ, far more so than is the case in classical authors. Ἴδιον in one place in the sense of *same*, the most usual meaning in modern Greek: ἴδιον καὶ παραπλήσιον ταῖς πόλεσι συνέβη. Here, however, the translation is doubtful. Ἀπὸ in the sense of worth or weight, as ἀπὸ δέκα ταλάντων, weighing

10 talents. So the Greeks of to-day say δός μοι ἀπὸ δέκα λεπτά, ἀπὸ μία δεκάρα. Εἰς τοὺς καθ' ἡμᾶς καιρούς, which is completely modern Greek, for ἐν τοῖς καθ' ἡμᾶς χρόνοις. This use of εἰς, as well as of καιρός, belongs equally to the New Testament. I will now add one or two examples of the modern phraseology of Polybius. Ὁ τῆς πραγματικῆς ἱστορίας τρόπος: i. e. the method of actual history. Πραγματικῶς διενοήθησαν, ii. 50. 5. Δικαιοδοσία, jurisdiction. xx. 6. 2; xxxii. 17. 19. Τρώγομεν for ἐσθίομεν, used, however, only in a proverbial expression. Λοιπὸν ἀνάγκη συγχωρεῖν τὰς ἀρχὰς καὶ τὰς ὑποθέσεις εἶναι ψευδεῖς, i. 15. Εἰς ἀληθινὰς ἐννοίας ἄγειν. Συμφωνοῦντες, in the sense of bargaining, already used in this sense by Xenophon, Hell. i. 3. 8. Κατὰ τὰς περιστάσεις, according to circumstances, κατὰ τὰς αὐτῶν προαιρέσεις. Ἀντίσπασμα, a diversion, xi. 18. Ἐκ τοῦ ζῆν ἐξεχώρησαν διὰ τὸν χρόνον. Id. 22, ἡ γὰρ λέξις αὕτη τοῦτο σημαίνει κυρίως. Εἰς φόβους συνεχεῖς καὶ ταραχάς, into continual fear and distress.

In the New Testament, among many others, we may notice the following modernisms:—Εἰς for ἐν, as εἰς τὸν κόλπον τοῦ πατρός, St. John i. 18. Ἵνα with the subjunctive is used continually for the infinitive, as Matthew iii. 3, εἰπὲ ἵνα οἱ λίθοι οὗτοι ἄρτοι γένωνται. Ἀνὰ μέσον, for among: ἄφες ἐκβάλω, the modern ἆς ἐκβάλω. Βρέχει for ὕει, Matth. v. 45. Ἔνοχος εἰς τὴν γέενναν for τῇ γεέννῃ. Ἐπάνω ὄρους. Περισσότερον for πλέον, as περισσότερον κρῖμα, 'greater damnation.' Δυσκόλως for μόγις or χαλεπῶς, 'with difficulty,' Luke xviii. 24. Αὐτὸς for ὅς or οὗτος passim. Ἐστάθην for ἔστην passim. The genitive for the dative as in modern Greek. Οὗ ἐγὼ οὐκ εἰμαι ἄξιος ἵνα λύσω αὐτοῦ τὸν ἱμάντα τοῦ ὑποδήματος. Ἰδοὺ for 'here,' the modern ἐδώ: Acts ii. 7, οὐκ ἰδοὺ πάντες οὗτοί εἰσιν οἱ λαλοῦντες Γαλιλαῖοι; Εὐχαριστῶ for χάριν εἰδέναι. Cf. Lob. in Phryn. on the word. Καθεὶς for ἕκαστος in Romans xii. 5. Such forms as γεμίζω, 'to fill,' ἐγγίζω, 'to approach,' are mostly Hellenistic and modern.

In Romans the phrase τῶν τὴν ἀλήθειαν ἐν ἀδικίᾳ κατεχόντων receives considerable light when it is known that κατέχω in many dialects of modern Greek is used for the more general ηξεύρω, 'I know,' formed from the aorist of ἐξευρίσκω, ηξευρον. Many another phrase, which to the mere classical scholar appears dark and strange, and in which critics of the school of Bengel think they hear the unearthly utterances of an oracle, would appear simple and natural to one versed in the vernacular of the modern Greeks. In leaving the New Testament we may remark finally how many words there are to which it has given a peculiar meaning which has now become the prevalent one, as διάβολος, κόλασις, θλῖψις, μετανοέω, αἰώνιος. Above all is it interesting to observe how the biblical word ἀγάπη has replaced the old expression ἔρως. The word is Hellenistic, and hardly occurs, I believe, in classical Greek, although the verb ἀγαπῶ does. Now the verb ἀγαπῶ implies the noun ἀγάπη, which must therefore have existed in the mouth of the common people long before it came to the surface in the Greek Bible. Ἀγάπη being derived from the root ἀγαυ-, as in ἀγαϝός, &c., is a far better word for Christian purposes than ἔρως, and indeed it would have served even Plato better in his more religious moments. Compare the Platonic ἔρως with the Pauline ἀγάπη in 1 Cor. xiii., and observe how this 'love' is with Paul, as the ἔρως with Plato, not only the religious sentiment, but more generally still, a certain upward and outward longing of the soul, a divine principle of development, which is at once the only eternal element in, as it is the common substratum of all belief and all knowledge alike, mounting ever upward, according to St. Paul, from that which is in part to that which is perfect, as in Plato, from beautiful sounds to beautiful forms, from beautiful forms to beautiful thoughts, from beautiful thoughts to that idea of good which mortal eye of man never but in part beheld.

With Polybius and the New Testament we pass within the Roman period. If any one desires to form an idea as to the state of the spoken language about 180 years after Christ, no book will be more useful than Lobeck's edition of Phrynichus' 'Eclogae' and Epitome. It is really astonishing to see how nearly every un-Attic form, against which Phrynichus protests, has established itself in the language of our own day. One may instance such forms as φαγᾶς and φακᾶς, νηρόν, now νερόν, for ὕδωρ, φλούδιον for φλοιός, κρύβω for κρύπτω, ἀπὸ μακρόθεν, a common New Testament and modern pleonasm, λιθάριον, σταθερός, βασίλισσα, γελάσιμον, ζωύφιον (and similar derivatives), ξενιτεύειν, κοράσιον, εὐχαριστῶ, ῥοίδιον for ῥοίδιον.

Passing on to the age of Diocletian let us stop for a few moments to read a Nubian inscription by a king Silco, Corpus Insc. iii. p. 486, which may serve as a type of the Greek spoken at that time in Aethiopia :—

Ἐγὼ Σιλκὼ βασιλίσκος Νουβαδῶν καὶ ὅλων τῶν Αἰθιόπων ἦλθον εἰς Τέλμιν καὶ Τάφιν, ἅπαξ δύο ἐπολέμησα μετὰ τῶν Βλεμμύων, καὶ ὁ θεὸς ἔδωκέν μοι τὸ νίκημα μετὰ τῶν ἐχθρῶν ἅπαξ, ἐνίκησα πάλιν καὶ ἐκράτησα τὰς πόλεις αὐτῶν, ἐκαθέσθην μετὰ τῶν ὄχλων μου· τὸ μὲν πρῶτον ἅπαξ ἐνίκησα αὐτῶν καὶ αὐτοὶ ἠξίωσάν με. ἐποίησα εἰρήνην μετ' αὐτῶν καὶ ὤμοσάν μοι τὰ εἴδωλα αὐτῶν, καὶ ἐπίστευσα τὸν ὅρκον αὐτῶν ὡς καλοί εἰσιν ἄνθρωποι· ἀναχωρήθην εἰς τὰ ἄνω μέρη μου. ὅτε ἐγεγονόμην βασιλίσκος οὐκ ἀπῆλθον ὅλως ὀπίσω τῶν ἄλλων βασιλέων ἀλλὰ ἀκμὴν ἔμπροσθεν αὐτῶν. οἱ γὰρ φιλονεικοῦσιν μετ' ἐμοῦ οὐκ ἀφῶ (cf. ἀφέωνται in New Testament) αὐτοὺς εἰς χώραν αὐτῶν εἰ μὴ κατηξίωσάν με καὶ παρακαλοῦσιν καθεσθῆναι. Ἐγὼ γὰρ εἰς κάτω μέρη λέων εἰμὶ καὶ εἰς ἄνω μέρη αἴξ εἰμί. ἐπολέμησα μετὰ τῶν Βλεμμύων καὶ Πρίμεως ἕως Τέλ[μ]εως ἐν ἅπαξ καὶ οἱ ἄλλοι Νουβαδῶν ἀνωτέρω ἐπόρθησα χώρας αὐτῶν, ἐπειδὴ ἐφιλονείκησαν μετ' ἐμοῦ. οὐκ ἀφῶ αὐτυὺς καθεσθῆναι εἰς τὴν σκιὰν εἰμὴ ὑποκλίνουσί μοι καὶ οὐκ ἔπωκαν νηρὸν ἔσω εἰς τὴν οἰκίαν αὐτῶν. οἱ γὰρ φιλονεικοῦσί μοι ἁρπάζω τῶν γυναικῶν καὶ τὰ παιδία αὐτῶν. For wildness of grammar this inscription is not equalled even by the Revelation of St. John, while for childishness of expression it stands unrivalled. The chief modernisms are ὅλων for πάντων, ἐπολέμησα μετὰ as passim in the Revelation, and ἐποίησα εἰρήνην μετ' αὐτῶν, ἀφῶ for ἀφίημι, ἔπωκαν, a hybrid aorist-perfect like εὕρηκαν and ἑώρακαν in the Septuagint, εὕρηκα and ἔθηκα in modern Greek, and ἔσω εἰς for ἐν, in modern Greek μέσα εἰς.

Other Nubian inscriptions give, as in Romaic, such forms as Ἰούλις for Ἰούλιος, with genitive ἰούλι, του as enclitic for αὐτοῦ, besides every possible extravagance in grammar and every conceivable error in spelling, the latter class of mistakes, however, invariably pointing to the identity of the pronunciation of that age with that of the present day; as ἤλκυσε for εἵλκυσε, τέκνυς for τέκνοις, ἴκωσι for εἴκωσι, ἀρχέως for ἀρχαίως, ἱερέος for ἱερέος.

From the age of Diocletian to the Byzantine Period is but a step, and the history of the development of modern Greek from that time is shortly told. Until the time of Ptochoprodromus, in the eleventh century after Christ, artificial Attic was still the language of literature; but the popular dialect, often referred to by authors, keeps coming from time to time to the surface; especially in such works as the 'Gospel of Nicodemus' (end of fourth century), the 'Apophthegmata Patrum,' 'Acts of the Council of Constantinople,' 536, 'Theophilus Antecessor and Joannes Moschus,' 620, Justinian's 'Constitutiones Novellae,' 565. In the 'Gospel of Nicodemus' and in Justinian we have a number of Latin words, not many of which, however, have survived. One of them, however, ἅρματα for *arma*, is a curious instance of Greek ingenuity in disguising barbarisms; for an 'armed man' is in modern Greek ἁρματωλὸς = ὁπλίτης, on the analogy of ἁμαρτωλός. See Sophocles' 'Glossary of Later and Byzantine Greek,' p. 59 of the Introduction.

The chief modernisms of this period are ὁ ἀββᾶς, τοῦ ἀββᾶ, pl. οἱ ἀββάδες, κοπάδιν for κοπάδιον, the modern κοπάδι (a piece); πολλὰ τὰ ἔτη, as a form of salutation; ἄμβων for βῆμα, ἔνι for ἔστι: and the combination τζ, as τζουμᾶς, τζαγγάρια. At the beginning of a word this is found only in barbarisms; but in all probability the combination existed in certain words even in classical times, as a necessary intermediate stage between the old Attic double σ as in κόσσυφος, and the later Attic ττ as in κόττυφος. It is interesting to know that the vulgar Greek of the present day gives us κότσυφος, or κότζυφος, sometimes pronounced almost κόdζυφος.

I subjoin a short specimen of the popular style adopted in this period from the 'Apophthegmata Patrum:'—

Ἠλθόν ποτε πατέρες εἰς Ἀλεξάνδρειαν κληθέντες ὑπὸ Θεοφίλου τοῦ ἀρχιεπισκόπου ἵνα ποιήσῃ εὐχὴν καὶ καθέλῃ τὰ ἱερά. Καὶ ἐσθιόντων αὐτῶν παρ' αὐτοῦ παρετέθη κρέας μόσχιον. Καὶ ἤσθιον μηδὲν διακρινόμενοι καὶ λαβὼν ὁ ἐπίσκοπος ἐν κοπάδιν ἔδωκε τῷ πλησίον αὐτοῦ γέροντι λέγων, Ἰδοῦ τοῦτο καλὸν κοπάδιν ἐστίν, φάγε ἀββᾶ. Οἱ δὲ ἀποκριθέντες εἶπον, Ἡμεῖς ἕως ἄρτι λάχανα ἠσθίομεν εἰ δὲ κρέας ἐστι οὐ τρώγομεν. Καὶ οὐκέτι προσέθετο οὐδὲ εἰς ἐξ αὐτῶν γεύσασθαι αὐτοῦ. A strange improvement on the Apostolic precept, 'ask no questions, for conscience' sake.' The meanness of the language is in striking harmony with the moral degradation of a religion of meats and drinks usurping the name of Christianity.

The next period in the history of the Greek language may be reckoned from 622, the date of the Hegira, to 1099. We have here before our eyes the transition in literature from the language of the grammarians to the language of the people.

Theophanes (758-806) gives us -άδες as the plural of nouns in -ας, Ἄς λαλήσωμεν for λαλήσωμεν, and ἆς εἰσέλθωσι for εἰσελθόντων. The perfect participle without reduplication, as σιδηρωμένος, καστελλωμένος, πυρπολημένος; ἀπὸ with the accusative, σὺν with the genitive, as well as ἅμα with gen. Malalas, whose age cannot be determined with certainty, gives us in addition -ες for -αι, as Πέρσες for Πέρσαι, ταῖς πλάκαις, metaplastic from ἡ πλάξ, as though it were ἡ πλάκα; κἂν in its modern Greek usage, οἶαι κἂν ἦσαν, 'whatsoever they were like.' Μετὰ with the accusative in the sense of *with*, as the mutilated modern μὲ (?). The nameless biographer of Leo Armenius uses the ending -ουν for -ουσι; ἐκ with the accusative, and εὐγενὸς for εὐγενής. Leo the Philosopher, 886–911, has ἴδικὸς = *proprium*, as in Romaic, and the ending -εσαι for -ει (second pers. sing. passive). Constantine Porphyrogenitus, who wrote all his works, with the exception of the Life of St. Basil, in a style purposely popular, gives us ἀλλάξιμον, gen. ἀλλαξίματος: cf. the form τὸ γελάσιμον, condemned by Phrynichus: μονογενῆ for the vocative of μονογενής; the ending -ικος, proparoxytone (possibly a Latinism); σᾶς for ὑμῶν, τῶν for αὐτῶν, ἵνα for ἕν, εἶσε for εἶ: εἶσε is probably from ἐσσὶ, just as εἶνε is from ἐντί: σου for σοι, as καλή σου ἡμέρα, 'good morning to you:' νὰ for ἵνα, and ἕως with the accusative.

An anonymous writer, known as Theophanes Continuatus, gives us Ἄλυ gen. of Ἅλυς, χρυσὸς for χρυσοῦς: Cedrenus, A.D. 1057, the numeral adverb ἑπτᾶι for ἑπτάκις. This would appear to be a relic of an old instrumental ending. Scylitzes gives us the following specimen of the common dialect, ἐῶ σὲ ἔκτισα φοῦρνε, ἐῶ ἵνα σὲ χαλάσω = in modern Greek ἐγώ σε ἔκτισα φοῦρνε, ἐγώ σε νά (sometimes used for θά) σε χαλάσω. Ἐῶ occurs in modern Greek as a dialectic form, as well as ἰώ, ἰών. Cf. Boeotian ἰών, ἰώνγα. Anna Comnena, who wrote a history of the Byzantine war about the year 1100, gives another example in the following verse:—

Τὸ σάββατον τῆς τυρινῆς,
Χαρῆς Ἀλέξιε, ἐνόησές το,

Καὶ τὴν δευτέραν τὸ πρωί
Εἶπε, Καλῶς γεράκιν μου.

Here we have τὸ σάββατον for τῷ σαββάτῳ, ἐνόησες for ἐνόησας, the enclitic το, χαρῆς for χαρείης used optatively, τὴν δευτέραν for τῇ δευτέρᾳ, Καλῶς as a form of salutation, still common in Greece, and the diminutive γεράκιν for γερόντιον, on the analogy probably of σκυλάκιον, diminutive of σκῦλος, or, properly speaking, of σκύλαξ. Γεράκιν is contracted for γεράκιον, and, in modern Romaic, would appear as γεράκι.

This closes the mediaeval period of Greek literature. The first writer who can be said to have used the popular dialect in its entirety was Theodorus Prodromus, nicknamed Ptochoprodromus; a monk who lived in the reign of the emperor Manuel Comnenus, and addressed to him a series of popular verses, στίχοι πολιτικοί, preserved to us by the grammarian Coray in the first volume of his 'Atacta.' The burden of these verses appears to be the poverty of learned men. They are written with great spirit, and remind us of Juvenal. The Greek language is now emancipated, and begins again to show its native power. We subjoin an extract taken from Mr. Sophocles' book above-mentioned:—

Τὴν κεφαλήν σου, βασιλεῦ, εἰς τοῦτο τί με λέγεις;
Ἂν ἔχω γείτονάν τιναν κέχῃ παιδὶν ἀγόριν,
Νὰ τὸν εἰπῶ 'τι, Μάθε το γραμματικὸν νὰ ζήσῃ;
Παρὰ κρανιαροκέφαλον πάντες νὰ μ' ὀνομάσουν.
Νὰ τὸν εἰπῶ 'τι, Μάθε το τζαγγάρην τὸ παιδίν σου.
Γείτοναν ἔχω πετζωτήν, τάχα ψευδοτζαγγάρην·
Πλὴν ἔνε καλοψουνιστής, ἔνε καὶ χαροκόπος.
Ὅταν γὰρ ἴδῃ τὴν αὐγὴν περιχαρασσομένην,
Λέγει ἂς βράσῃ τὸ κρασὶν καὶ βάλε τὸ πιπέριν·
Εὐθὺς τὸ βράσειν τὸ θερμὸν λέγει πρὸς τὸ παιδίν του
Νά το, παιδίν μου, ἀγόρασε χορδόκοιλα σταμένου,

OF MODERN FROM ANCIENT GREEK.

Φέρε καὶ Βλάχικον τυρὶν ἄλλην σταμεναρέαν,
Καὶ δός με νὰ προγεύσωμαι, καὶ τότε νὰ πετζόνω.
Ἀφ' οὗ δὲ φθάσῃ τὸ τυρὶν καὶ τὰ χορδοκοιλίτζια,.

*   *   *   *   *

Κἂν τέσσερα τὸν δίδουσιν εἰς τὸ τρανὸν μουχρούτιν·
Καὶ παρευθὺς ὑπόδημαν ἐπαίρει καὶ πετζόνει.
Ὅταν δὲ πάλιν, βασιλεῦ, γέματος ὥρα φθάσῃ,
Ῥίπτει τὸ καλαπόδιν του, ῥίπτει καὶ τὸ σανίδιν,
Καὶ λέγει τὴν γυναῖκά του, Κυρὰ καὶ θὲς τραπέζιν·
Καὶ πρῶτον μίσσον (Lat. *missus*) ἐκζεστόν, δεύτερον τὸ
σφουγγάτον,
Καὶ τρῖτον τὸ ἀκριόπαστον ὀφθὸν ἀπὸ μερίου.
Καὶ τέταρτον μονόκυθρον, πλὴν βλέπε νὰ μὴ βράζῃ.
Ἀφ' οὗ δὲ παραθέσουσιν καὶ νίψεται καὶ κάτσῃ,
Ἀνάθεμά με βασιλεῦ καὶ τρισανάθεμά με,
Ὄνταν στραφῶ καὶ ἴδω τον λοιπὸν τὸ πῶς καθίζει,
Τὸ πῶς ἀνακομπόνεται νὰ πιάσῃ τὸ κουτάλιν,
Καὶ οὐδὲν τρέχουν τὰ σάλια μου, ὡς τρέχει τὸ ποτάμιν.
Καὶ ἐγὼ ὑπάγω κ' ἔρχομαι πόδας μετρῶν τῶν στίχων·
Εὐθὺς ζητῶ τὸν ἴαμβον, γυρεύω τὸν σπονδεῖον·
Γυρεύω τὸν πυρρίχιον καὶ τὰ λοιπὰ τὰ μέτρα.
Ἀλλὰ τὰ μέτρα ποῦ 'φελοῦν 's τὴν ἄμετρόν μου πεῖναν;
Πότε γὰρ ἐκ τὸν ἴαμβον νὰ φάγω κοσμοκράτορ;
Ἢ πῶς ἐκ τὸν πυρρίχιον ποτέ μου νὰ χορτάσω;
Ἔδε τεχνίτης σοφιστὴς ἐκεῖνος ὁ τζαγγάρης.
Εἶπε τὸ Κύριε 'λέησον, ἤρξατο ῥουκανίζειν.

The language here is essentially modern Greek, though middle voice appears not quite extinct, as we have προσωμαι, ἤρξατο, &c.; and ν sometimes etymologic, sometimes ιelcystic, is written after a number of words where it is w left out, as ὑπόδημαν, παιδίν. Ἔδε for ἴδε strengthens the mology of ἰδῶ from ἰδοῦ. Οὐδὲν is written for the modern The form ὄντε we have referred to on p. 79.

For the subjoined translation I am responsible:—

'By your own head, O king, I swear, ~~I do not know your meaning.~~
Suppose I have a neighbour now, blessed with a boy in breeches,
Shall I go tell him, "Teach your son his letters for his living"?
Sure all the world would dub me then a most consummate blockhead.
Nay, I should say, "Go, teach your son a bootmaker's profession."
One of my neighbours cobbles shoes, perhaps pretends to make them;
Now there's a famous manager, who understands good living.
No sooner does he see the dawn streaking the sky to eastward,
Than straight he cries, "Let boil my wine, and sprinkle in some pepper."
Scarce has the hot potation boiled, when thus he hails his servant:
"Here boy! a shilling's worth of tripe go bring me from the market:
A shilling's worth of cheese besides, Thessalian cheese, remember.
If I'm to cobble shoes to-day, I first must have my breakfast."
And when the cheese comes with the tripe in dainty little clusters,
Four times they fill him to the brim a mug of vast dimensions.
And then he takes a shoe in hand and cobbles at his leisure.
But when the dinner-time comes round, why then, my lord and master,
Away with last and cobbling-board, the time has come for eating.
"Good wife," he cries, "come lay the cloth, and get the dinner ready.
Bring me the broth, that's the first course, the second is an omelette,
The third a haunch of venison pie, browned nicely in the oven,
A mess of hotch-potch for the fourth; take care it don't boil over."
When all is served and he has washed, and seats himself at table,
Curse me, your gracious majesty, not once, but three times over
If—as I look and contemplate the way he sits at dinner,
Unbuttoning his waistcoat first, to hold his spoon the easier—
It does not fill my hungry mouth with water like a river.
And I; I go and come again, and measure feet for verses,

Now hunting for a short and long, now for two longs together;
And now for two short syllables, with all the other measures.
Alas! what help the measures my unmeasurable hunger?
When, mighty prince, will shorts and longs provide me with a dinner?
Or how with two short syllables am I to fill my belly?
Behold a shoemaker indeed, a skilful craftsman truly;
A blessing asked, he straight proceeds to polish off the victuals.'

CHAPTER VIII.

Dialects of Modern Greece.

PROFESSOR MULLACH divides the existing dialects of modern Greece into six main varieties, besides Tsakonian and Albanian, whose claim to be considered Greek dialects will be separately considered. These six varieties he designates as follows:—1. That of Asia Minor, ἀνατολικὴ διάλεκτος. 2. Chiotic. 3. Cretan. 4. Cyprian. 5. Peloponnesian. 6. That of the Ionian Islands.

1. DIALECT OF ASIA MINOR.

The chief feature of this dialect is the substitution of τ for θ, as τέλω for θέλω, and κ for χ; in general a preference for unaspirated tenues. The dialect of Trapezus seems to have preserved us several Homeric forms, as ἄθε = ἔθεν, and ἆμον = ἦμος: for the substitution of ν for ς we may compare ἴχομες, ἴχομεν, &c., where the ς is first dropt, and then its place filled up by ν ἐφελκυστικόν.

In the same dialect, i. e. of Trapezus, δίκλοπος for ἀπατηλὸς has a very archaic sound. Ἔνι and ἐν still stand for ἐστί, i. e. ἐντί. Ἔλλενος = *robustus*. Ἐξεπάγη appears as ἐχπάγεν, θυγάτηρ as θαγατέρα. 'Κ stands for οὐκ instead of the modern

Greek 'δίν. Κὰ = κάτω. Μαξίλας = ῥάπισμα, perhaps a blow on the mouth, possibly connected with *maxilla*, of which, however, the common modern Greek form is μάγουλον. Οἰνιάριν, from ὄἶς, is in place of the modern κρέας πρόβιον, or προβάτινον. Οὔς stands for ἕως. Πόστιν = δέρμα, cf. πέσκος. Τὸ πρόβαν = τὸ πρόβατον. Ποδεδίζω = δέομαι, cf. γονατίζω.

2. THE CHIAN DIALECT

is said to preserve the Homeric κε, which appears also in Pontus as κες, but I have never been able to discover an example in any of the Chian poems which I have read. 'Αδανὰ is explained by Mullach ἤδη νῦν. Δὰ certainly stands for δὴ in modern Greek, as ἴλα δὰ = exactly ἄγε δή, ἴλα being imperative present from ἐλάω or ἐλάϝω, the root form of ἐλάϝνω = ἐλαύνω. So too κάμε δά, ὄχι δά, (for οὐχὶ δή).

3. THE CRETAN DIALECT

abounds in peculiar forms and archaic usages. In the pronunciation the most marked feature is the sound of κ as *ch* in *cherry* before ε and ι sounds. Ὑσεῖς is said to stand for the modern σεῖς, ἐσεῖς = ὑμεῖς. The omission of the augment and the use of ὁ, ἡ, τὸ as a relative strongly remind us of the Epic and Ionic dialects: e. g.

τὰ κάμαν καὶ τὰ φέραν.
In Epic, τὰ κάμον καὶ τὰ φέρον.

In Cretan we also get the dialectic form μούθε for μήτε.

4. THE CYPRIAN DIALECT

appears, in common with that of Rhodes, to leave out in many instances the semivowels δ and γ, as μεάλος = μεγάλος for μέγας, ἰὼ ἐν τὸ ἀλλάσσω for ἐγὼ δὲν τὸ ἀλλάσσω. Mullach well compares ὀλίος Sicilian for ὀλίγος, ἰών, ἰώνγα Boeotic for ἔγωγε, εἴβω Epic for λείβω, and τοί, ταί for τοδὶ and ταδὶ in the Elian Rhetra. 'Corpus Inscript.' 11. Λίος for ὀλίγος is a Cyprian form. We have also the Pindaric ὄρνιχα for ὄρνιθα, and also βάχος for βάθος. In Μεσαϝουρία, or Μεσαβουρία, the digamma is preserved. Γ stands for the consonantal ἰῶτα, as χωργὰ for χωριά, σαρανταργὰ for [τεσ]σαρα[κο]νταριά. The termination ιον of diminutives appears as ιν, as in Ptochoprodromus and later Roman period (whereas in the common dialect of Greece it appears as ί); e. g. βουνίν, παιδίν, μελίσσιν : also τοῦτον for τοῦτο; cf. in Attic ταὐτὸν for ταυτό, and τοιοῦτον for τοιοῦτο : the latter form belonging also to Herodotus and the Odyssee. Λάμνω stands for ἐλαύνω, as σεμνὸς for σεβνός : π and μ seem also interchangeable, as we get μλοῖον for πλοῖον and πνῆμα for μνῆμα. Ποῦ νὰ ῥέξομεν τώρα ; *whither shall we now tend?* ῥέζομεν being connected with ὀρέγομαι. We get also the metathesis δάρκυα, τρεπνός, for δάκρυα, τερπνός. Τρέπομαι and τέρπομαι are possibly the same root, in which case τρέφω alone would be referable to the Sanscrit *trip, tripáyámi*. This metathesis leads us to connect τάρβος, ταρβέω, ταρβύζω with the modern Greek τραβέω, ἐτράβιξα, *to turn* or *to go away*, which doubtless was the original signification of ταρβέω. In Cyprus as well as in Crete the enclitic seems to be preferred to the proclitic construction, εἰδά τον to τὸν εἶδα.

5. The Peloponnesian Dialect

in general seems to prefer verbs in an uncontracted form, as τιμάω, τιμάεις, τιμάει. It appears to use the nominative for the accusative in such words as ἐφημερὶς for ἐφημερίδα, but this may be a matter of pronunciation only. By a curious metathesis τσῆ stands for τῆς as well as for τούς. This is also found, I believe, in the dialect of the Ionian Islands, and certainly in that of Crete.

In addition to these general divisions, Mullach notices especially the dialect of Thera as peculiarly harsh and singing, and draws attention to the archaism πῶς ἀκούεις for πῶς ὀνομάζεσαι. Δίδωμι, in modern Greek δίδω or διδόνω, appears as δόνω. Τὰ πράτη = τὰ πράγματα, from τὸ πράτος. This must stand for τὸ πράκος, and strengthens the theory of philologers that πραγ-, τὸ πράγος &c. are weakened for πράκ-. Χρηματάω = χρηματέω, which in the common dialect means only, 'I employ myself, spend my time,' &c., as ἐχρημάτησα δύο ἔτη εἰς τὸ γραφεῖόν του, 'I was employed two years at his office,'—is idiomatically used, according to Mullach, for χρησιμεύω, among the Theraeans.

In Cythnus, Psyra, and Chios, εὖντας, εὖντα is used for τίς, τί, which appears to be a transposition for τίνας, metaplastic from τις (compare ὄντα[ς] or ὄντα[ν] for ὅταν); and as such should be written ἴντας, ἴντα. Yet ὄνταν looks very like ὄντε ἂν [χρόνον], especially when we remember that ὄντε = ὅτε occurs, as well as ὄνταν for ὅταν. In Cythnus too the termination νε seems to be added on to certain words with no meaning at all, as χήρα-νε γίνε-νε, μαῦρα φορέθη-νε, i. e. χήρα ἐγένετο, μαῦρα ἐφορέθη, where it would seem we have the archaism of a neuter plural being used with a singular verb. In Cythnus ἔρχομαι makes ἤρχα, instead of ἤρθα or ἦλθα, an additional ground for connecting in one root ἔρθουμαι, ἔρχομαι, ἦλθον, ἦνθον, and ἤρθα.

In Siphnos, Naxos, and Thera, the forms ἔχουσι, εἴχασι are preferred to ἔχουν and εἴχαν. They are also common in Crete.

In Amorgos, Calymnos, and Astypalaea, χ palatal is pronounced as *sh*, e. g. ἔχει *ishi*. The augment is lengthened, as ἤγραφα for ἔγραφον: cf. the common form ἤπια for ἔπιον. The same thing occurs in ancient Greek in θέλω, ἤθελον; and as ἤθελον implies a form ἐθέλω, so probably ἐπίνω, ἐγράφω are obsolete forms from which ἤγραφα and ἤπια have arisen. In these islands ὄτοιμος and ὀλεύθερος occur for ἕτοιμος and ἐλεύθερος. Compare the common form ὄμορφος for ἔμορφος, i. e. εὔμορφος.

In Patmos the Aeolic accent, ἀλήθης, καῦρος, νέρον, κόντα, κάλος, βρόχη, obtains.

In Rhodes, Carpathos, and Calymnos, εἴχνω, ἔειξεν, οὐλεύω stand for δείχνω (i. e. δεικνύω), ἔδειξεν, δουλεύω. Also γνωρίω and συνάω for γνωρίζω and συνάζω, implying the forms γνωρίδ-ω and συνάγω: afterwards, by the insertion of ἰῶτα = y, made into γνωρίδγο, συνάγγο, and hence γνωρίζω, συνάζω.

Here too, as in Asia, κ appears to supplant χ, as ἴκω, στοκάζομαι, ἔρκομαι, τεκνίτης. Here κ may sometimes be the earlier sound. Τέχνη is really aspirated from τέκνη, compare τέκτων, τίκτω, ἔτεκον. So in modern Greek δείκνω becomes δείχνω; διώκνω, διώχνω, and in ancient Greek ἐξαπίνης is contracted to ἐξαίφνης. Ν appears to have an aspirating influence on a preceding tenuis. At the beginning of a word χ sounds like h, as hάρις for χάρις.

In Carpathos we get τέτσαρες for τέσσαρες, an intermediate form between τέσσαρες and τέτταρες, as κότσυφος is between κόσσυφος and κόττυφος: and I cannot doubt the feminine termination ίτσα, common in modern Greek, to be intermediate between ισσα and ιττα, as seen in μέλισσα, μέλιττα, notwithstanding the accent, which may arise in modern Greek from a Doricized Ionicism, i. e. ἴση, ἴτσα.

In Rhodes, α is often weakened to ε, as σιτέριν, σφογγέριν for σιτάριον, σπογγάριον (here too notice the termination ιν), ἔνοιξε for ἄνοιξε; γελανής appears in ancient Greek for γαληνός; γαλήνη plainly means 'the smile of the sea.' Compare too ὕελος, πύελον, πιέζω, and their corresponding forms ὕαλος, πύαλον, πιάζω.

In Carpathos, similarly, we have πεντικὸς and καθέλου for

ποντικός and καθόλου. Ὄλυμπος is called Ἔλυμπος at the present day.

Professor Mullach observes that fewer diminutives are found on the islands than on the mainland: the old forms τράγος, σκύλος, and κριός, have not yielded to τραγί, σκυλί, and κριάρι.

We have now to consider a very singular phenomenon in the shape of the Tsakonian dialect, the language of the inhabitants of the ancient Cynuria. We can at present do little more than state a few peculiar forms and grammatical vagaries on the authority of Professor Mullach. First, then, we have undeniable Doricisms and antique forms which seem to carry us back to that period when Greek had scarcely parted from Latin. As Doricisms (partly Boeotic) let us notice φωνά for φωνή, κτουπῶ for κτυπῶ, cf. γδοῦπος, γδουπῶ in Homer. An apparent tendency to use the vocative for the nominative, as βότσχυ for βότρυς, δεινούμενε for δυνάμενος, καπνέ, ἀετέ, χορέ, which in the forms νόμο, σοφό seems to explain itself partly as a dislike to s as a termination, is paralleled by certain forms in Homeric Greek. Compare ἱππότα, νεφεληγερέτα with the Tsakonian πολίτα, ναύτα, ἐριμήτα, τεχνίτα, προφήτα. Other peculiar forms are as follows:—κρίε = κρέας, ἐκάνου = ἱκάνω, an undoubted archaism; γουναίκα = γυνή, κοῦε = κύων, νιοῦτα = νύκτα, i. e. νύξ, νύχα = δνυχ-s, cf. νύσσω, i. e. νύχγω, πᾶσχα = πᾶσα, ἔνθσχε = ἔνθεν (another archaism), τσχί = τί: φοζούμενος = φοβούμενος, and φύζουμεν = φύγωμεν, cf. φύζω. Ζεῖος stands, according to Mullach, for θεῖος, but he does not inform us for which θεῖος, whether in the sense of *uncle*, or in the sense of *divine*. If it stand for the latter, I should derive it not from θεῖος, but from δῖος, and write ζῖος, which might be compared with ἀρίζηλος and ἀρίδηλος, &c. z stands in Tsakonian instead of κ before ε and ι sounds, which is only to be explained, so far as I see, by assuming that κ was first softened to γ. Thus καὶ, γαὶ = γιὲ = ζέ. Κ is found for π, as κιάνω for πιάνω. Ρ for λ, as γροῦσσα for γλῶσσα. Δάκτυλος becomes δάτυλο, πρόβατα προύατα, the semivowel changing to a vowel, πόδα, ποῦα; θέλω, θέου and τσχέου; δίδω-μι, δίου (observe the tendency, noticed elsewhere in Greek, to drop δ and λ); κύνες becomes κοῦε, κεφαλὴ ζουφάλα, θυμόνω θυμούκου, ἀγαποῦσα ἀγαποῦα; ἄρουρα (another archaism) appears as ἄγουρα; ἄνθρωπος ἄθρωπο, σκιά ζία, ἁρπάζω = ἀβράγω, i. e. ἁρπάγω: γὰ is for γάλα, like κρῖ, δῶ, ἔρι, βρῖ, ἄλφι. Ἄνθε is for ἄρτος, which I have above connected with ἀλθέω, ἀλέθω, ἄλφιτον, ἄλευρον, &c. I therefore dissent from Professor Mullach in regarding ἄνθε as a word unknown elsewhere in the Greek language. Πόρεσχε (= νῦν), to which Dr. Mullach can assign no etymology, appears to me to be evidently πόρρωθεν, i. e. *henceforth, further*, as the Greeks say τώρα πλέον in the 'common dialect, and the Germans *nunmehr*. Ἔνθεν becomes ἔνθσχε, and θέλω τσχέον, therefore πόρρωθεν would naturally become πόρρωθσχεν, while ω and ο, as we have seen, readily become ε, as in κοῦε, καπνέ. We thus get πόρρεθσχεν, the ν of which may of course be dropped at pleasure; and this is quite near enough to πόρεσχε to leave no doubt in my mind as to the derivation. The declension of the pronouns presents us with some very extraordinary phenomena:—

ἐγὼ = ἐσοῦ		ἡμεῖς = ἐνύ, ἐμὺ	
ἐμοῦ	μὶ	ἡμῶν	νάμου
ἐμοὶ	μὶ	ἡμῖν	νάμου
ἐμὲ	ἐνίου	ἡμᾶς	ἐμούνανε

σὺ = ἐκιοῦ, G. τί, D. νί, A. κίου.
Pl. ἐμού, G. νιούμου, D. νιούμου, A. ἐμού.

Of the third person only the following cases are known:—

G. σί, D. τι, A. σι.
Pl., G. and D. σού.

Here ἐκιοῦ is plainly for ἐ-τιοῦ = τιοὺ = τύ. Cf. the Boeotian Λιουσίας for Λυσίας, &c.; for the κ, κιμῶ, &c.

Ἐκεῖνος is declined as follows:—

    N. ἐτείνερε, ἐτειναῖ, ἔκεινι.
    G. ἔτεινου, ἔτειναρι, ἔτεινου.
    D. wanting.
    A. ἔτεινενι, ἔτεινανι, ἔκεινι.

It is difficult to conceive how these words can be accented as Professor Mullach writes them. No less extraordinary is the change from τ to κ in the Nom. and Acc. neuter.

The formation of this declension, so far as it can be traced, is evidently barbarous, and proves to my mind that the Tsakonian is no pure dialect, but a jargon or lingua franca; and I think we shall be able to trace certain Semitic elements in the structure of the conjugation. Here ἐτείνερε seems to me to stand barbarously enough for ἐκεῖνος ὁ, in broad Laconian ἐκείνορ ὁ ἔτειναῖ for ἐκείνα ἡ, and ἐτείναρι still more barbarously for ἐκείναρ ἡ. Yet the ι *may* be in all these cases merely the well-known demonstrative termination; and perhaps in that case ἐτείνερε should be ἐτείνερι.

For οὗτος we get the inexplicable form:—

    N. ἔντερι, ἐνταῖ, ἔγγι.
    G. ἔντου, ἔνταρι, ἔντου.
    D. wanting.
    A. ἔντενι, ἔντανι, ἔγγι.
    Pl. N. ἐντεῖ for all genders.
    A. Masc. ἔντου.

τις and τι = respectively τζί and τζίs or τσχί. Ὅς, ἥ, ὅ, is ὅπουε, ὅπουα, ἔτεινερι; where we have a clear case of barbarism, inasmuch as the masculine and feminine endings ε (for ος) and α are added on to the modern Greek indeclinable relative ὅπου.

Εἰμὶ is conjugated thus in the present, ἔνι, ἔσσι, ἔννι; ἔμμε, ἔτε, ἴννι; and in the imperfect, ἔμα, ἔσα, ἔκι; ἔμμαῖ, ἔταῖ, ἴγκιαῖ.

These forms are hopelessly barbarous, but it is pretty plain that ἔ-κι is formed by adding a fragment of ἐκεῖνος, κεῖ on to the prevailing vowel of the root, while in κι-αῖ we have two suffixes, one to show the third person, the other to mark the plural, viz. ι, which runs all through the imperfect plural, and is probably nothing else than the article οἱ added on. This again is just what we should expect from a Semitic race trying to learn Greek. The further formation of tenses is equally remarkable: ἐγαμῆκα and ἐμποῖκα are formed as a kind of aorist-perfects in Greek fashion, but the present and imperfect are expressed by the participle and the substantive verb joined by the letter ρ, which perhaps stands for σ, in which case we must assume that to simplify matters γράφων became γράφος, Laconian γράφορ, and that ρ was written by analogy after α, where however, agreeably to our theory, it may be optionally left out. What is plain is, that these foreigners who were trying to learn Greek looked at each termination as a separate word, and probably regarded the root γραφ- as in itself the participle, in accordance with Semitic principles of grammar. However that may be, γράφω is in Tsakonian γραφ-ου-ρ-ένι or γραφ-α-ρ-ένι, according as the subject is masculine or feminine, and so forth. The substantive verb may also be prefixed, ἔνι γράφου, ἔνι γράφα, &c. So, too, the imperfect, ἔμα γράφου, or γραφουρέμα, &c.

The present passive is similarly formed: γραφούμενερένι, &c., or ἔνι γραφούμενε, &c., i.e. γραφόμενός ἐστι, &c.

The future is thus expressed: θέου νὰ ἔνι γραφτέ, i.e. θέλω νὰ ἦμαι instead of θέλω εἶσθαι γραπτός; the verbal adjective supplying the place of the perfect participle.

With the periphrastic present and imperfect we cannot avoid

comparing the Spanish *estoy escribiendo*, and drawing attention to the fact that Spanish and Portuguese, the only Neo-Latin languages which were subjected to Semitic influences, are likewise the only ones in which this idiom is found. In Hebrew there is no present tense, and, properly speaking, no imperfect, but the meaning is given by the participle and the pronoun, which are in force exactly equivalent to the participle + substantive verb in an Indo-Germanic language. It is plain that the Tsakonian language did not develope, like other dialects of Greece, in a natural way. It is the language of a foreign race, adopting and adapting the materials of the Greek language, not once and for all, but gradually, partly during the time that Greek was still ancient Greek, and partly after it had become modern. The old Doric forms ἱππότα, ἁ, &c., show that this foreign, as I think Semitic, tribe was settled in Cynuria before dialectic distinctions had been obliterated by the κοινὴ διάλεκτος: yet as we cannot with certainty assert that they ever were quite obliterated, it is hard to say how early or how late the settlement may have been formed. Again, ἱππότα, &c. may not be so old as Homer, for it may only be mutilated for ἱππότας, as all words ending in ς are. But at any rate, the Tsakonian dialect has preserved many ancient Greek words, as ὡρᾶκα for εἶδον, ἐμποίκα for ἔκαμα. Ὁράω and ποιέω are not found in the language of the common people in the present day. Again, the distinction between dative and accusative is still partially preserved. The word ἐκάνου = ἱκάνω seems to take us back nearly to Homer. Τὸ κῶλε for τὸ ξύλον and ἄγουρα = ἄρουρα point back to a time far anterior to the later period of ancient Greek, certainly as far back as heathen times. On the other hand, many of the forms and constructions are plainly corruptions of modern Greek.

That there has been then from time immemorial settled in Cynuria a foreign tribe which has mangled the Greek language, and clung to it in its mangled form with a tenacity which is astounding, I think I may assume has been made out. But what was this foreign tribe? I know of but one people who are capable of doing what the Tsakonians have done, and that people is the Jewish race. They alone choose by a natural instinct the very broadest and harshest dialect of the people among whom they settle; they alone seem capable of giving to each word the most barbarous and mutilated form which the imagination can conceive; they are the only race which, though they live for centuries among strangers, will never learn to speak their adopted tongue correctly. Some Semitic element must certainly be at the bottom of the Tsakonian dialect, and what Semitic race so likely to have founded inland colonies but the Jews? In the Tsakonian words for *brother* and *sister*, ἀθἰ and ἀθία, I cannot but recognise a genuine Hebrew formation. *Brother* in Hebrew is אֲחִי (in the construct form), and אֲחִיָּה seems a possible, though not in classical Hebrew an actual form, for the feminine of אֲחִי, i.e. *sister*. In the plural of the first personal pronoun we see, I think, a grotesque attempt to combine the vowels and consonants of the Hebrew and Greek. In the nominative אֲנוּ *anu*, we have the two forms ἐνὺ and ἐμύ, of which the first form is little more than an iotacized transcription of the Hebrew; while the other has a little more resemblance to the Greek form. The genitive and dative νά·μου, seem to be made up of the Hebrew fragmentary suffix נוּ, and a similar fragment of the Greek ἡμῶν. We have already seen by various examples, as γράφου = γράφων, κιμοῦ = τιμῶν, &c., that ου stands for -ων, and knowing that α = ου, e.g. ἔμα = ἤμουν, we have no difficulty in writing νάμου into the required form νού-μων, at once. In the accusative ἐμούναντ, which could scarcely have attained so extraordinary a length except on some such theory as that here advanced, we seem to have the elements ἐμ-άναχνου = ἐμ-

אֲנַחְנוּ softened first into ἐμάνανον, and then, the final ον becoming weakened into ι, and compensated in the second syllable, ἐμούνανι, and hence ἐμούνανε, the ι being weakened in its turn into ε, as in λέγουνε, εἶνε, &c., &c. The accusative singular ἐνίου is evidently אֲנִי = ἐνὶ and the fragment ου, which is either a part of ἐσοῦ = in Tsakonian ἐγώ, i.e. ἐγγώ = ἐσσώ, or more probably is simply the ending of the first person of verbs in ω which in Tsakonian = ου, and would of course by a Semitic race be regarded as a pronominal suffix, as indeed, in its original form, it really was. The foreigners whose settlement in Cynuria we were supposing, seem to have been rather puzzled by the fact that with the slight difference, unheard perhaps among the Greeks even in very early times, as now, and in any case barely distinguishable to the Semitic ear, between ἠ and ὐ, the first and second persons plural were the same, i.e. ὑμεῖς and ἡμεῖς. Having formed ἐμούνανε = ἡμᾶς, they left out the νάνε, which seemed to them the part of the word most clearly indicative of the first person, and used the mutilated ἐμού for both the nominative and accusative of ἡμεῖς, the more so as ἐμού came nearer their pronominal fragment כָּם than did ἐνί.

The genitive and dative νούμου, seem to be for ἰουμῖν and ἰουμῶν = ὑμῖν and ὑμῶν, but with some prefix, probably לְ and מ = λε and μι: μι regularly becomes ν in Tsakonian, e.g. νία = μία, &c.; while λ might very well become so. In any case the analogy of modernizing Greek would soon make the dative take the same form as the genitive.

The way in which ά (= הָ) is added as a feminine termination on to an indeclinable base, as in ὄπουα, as well as perhaps הִי in ἔτεινaί, the correspondence of the frequently recurring masculine termination ε with זֶה and ου with הָאוּ, all point to a complete confusion of Greek and Hebrew grammar; a phenomenon the more interesting, as I believe it is held by Professor Max Müller to be an impossibility.

I copy out for the perusal of the reader one or two short specimens of the Tsakonian dialect, given by Professor Mullach in his 'Grammatik der Griechischen Vulgarsprache,' taking the liberty to emend his text, where such emendation appears obvious.

1.

Νία γουναῖκα ἔχα νία κόττα · ὅπουα καθαμέρα ἔκι γεννοῦα
Μία γυνὴ εἶχε μίαν κότταν (ὄρνιν) ἥτις. καθημέραν ἐγέννα
ἕνα αὐγό. ἔκι νομίζα ἂν νιδῖ τὰν κόττα πᾶσχε κρίσι θὰ γεννάει
ἐν αὐγόν. ἐνόμιζε ἂν δώσῃ τῇ ὄρνιθι πολὺ κριθίον θὰ γεννᾷ
δυβολαὶ κατ' ἀμέρα ζὲ νὶ ἐμποῖζε. Ἀλλὰ ά κόττα, ἀπὸ
δύο βολὰς καθ' ἡμέραν καὶ τῇ (τὸ) ἔκαμε. Ἀλλὰ ἡ ὄρνις, ἀπὸ
πάσχου πάχου δὲν ἐμπορίζε πλία νὰ γεννάῃ κανένα αὐγό.
πολλοῦ πάχους δὲν ἡμπόρεσε πλέον νὰ γεννᾷ κανέν αὐγό.

The translation underneath is in modern Greek. Note that ἐμποῖζε = ἐποῖκε, as καὶ = ζε.

2.

Περοῦ ἕνα κούε ἀπὸ τὸ ποταμὸ μὲ τὸ κρίε 'ς τὸ τοῦμα
Περῶν εἰς κύων ἀπὸ τὸν ποταμὸν μὲ τὸ κρέας εἰς τὸ στόμα
ζὲ ὁροῦ τάσου (Heb. τάχαθ?) τὸ ύο τὸ [τῇ?] νακόθ-
καὶ ὁρῶν ὑποκάτω τοῦ ὕδατος τὴν ἀπο-
σχασι ἔκι νομίζου ποῦ τὸ κάτω ὁρούμενε ἔκι ἄλλε
σκίασιν = τὴν εἰκόνα ἐνόμιζε πῶς τὸ κάτω ὁρώμενον ἦτο ἄλλος
κούε π' ἔκι ἔχου κρίε σ' τὸ τοῦμα. τότε ἀφῆζε τὸ ἀληθινὸ διὰ
κύων ὅπου εἶχε κρέας εἰς τὸ στόμα. τότε ἀφῆκε τὸ ἀληθινὸν διὰ
νὰ πάρε τὸ ὁρούμενε, καὶ ἔκι ζὲ ἀπὸ τὰ δοὑο στερουτέ.
νὰ πάρῃ τὸ ὁρώμενον, καὶ ἐστερήθη καὶ τῶν δύο.

3. THE LORD'S PRAYER.

Ἀφέγγα [Αὐθέντα ?] νάμου, π' ἔσι 'στὸν οὐρανέ, νὰ ἔνι ἁγιαστέ τὸ οὔνομάν τι, νὰ ναθῇ τὸ θέλημάν τι, νὰ μόλῃ ἁ βασιλείαν τι 'σὰν 'σ τὸν οὐρανέ, ἔζρου ζὲ ἐς τὰν ἰγῆ· τὸν ἄνθε τὸν ἐπιούσιον δὶ νάμου νι [νιν ?] σάμερε· ζὲ ὄφε νάμου τὰ χρίε νάμου καθοῦ ζὲ ἐνὺ ἐμμαφίντε τὸν χρεουφιλῖτε νάμου, ζὲ μὴ νὰ φερίζερε ἐμούνανε 's κειρασμὸ, ἀλλὰ ἐλευθέρου νάμου ἀπὸ τὸ κακό. Notice the archaism μόλῃ. I remember seeing the form ἰγῆν or ἰγιν as a Judaeo-Greek form in a specimen of Hebraistic modern Greek, but where I saw it I cannot now recall to mind. I cannot think of any Greek derivation for ἔζρου: the first part may be the Hebrew אָז. Comparing ἔζρου with καθοῦ, we see that it stands for ἔζρως: cf. also above, ποῦ for πῶς. Ἔζρως would be the Greek writing of אָזראשׁ = *then first; dann erst* German, *tum demum* Lat.; the sense being, 'as in heaven, so afterwards on earth.' The omission of σ in τοῦμα for στόμα is also Hebraistic, the combination στ at the beginning of a word not being tolerated. Observe no Spanish word begins with *st* or *sp*.

On a review of all the evidence, we find ourselves quite unable to say with Dr. Mullach, 'Die Sprache der Zakonen ist für uns ein noch unentwickelter Zweig der ältesten Gestaltung des Hellenismus (!) und ein Schlüssel zu verschiedenen Erscheinungen sowohl der alten und heutigen Dialecte, als der verwandten Sprachen.'

It is true that some light may be thrown on other languages, especially those in a transition state or in a process of amalgamation, by means of the Tsakonian dialect. For the rest we are sure that it can be no primitive or undeveloped form of Greek, because we know that the greater part of Greek accidence was ready made before ever the Greek nation rose into existence.

I cannot agree with the derivation Τσάκωνες from Καύκωνες: κ might become τσ, pronounced almost as *ch* in *church*, before palatal vowels; but I know no instance in Greek of such a change before a guttural vowel. The other derivation, Λάκωνες, is yet more improbable.

In conclusion, I must leave the question to Semitic scholars. I feel confident that the more the matter is investigated, the more clear it will become that Tsakonian is a hybrid production of Greek and some Semitic language; whether Hebrew or not I will leave to others to determine.

I will pass on to consider as briefly as possible the Albanian language in relation to Greek. The popular notion of the Greeks themselves that the Albanians are the ancient Pelasgians, may be after all not very far from the truth. Certain it is, that in Albanian, in spite of its corrupt or modernized state, as seen in the poverty of its case endings, &c., we do undoubtedly find the meeting point of Greek and Latin. Albanian is neither more nor less than modern Graeco-Italic; and no greater service could be rendered to Comparative Grammar than an ideal reconstruction of ancient Albanian.

I can now do no more than barely indicate a few instances of the connection of Albanian with Greek on the one hand, and Latin on the other. First, then, the very alphabet is mixed in Albanian. We have both *d* and *δ* as well as *t* and *θ*; we have again both ε and ē, and *b* as well as β. Besides this we have, as in Sanscrit, a palatal ν written ṅ, and a palatal *r* = ṙ, like *ŕi* in Sanscrit. Again, the palatal γ and κ, which in modern Greek are used only before palatal vowels, have in Albanian an independent existence, like *jă* and *chă* in Sanscrit, which are only modifications of palatal *g* and *k*. In a word, there is a far greater wealth of both vowel and consonantal sounds in Albanian than in Latin and Greek; and it is plain that when Graeco-Latin separated into Latin and Greek, the Greeks took along with them ζ, β and δ, &c., the Latins *b* and *d*, &c., while many sounds, as for example *sh*, *zh*, they left behind them as far as we know altogether.

The fact that we find in Albanian the Greek and Latin sounds combined, proves the general identity of the modern with the ancient Greek pronunciation to something very like demonstration.

To proceed to the grammar. The first thing that strikes us is the preservation in Albanian of the infinitive endings ἔναι, ἄναι, and ἐμέν-αι, corresponding to the Latin substantive terminations *en-i* or *en-e*, and *men-i* or *men-e* : cf. *pecten-e, nomen-e, specimen-e*, &c. In Albanian we have these substantive endings, as in Greek, but the infinitive mood is expressed not by a case-ending or suffix, but a separate word prefixed; e.g. φάν-αι = μὲ θάνουν, λυσέμεν-αι = μὲ λύσουμουν. The termination -ουμουν slightly varied actually appears in Albanian as a substantive ending, e. g. ἄρδεμεν = ἔλευσις, πρεδίκιμεν = *praedicatio*. Albanian gives us again the transition between -μι and ω, in the form ομ, φημὶ = θόμ.

Albanian preserves the ablative termination *t*, which it uses for the genitive case; e.g.

   vdè dìττ tè μρρέτιτ ἱρόditt.

Explanation:—*in(de) diebus* τοῦ *imp'rátov* = *imperatoris* Herodis, with Greek termination η-s for -*or*.

T as the sign of the third person singular in verbs is likewise preserved in Albanian, as θῶτ = φατί = φησί. But this *t* is often weakened into ν, both in the third person singular and the second plural.

I will give a few paradigms illustrating the relation between the verbal terminations in Albanian and Greek.

Present.

θὸμ	= φαμὶ	= φημὶ	θόνα	= φαμὲν	
θούε	= φασὶ	= φῆς	θόνι	= φάτε	
θῶτ	= φατὶ	= φησὶ	θῶν	= φασὶν, i.e. φαντί.	

K

Aorist.

θāξ = ἔφην (ἔφᾱσα).
θᾶν = ἔφασαν.

Imperfect.

θόσ̓τε = ἴ-φασκε.
θώσ̓ιν = ἔφασκον.

Θώσιν in form is to be compared with ἦσαν, Albanian ἦσιν. With θόσ̓τε = ἔφασκε compare ἴστε = ἔσκε.

Ἔρδα = modern Greek ἦρθα, classical ἦλθον; root, perhaps Sanscrit *ard-* 'to come;' ἔρδεμ = ἤλθομεν, ἤρθαμε; ἀρθτ = ἐλθέτω; ἄρδουν = ἐλθεῖν, i.e. ἐλθέμεν.

Εἰμί, &c. = ιάμ, ιέ, ᾶστ, ιένα, ιένι, ιᾶν.

Albanian explains to us the meaning of the termination κα, which is so common in Greek both as an aorist and perfect termination, as we see in ἔ-θη-κα, ἔ-δω-κα, δέ-δω-κα, and in modern Greek in εὔρηκα, ὠράκα (Tsakonian), ἐγράφηκα, &c. In Albanian κὰμ = ἔχω, of which one form seems to have been ἔκω.

Now the perfect in Albanian is thus formed:—

κὰμ	δάνουν		κένα	δάνουν.
κὲ	δάνουν		κένι	δάνουν.
κᾶ	δάνουν		κᾶν	δάνουν.

Literally ἔχω δοῦναι, &c., as in modern Greek ἔχω δώσει. In δέ-δωκα, and ἔ-δωκα, the root of the verb is put for the infinitive, and κὰ = ἔχω is used as a suffix.

The Albanian for *and* is ἔδε, plainly the Homeric ἰδέ and ἠδέ.

Ποῦ and που are in Albanian κου, the original form: τίς and τί are κῖ and κά; Sanscrit *kah, ká, kim,* Latin *qui, quis,* &c.

DIALECTS OF MODERN GREECE.

I will now illustrate the language further by a few sentences and words:—

Ἔρδε μbὲ τί σαγατ, ἴδε τί σαγατ νοῦκ ἐ πρίτέν.
Ἦλθε ἀμφὶ τὰ *sua* ἠδὲ ἰὰ *sua* νη-οὐκ ἐ παρέλαβον.
Οἷ θὰ.
Οἷ ἔφα.

'Ατοῖ = αὐτῷ. Cf. αὐτὰρ and ἀτάρ, modern Greek ἀτὸς and αὐτός.

Οὔδουκ.
Ἐ-δόκ-ει
Οὐδείφτουε.
Ἐ-δείκνυε.
Σὶ ἔρδέν.
Si = ὅτε, ἤρθαν.
Ν*dὲ* ὀτέπη.

Inde σκέπην = ὅτε ἦλθον εἰς τὴν οἰκίαν. Ν*dὲ* appears to be the Latin *indu-*, *indi-*, or *inde-*, and μbὲ *above*, the Latin *ambi*, Greek ἀμφί; μbὶ (= ἐπὶ) is probably only another form of the same word.

Vοειτέν, ἐ-φοίτη-σαν.
Vόρφέν, i.e. Fορφέν = ὀρφανός.
Ν*d*ιίκιν, διώκουν; ν*d*όκέν, ἐδίωκ-σαν.
Βὲτ or Fὲτ = Fέθεν (?).
Κουρfένια = πορνεία, and would suggest an older form, κορβνεία or κορfνεία.
Μ*b*αλαφάκε = ἐν τῷ φανερῷ. The etymology is plainly *in palâ facie* (palus = *open*, implied in *palam*).
Μίκου = *amicus*; νέμίκουν, *inimicum*.
Κούλουτέ = ἀπόλυτοι quasi ἀκόλουτοι (?).
Μὼς *b*άῃς, μὴ ποιῇς.

"Ασπακ, ἅπαξ (?).
Οὐ-ϧάφτ, ποιηθήτω.
Δέου = γαῖα, δαῖα, γῆ.
'Ατιέ, ἐκεῖ.
Βιέδιν, βιάζουσιν, βιάζουν.
Κρίλε, κάρα.
Πούλ = ἐγέννησε. In modern Greek πούλος is a patronymic termination. Cf. Latin *pullus*, Greek πῶλος, also *-pulus* in *disci-pulus*, Albanian διϧἔπουλι.

The word for God in Albanian is Πέρνδια Πέρνδι, gen. Πέρνδιε or Πέρνδιστέ, acc. Πέρνδινέ. Does this word contain the same elements as *Diespiter*, reversed?

The view that δειλινόν and ἥλιος are connected is somewhat strengthened by the Albanian for ἥλιος, which is δίλι. "Ετος is in Albanian Fίτ, cf. Latin *vetus*, Sanscrit *vatsas*. Fίτ becomes in the plural Fιἔτϧ.

It is interesting to find in the modern Greek ἐφέτος, i.e. ἐπὶ ἔτος, the relic of the F in the form of the aspirate. In 'Ενιαϝτός, ἀϝτός is probably only transposed for Fατός, and this helps us to understand Fέhτεν, the Albanian for αὐτόν in ἑαυτόν, ἐ Fέhτεν being equal to ἐ-αὐτόν. I have written β here and elsewhere as F, because it seems almost always to represent that letter. But the literal changes in Albanian seem by no means regular: *h* for instance represents sometimes χ, and sometimes φ, though it must be borne in mind that these letters are interchangeable in Greek. Thus we have *hῑρ*, χάρις; *hερέ*, φορά; *ἀτέ-hερέ* = αὐτῇ φορᾷ, i.e. νῦν, *dü hερέ* δύο φοράς, modern Greek for δίς. Also *ha* τρώγω, connected with root φάγ-; *hάγρουν*, φαγεῖν. (Is *hunger* connected with this form?)

Two Latin particles receive great light from Albanian, viz. *re* and *se*. 'Pέ in Albanian means *new*, and σ'. in composition σέ, means *not*, e.g. σ'μούνδετ, οὐ δύναται, σέμουνδέ = ἀδύνατοι, i.e. ἀσθενεῖς, ἄρρωστοι, νοσοῦντες.

DIALECTS OF MODERN GREECE.

A passive verb is changed into an active in Albanian by prefixing the syllable ού, e.g. δάνουν = δοῦναι, οὐδάνουν = δοθῆναι.

The future tense is formed, like the perfect, by means of κὰμ (= ἔχω) and the infinitive, but in the future the preposition μὲ is inserted: examples, κὰμ μὲ πέργιάίτουν, ὁμοιώσω, κὰμ περγιάίτουν ὡμοίωκα, κὰμ μὲ οὐπεργιάίτουν, ὁμοιωθήσεται.

The pronouns in Albanian present some very remarkable phenomena:—

Greek.	Albanian.
N. ἐγών, ἰὼν	οὐν.
A. μὲ	μέ enclitic, μοῦε emphatic.
G. μοῦ, μεῖο	μέγε, μέγει.
D. μοὶ	μέ, μέγε.

With the plural it is better to compare the Latin:—

N. nos	νά.
A. nos, Sanscrit naḥ	νά, emphatic νέ.
G. Sanscrit naḥ	νέ.
D. nobis, Sanscrit naḥ	νέfε, enclitic νά.

In this νέfε, written also with the ablative termination νέfεr, we have the Latin *bis* or *bus*, the Sanscrit *bhiḥ*, the Greek φι; or rather we have the Sanscrit *bhi*, the common element in *-bhiḥ, -bhyam, -bhyaḥ*, &c., for ν- has not only a dative, but more often an ablative, i.e. genitive force, as in ἀτύνεfε = ἐκείνων, τὲ Γιούδέfεr, τῶν Ἰουδαίων.

Greek.	Albanian.	Sanscrit.	Albanian.
N. Σύ, τύ	τὶ	*yúyam*	*yoû*.
A. Σὲ	τὲ	*yushmán*	*yoû*.
G. τεῖο	τέγε, τέγετ	Gen. *yushmákam*	*yoûš*.
D.	τὰ, and τέγε	Dat. *yushmabhy-am*	*yoû-fε*.

Αὐτῆς is in Albanian ἀσᾶι, which in signification is as often dative as genitive. This comes very near the Sanscrit *asyáh* (gen.), *asyai* (dat.). The nominative is ἄyŏ, cf. Sanscrit *iyam*. Κἰτέ, τοῦτο may be compared with haec-*ce*, *ci*-tra.

The possessive pronouns are extremely puzzling. Ὥρα ἴμε (= ὥρα ἐμή) seems straightforward enough; but when we come to Ἄτι γοῦί, of which the genitive is Ἄτιτ τοῦ, we see that the possessive pronouns have the peculiarity of taking the case-endings as prefixes, instead of suffixes. This same case-ending τ appears in the possessive pronouns to be accusative, as well as genitive or ablative in force. Is not this so also in the Latin personal pronouns *tete*, *nosm-et*, *vosm-et*? Examples in Albanian are, Fέλᾱ ἷτ, ἀδελφός σου, τῦτ-fέλᾱ ἀδελφῷ σου, ἀδελφόν σου. But this is not all: not only are the case-endings prefixed, but sometimes, at least, the differentiating signs of gender also; so that nothing remains of the original pronoun but a single consonant. Thus ἷτ = σός, γότε = σή. That *yo* is a feminine termination we have seen in ἄyŏ, *she*, *it* we have in κίι = οὗτος. Υότε seems moreover to have a double feminine termination, if we regard ἴμε as = ἐμή. Υότια is plural, and, so far as I can see, for all genders.

Ἐμὴν is τέμε; ὑμετέραν, τούγέη and τοῦι; ἐμά, ἐμία; ἡμέτερος, ὗν and ὕνε; ἡμετέραν, τῶν or τόνί; ἡμέτερα, τόνα; ἡμετέρων, τῶν.

Internal changes of the vowel sound also take place, as Ἰμ-ἅτ πατήρ μου, τέ τιμ-έτ τοῦ πατρός μου, τεμ-ἅτ πατέρα μου. When, however, the possessive pronoun is used substantively, it has a much simpler form, as

γίθε τέ μίατ λᾶν τέ τίατ
πάντα τὰ ἐμὰ εἰσὶν τὰ σά.

For the oblique cases of σός, one form used is τάνδ and τάνδε, of which τάνδε appears to be the feminine. The difference between τάνδε and τῦτ seems to be that the one is used with a preposition, the other with a verb, as μὲ τῦτ-fέλᾱ (μὲ τὸν ἀδελφόν σου in modern Greek), but Doùi fίκινέ τάνδ, ἴδε

DIALECTS OF MODERN GREECE. 135

ki μενϊ ἀνέμἰκουν τάνd, i.e. *Ames vicinum tuum et oderis inimicum tuum.*

We will conclude this account of the Albanian language with a few prepositions and numerals:—

Μὲ = *with*, modern Greek μέ and μὰ, ancient Greek μὰ, μὰ τὸν Δία.
Πρέϊ = *from*, Greek παρά.
Πέρ = *through*, Latin *per*.
Κούνδέρ = *contra*.
Νdὲ = *in*, Latin *indu-*, *indo-*, Greek ἔνδο- and ἔντο-.
Μδὲ and μδὶ = *on*, Latin *ambi* (?), Greek ἀμφί.
Σιπέρ = *super*.

1. νὶ, f. νῖ.
2. dü.
3. τρὲ, f. τρί.
4. κάτερ.
5. πέσε.
6. γιάστε.
7. ὀτάτε (Sanscrit *sápta*).
8. τέτέ.
9. νάνdέτ.
10. δέτέ.
11. νιμbεδέτέ, i.e. εἰς κ.τ.λ. ἐπίδεκα.
12. düμbεδέτέ.
20. νίζετ.
30. τρίδετέ,
40. κατερδέτέ.
50. πεσεδέτέ, &c.
100. κίνd, Latin *centum*.
1000. μίy.

It is observable here that Latins, Greeks, and Albanians count together as far as 10, although the form νάνdέτ presents some difficulty. Afterwards, however, the agreement ceases. Latin and Greek coincide in 11 and 12, but the exact coincidence goes no further. Where the ancient Greeks said τρεισκαίδεκα the Romans said *tri-decem*. The agreement between Latin and Greek is, however, resumed in *viginti*, είκοσι = είκοντι or ϝείκοντι; while in Albanian, *νί-ζετ* is plainly a different formation, and seems to be compounded of νι-, *one*, and ζέτ, which must mean a *score*, whatever its derivation. Afterwards, τρίδετέ, &c. = not τρί + δέτέ, but τρι × δέτέ, and so on. Yet the coincidence is again resumed in κίνδ = *centum*, and μίγ = *mille*. The fact is, numerals after 10 afford no historical evidence as to the independence of different races, though their agreement, however occasional, does supply most indubitable proof of their having sprung from one stock.

The same race may have two modes of counting beyond 10, and one may be more fashionable than the other, or both may meet with equal favour. The ancient Greeks themselves said δεκαπέντε as well as πεντεκαίδεκα, and the modern Greeks say not only δεκαπέντε, but δεκατρείς, δεκατέσσαρες, δεκαεπτά, δεκαοκτώ, δεκαεννέα. In the Teutonic languages 11 and 12 exhibit a similar divergence, while in English we say twenty-three, three and twenty, sixty or three score, &c. French, Italian, and Spanish count together as far as 60, after which they diverge, though only to coincide again afterwards. The numerals, therefore, give us no grounds for doubting our original hypothesis, that Albanian presents us, in a mutilated shape, with the Graeco-Italic language before it had split into Greek and Italic.

With regard to νάνδε or νάνδετ, I question whether we have not the same word in the Latin *nundinae*, *-inae* being simply a termination. With regard to the derivation of *νίνδετ*, I would suggest that as *ûnavimśati* in Sanscrit means *less than twenty*, i.e. *nineteen*, so *ûnadaśa* might be another form for *nine*, of which ἀνδετέ or ἀνδετ might be a contracted form. The influence of the ν would naturally convert δ into d, and we should then get ἀνδετ = 10, rendered more definite in Albanian by the prefix νὶ = 1, hence νάνδετ, νάνδετ.

We have already seen that Albanian preserves many of the Sanscrit forms which Latin and Greek have lost, and we will conclude this rapid sketch with one more example.

In Sanscrit, the two words *anya* and *itara* are used respectively in the sense of 'the one' and 'the other,' being combined in the compound *anyatara*, 'either.' Now in Greek we have ἕτερος, and in Latin *caeterus*, both of which words *may* contain the same root as *itara*. But in Albanian we have both, opposed to each other, in νι-άνι, 'the one,' and τι-έτρι, 'the other;' the prefix being in one case the indefinite, in the other the definite article. Here, too, we find νι actually added to ἄνι, just as we have supposed it to be added to ἀνδετ.

CHAPTER IX.

Modern Greek Literature.

We must distinguish, in the outset, between modern Greek literature and the literature of the modern Greeks. The name of modern Greek literati is legion, but the names of those who wrote anything worthy of record in modern Greek before the present century are very few. It is with the latter alone that we are at present concerned.

The first modern Greek writer was Theodorus Ptochoprodromus, 'the heaven-sent poor forerunner' of modern Greek literature, a satirist of no mean power, whose happiest verses were extorted by the pangs of hunger. A specimen of his style concludes Chapter VII. His date is given by Mr. Sophocles as 1143—1180.

Almost contemporary with him was Simon Sethos, a chronicler, who is the first *prose* writer in modern Greek.

Next in order comes the 'Book of the Conquest of Romania and the Morea,' or Τὸ πῶς οἱ Φράγκοι ἐκέρδησαν τὸν τόπον τοῦ Μωρέως, supposed by Buchon (in the second volume of his 'Recherches Historiques') to be a translation from a French account of the same events. Elissen ably controverts this opinion by a comparison of the two works, in which he fully justifies the superior reputation of German over French criticism. The 'Book of the Conquest' may be best described as a rhyming chronicle, which might deserve the name of poor verse were it not so prosaic, or of bad prose were it not written in metre. It belongs to the fourteenth century.

To the same period probably belongs the poem entitled 'Belthandros and Chrysantza,' a romance of knight-errantry, in which we can plainly trace the effects of the crusades in Greece. The heroes of Greece are henceforth knights-errant, but the Greek of the age is so far true to himself as to be more susceptible of chivalrous than religious enthusiasm. The mistress of his heart is very prominent, while Mother Church is kept quite in the background. The plot of 'Belthandros and Chrysantza' is simple but imaginative. The hero is Belthandros (a Graecism for Bertram), the son of Rhodophilus, king of Romania, who has two sons, Bertram and Philarmus, one of whom he loves, and the other of whom of course he hates. Belthandros, the unfortunate object of his father's displeasure, accordingly takes a journey eastward, and after heroic exploits performed at the expense and on the persons of his father's men-at-arms, who are dispatched to bring him back, he reaches Armenia, and the fortress of Tarsus. Riding by the side of a small stream, he espies a gleam of light in the running waters, and follows up the course of the rivulet a ten days' journey. It leads him to a magic building called the Castle of Love, built of precious stones, and surrounded and filled with every imaginable form of wonder in the way of automaton birds and beasts of gold, reminding us of Vulcan's workmanship. Then follows an introduction to the King of the Loves, the owner of the enchanted palace, who gives him the task of choosing the most beautiful out of forty women. He first selects three, and having thus equalized the problem to that which Paris had solved of old, he proceeds to award the palm to Chrysantza, who turns out to be the daughter of the King of Antiochia, and whose subsequent appearance at the Court of Rhodophilus reconciles the father, and terminates the story with the slaying of the fatted calf.

The following is an attempt to render the metre and the meaning of some of the most beautiful lines in this unequalled poem:—

> 'Thus then together journeying, they reached the Turkish border:
> This passed anon, they entered next upon Armenia's frontier;
> And last of all approached the town of Tarsus, and its stronghold.
> And while Belthandros wandered through the country with his followers,
> He found a rivulet, and lo! beheld among its waters
> A sheen as of a falling star that leaves its track in heaven.
> There in the water's midst it gleams, and he in haste pursues it:
> Stream-upwards he betakes him, if perchance he may discover
> Whence erst was born that liquid flame that glitters in the streamlet.
> Ten days' full space he wandered on, and when the tenth was ended,
> He found a castle large and high, and goodly was the vision,
> Of pure sardonyx well hewn out, most cunningly proportioned.
> And high upon the summit of that fair and shining building,
> In place of catapults were ranged a marvellous assemblage
> Of heads of griffins carved in gold, full curiously fashioned,
> Wrought by a cunning master's hand, with great and wondrous wisdom:
> And from their open jaws amain, most direfully resounded
> Furious and terrible and shrill a grimsome noise of roaring;
> And thou wouldst say they moved as though the breath of life were in them.'

The imaginative power and mastery of language which the author shows, bespeak a genius of the highest order. Like many another genius, he is among the nameless dead.

His creative power reminds us sometimes of the 'Divina Comedia,' sometimes of the second part of 'Faust.' Even his *sesquipedalia verba*, or, as the Greeks call them, λέξεις σχοινοτενεῖς, rather excite our admiration by the boldness and the beauty of their composition, than our impatience by their length. Ῥοδοκόκκινος, στρογγυλομορφοπήγουνος, μοιρογράφημα, σωματούργησες, ὁλοσωματωμένη, οὐρανόδρομος, κρυφοκάμωμα, however they might raise the bile of a Phrynichus, have a power of harmony and a perfection of taste for which that poor pedant had neither eyes nor ears.

Did the modern Greek language possess but this single Epic, to say that it is destitute of literature were a calumny indeed.

The next writer we shall notice is Emmanuel Gorgilas, who forms the bridge between the Byzantine and the Turkish period of modern Greek literature. He was a native of Rhodes, and lived at the time of Constantinople's fall.

The following works are attributed to him:—

1. Διήγησις εἰς τὰς πράξεις τοῦ περιβοήτου στρατηγοῦ τῶν Ῥωμαίων μεγάλου Βελισαρίου (ἐξεδόθη ἐν Βενετίᾳ τῷ 1554 ὑπὸ Φραγκίσκου Ῥαμπατσέτου εἰς 4 τόμους), in which Belisarius appears as an almost mythical character, a kind of Alexander redivivus, upon whom every kind of possible and impossible exploit is fathered. The work is metrical.

2. Τὸ θανατικὸν τῆς Ῥόδου (ἀνέκδοτον ἐν τῇ Παρισιανῇ βιβλιοθήκῃ).

3. The celebrated Θρῆνος τῆς Κωνσταντινουπόλεως, which has been compared by its admirers to the Iliad; whether from its length or from its merits, I am unable to say. The latter, and fortunately the former also, fall far short of that great original. A certain well sustained glow of patriotism, and a prophetic yearning of hope, are its only claims to be considered in any sense a poem, and even these features are not sufficient to redeem it from wearisomeness. For curio-

's sake I will give two short extracts, the one from the
jvos, and the other from the Θανατικὸν τῆς 'Ρόδου.

I.

Τὸν Τοῦρκον ἂν ἀφήκετε τὴν πόλιν νὰ κρατήσῃ,
Θέλει γὰρ πάλιν τὸ θεριὸν καὶ θέλει δυναμώσει,
Καὶ θέλει καταπ'τεῖ πολλοὺς ὁ σκύλος ὡσὰν δράκος·
Λοιπὸν πανυψηλότατοι αὐθέντες μου ῥηγάδες,
'Αγάπην ὅλοι κάμετε νὰ πᾶτε 'στοὺς ἐχθρούς σας,
Καὶ τὸν σταυρὸν σηκώσετε σημάδι στ' ἅρματά σας,
Νᾶνεν ἐμπρὸς καὶ 'πίσω σας σημάδι 'στὰ κορμιά σας·
Νὰ βγάλλετε τοὺς ἀσεβεῖς ἀπὸ τὰ γονικά σας,
Μέσα ἀπὸ τὰ σπίτια σας, κ' ἀπὸ τὰ γονικά σας.

II.

Αἱ πικραμὸς, αἱ συμφορὰ πόσονε τὸ κακό μου·
'Αφῆκε με τὸν Γεωργιλᾶν καὶ Γεώργι τὸν υἱόν μου.
Κ' ἔπινον, πίνω, καὶ νὰ πιῶ ὁλονῶν (= ὅλων) ταῖς πικράδαις·
Καὶ δύο καὶ τρία ὀρφανὰ ἀπὸ κόρην καὶ μανάδες,
Παιδιὰ ἀπὸ τὰ μέλη μου, καὶ ἀπὸ ταῖς ἀδελφάδες.
Καὶ κλαίω πῶς ἐγδέχουνται μῆνες καὶ ἑβδομάδες.
Τέτοιαις (τοίας) δὲν θέλουν νὰ διοῦν (νὰ ἴδωσι) ἀλλ' οὐδὲ νὰ γευθοῦσι,
Διότι ὥστε νὰ λυπηθοῦν, πολλὰ νὰ πικραθοῦσι.

One scarcely knows whom most to commiserate, the man
the poet.
In the sixteenth century we have no poet of eminence.
kobos Triboles is a writer of most wretched doggerel.
There were always plenty of preachers, like Cyrillus
ucaris, Meletius, &c., but their works have not for the most
ırt come down to us. Almost the only examples of
odern Greek in the sixteenth century consist of letters and
agments of speeches, chiefly the utterances of ecclesiastics.

The great work of the seventeenth century is one which almost unknown: the work of one Chortakes, a Cretan; titled 'Erophile,' and written in the Cretan dialect. It is a gedy, and opens with a monologue of Charon, the impernation of Death, who speaks as follows:—

'Η ἄγρια κ' ἡ ἀνελύπητη κ' ἡ σκοτεινὴ θωριά μου,
Καὶ τὸ δρεπάν' ὅπου βαστῶ, καὶ ταῦτα τὰ γυμνά μου
Κόκκαλα, κ' ἡ πολλαὶς βρονταὶς, κ' ἡ ἀστραπαὶς ὁμάδι,
Ὅπου τὴν γῆν ἀνοίξασι, κ' ἐβγῆκ' ἀποῦ τὸν Ἅδη,
Ποιὸς εἶμαι μοναχά τωνε[1] δίχως μιλιὰ μποροῦσι
Νὰ φανερώσουν σήμερον 'ς' ὅσους με συντηροῦσι[2].

* * * * * *

Ἐγώμαι κεῖνος τὸ λοιπὸν ἀπ' ὅλοι με μισοῦσι,
Καὶ σκυλοκάρδη καὶ τυφλὸ κ' ἄπονον με λαλοῦσι.
Ἐγὼμ' ἀποῦ τζὴ βασιλεὺς[3], τζὴ 'μπορεμένους οὐλους,
Τζὴ πλούσιους κ' ἀνήμπορους, τζ' ἀφέντοις καὶ τζὴ δούλους,
Τζὴ νέους καὶ τζὴ γέροντας, μικροὺς καὶ τζὴ μεγάλους,
Τζὴ φρόνιμους καὶ τζὴ λωλοὺς, κ' ὅλους ἀνθρώπους τζ' ἄλλους,
Γιαμὰ, γιαμὰ ὄντε[4] μοῦ φανῇ ρίχνω καὶ θανατόνω,
Κ' εἰς τὸν ἀθὸ[5] τζὴ νιότης τους τζὴ χρόνους τους τελειόνω.
Λυόνω τζὴ δόξαις καὶ τιμαὶς τὰ 'νόματα μαυρίζω·
Τζὴ δικιοσύναις διασκορπῶ, καὶ τζὴ φιλιαὶς χωρίζω,
Τζ' ἄγριαις καρδιαὶς καταπονῶ, τζὴ λογισμοὺς ἀλλάσσω,
Τζ' ὀλπίδες ρίχνω 'ς μιὰ μεριὰ, καὶ τζ' ἔγνοιαις[6] κατατάσσω·
Κ' ἐκεῖ ποῦ μὲ πολὺ θυμὸ τὰ 'μάτια μου στραφοῦσι,
Χώραις χαλοῦν ἀλάκαιραις[7], κόσμοι πολλοὶ βουλοῦσι.

μοναχά τωνε, by themselves; so ποτέ μου, in my life; μόνος μου, by self; further down ποτέ τους: a peculiar modern Greek idiom.
συντηροῦσι, observe, for the more common παρατηροῦσι.
τζή βασιλεύς, i. e. τοὺς βασιλέfς, contracted for τοὺς βασιλέfας.
Γιαμά, γιαμά ὄντε, as soon as; etymology δι' ἄμα ὄντε (χρόνον).
Ἀθό, the ancient ἀθήρ with a different termination.
ἔγνοιαις = ἔννοιαι.
ἀλάκαιραις, Cretan for ὁλόκληραι. Italian and Albanian both offer

Ποῦ τῶν Ἑλλήνω ἡ βασιλειαίς; ποῦ τῶ Ῥωμιῶν ἡ τόσαις
Πλούσιαις καὶ μπορεζόμεναις χώραις; ποῦ τόσαις γνώσαις;

*   *   *   *   *

Φτωχοὶ στὸ λάκκο κατοικοῦν, βουβοὶ μὲ δίχως[8] στόμα
Ψυχαὶς γδυμναὶς[9] δὲν ξεύρω ποῦ στὴ γῆ λιγάκι χῶμα.
Ὦ πλήσια[10] κακορρίζικοι καὶ γιάντα δὲ θωροῦσι
Τζὴ μέραις πῶς λιγαίνουσι, τζὴ χρόνους πῶς περνοῦσι;
Τὸ ψὲς[11] ἐδιάβη, τὸ προχθὲς πληὸ δὲν ἀνιστορᾶται,
Σπίθα μικρὴ τὸ σήμερο στὰ σκοτεινὰ λογᾶται.
Σ' ἕναν ἀνοιγοσφάλισμα[12] τῶν ἀμματι' ἀποσώνω
Καὶ δίχως λύπησι καμιὰ πᾶσ'[13] ἄνθρωπο σκοτώνω·
Τὰ κάλλη σβύνω, κ' ὄμορφο πρόσωπο δὲ[14] λυποῦμαι,

some analogy, e. g. κλαίω, κλά-μεν, Albanian κιάμουν, Latin cla-mare, Italian chiamare.

[8] μὲ δίχως, the μὲ is pleonastic; compare the English without, and the vulgar German heard only in London, mitaus, e. g. 'Ich gehe aus, mitaus Sie zu mir kommen,' instead of 'ohne dass Sie zu mir kommen.'

[9] γδυμναὶς, for γυμναὶς. If this be the oldest form of the word, it points to the derivation γδύω, vulgar modern Greek for ἐκδύω, being, in fact, a participial adjective: for the accent, compare δεξαμενή (a reservoir), which is nothing but a participle used as a substantive. With γδύω for 'κδύω one may compare γδοῦπος for κδοῦπος, i. e. κτοῦπος = κτύπος.

[10] πλήσια = μάλα, same root as πίμπλημι, &c. κακκορρίζικοι, ill-fated. τὸ ῥίζικὸ is modern Greek for Fate, generally derived from risebio Italian; but neither the accent, the form, nor the sense, agree with this derivation. The idea seems rather to be the same as in πεπρωμένον, εἱρμαρμένη, 'that which is deep fixed like a root in the ground,' ῥίζα.

[11] τὸ ψὲς, yesterday evening; formed on the analogy of χθές, the root being ψε, as in ὀψέ, ἀπόψε, ὀψιμαθής, &c.

[12] ἀνοιγοσφάλισμα, from ἀνοίγω and σφαλίζω, i. e. ἀσφαλίζω, to make fast, hence to shut.

[13] πᾶσα, for πάντα, as -ασι for -αντι, -ουσι for -οντι, &c.

[14] δὲ, for δὲν = οὐ; either contracted for οὐδέν, or the word δὲν (neuter of δεὶς) used negatively, as is the case in modern Greek with τίποτε, ποτέ, κανέν, διόλου, and in French with jamais, du tout, &c.

MODERN GREEK LITERATURE.

Τοὺς ταπεινοὺς δὲ λεημονῶ, τοὺς ἄγριους δὲ φοβοῦμαι.
Τοὺς φεύγουν[15] φτάν' ὀγλήγορα, τοὺς μὲ ζητοῦν μακραίνω,
Καὶ δίχως νὰ μὲ κράζουσι συχνὰ τζὴ γάμους 'μπαίνω.

* * * * * *

Φτωχοὶ τ' ἁρπᾶτε φεύγουσι, τὰ σφίγγετε πετοῦσι,
Τὰ περμαζόνετε σκορποῦν, τὰ κτίζετε χαλοῦσι.
Σὰ σπίθα σβύν' ἡ δόξα σας, τὰ πλούτη σας σὰ σκόνη
Σκορπούσηνε καὶ χάνονται, καὶ τὄνομά σας λυόνει
Σὰ[16] νᾶτον μὲ τὸ χέρι σας γραμμένο εἰς περιγιάλι
Στὴ διάκρισι τζὴ θάλασσας, γὴ[17] χάμαι[18] στὴν πασπάλη.

His apostrophe to Joannes Murmures, a celebrated lawyer and a friend of the poet, is quite in the spirit of Dante or of Lucretius:—

Σ' ἐδιάλεξα εὐγενέστατε Μουρμούρ' ὑψηλοτάτε,
'Ρήτορα 'π' ὅλαις τζ' ἀρεταῖς καὶ τζὴ τιμαῖς γεμάτε,
Μὲ τὄνομά σου τοῦτο μου τὸν κόπον νὰ στολίσω,
Καὶ χάρι ἀπὸ τζὴ χάραις σου πλήσα νὰ σου χαρίσω.
Γιατὶ ὅσο σὲ θωρῶ ψηλὸ, σὲ βλέπω κἄλλο τόσο
Μὲ σπλάγχνος ἀνεξίκακο, κἄμετρη καλοσύνη.
Κεῖσαι 'π τὴν 'περηφάνησι μακρὰν τοῦ κόσμου κείνη
Τὴ σκοτεινὴ, ποῦ δὲ γεννᾷ λάβρα, οὐδὲ φῶς χαρίζει
Μὰ τζίκνα[19] μόνο καὶ καπνὸ τὰ τρίγυρα γεμίζει.

---

[15] Τοὺς φεύγουν, i.e. οὓς φεύγουσι, for οἱ φεύγουσι. A curious instance of attraction, rare in ancient Greek, from the nominative to the accusative.

[16] Σὰ='σαν, i.e. ὡσάν.

[17] γή, Cretan (also Chian) for ἤ.

[18] χάμαι, Cretan for the modern χάμον, the ancient χαμαί. The accent need not perplex us, as the reader will perceive the accentuation in Crete is extremely variable and uncertain, and often diverges from the usual system. A little further down we have ἄνεμοι for ἄνεμοι.

[19] τζίκνα, a curious corruption and metathesis for κνίζα. Κνίζα itself, however, seems to be a mere onomatopoeic form, like *sniff*, *snuff*, *schnupfen* (Germ.), &c., and τζίκνα may be the same.

*   *   *   *   *   *

Γίν' ὁδηγὸς τζὴ στράτας μου, νὰ φύγω τοῦ χειμῶνα
Τζ' ἀνεμικαῖς, κ' ὡς πεθυμῶ ν' ἀράξω στὸ λιμιῶνα,
Γιατὶ ὅσαις θέλουν ταραχαῖς, κ' ἀνέμοι νὰ γερθοῦσι,
Κ' ὅσα φουσκώσουν κύματα, στὸ βράχος δὲν μποροῦσι
Ποτέ τους νὰ μὲ ῥίξουσι, γ' ἀλλοιῶς νὰ μὲ ζημιώσου,
Θωριῶντας μόν' ὡς Ἄστρο μου λαμπρὸ τὸ προσωπύ σου.
Κἂν εἶναι κἀποκότησα[20] χάρισμα νὰ σου δώσω,
Ἄξιο, καθὼς ἐτύχαινε, καλὰ[21] δὲν εἶναι τόσο,
Τζὴ Τύχης δὸς τὸ φταίσιμο, κὄχι τοῦ θεληματου·
Γιατὶ ψηλαῖς τζὴ πεθυμιαῖς πᾶσα καιρὸν ἐκράτου.
Μὰ κείνη χάμαι τζ' ἔρριξε, καὶ τὰ φτερὰ ποῦ σῶνα
'Σ' ὄρος νὰ μ' ἀναιβάσονσι ψηλὸ ποῦ τ' Ἑλικῶνα
Μοῦ κόψ' ὄντα ἀρχήσασι καὶ χαμηλοπετοῦσα,
Κὴ ὄρεξι μ' ἀπόμεινε μόνο, σὰν πρῶτας πλοῦσα.
Κἀντὶς τὰ θάρρειε κ' ἔλπιζε, κ' ἔδειχνε, κ' ἔτασσέ μου,
Κεὶς τζ' οὐρανοὺς συχνότατα τὸ νοῦν ἀναιβαζέ μου,
Μοῦ κτίζει πύργους 'στὸ γιαλὸ περβόλια στὸν ἀέρα
Κ' ὅ, τι τὴν νύκτα μεριμνῶ, χάνεται τὴν ἡμέρα.

The following is an almost literal translation, in which, however, I have taken the liberty of shortening the metre by one syllable, except in one or two cases :—

'My visage fierce and pitiless, my dark and ghastly stare;
The sickle which I carry; my fleshless bones and bare;
The lightning, with the thunder claps that shake the air around,
Forth bursting from the jaws of hell, and rending all the ground,
These things may tell you who I am; it needs no words of mine:
Whoso but looks on me to-day, my name may soon divine.

[20] ἀποκότησα = ἔτλην: ἐτόλμησα, cf. κοτέω, κοτέομαι, κότος. The notions of wrath and daring are not far removed from each other. Compare μένος with its cognate words, and kindred varieties of meaning: μενῖ in Albanian means *hatred*.

[21] καλά = τάχα, ἴσαν: so ἀγκαλά, ἂν καλά = el καί: cf. German *wol*, 'perhaps;' *obwol*, 'although.'

Yes, I am he whom all men hate, and call with one consent
Hound-hearted, blind, and pitiless, whose soul can ne'er relent.
I spare nor kings, nor potentates, the mighty of the earth,
The master and the slave alike; in plenty or in dearth;
The young, the old, the great, the small, the simple and the wise,
Whene'er I please I lay them low, never again to rise.
Even in the flower of their youth their fleeting years I number;
Glory and praise and fame I whelm in dark eternal slumber;
The memory of righteous deeds swift to the winds I scatter;
The closest bonds that friendship knits, I sunder and I shatter;
The fiercest heart I quickly tame, sage counsels I confound;
Fair hopes I blight, and lofty thoughts lay even with the ground.
And wheresoe'er my eyes are turned with fell destructive power,
Whole countries sink, whole worlds decay, and vanish in an hour.
Where is the sovereignty of Greece; where is the wealth of Rome;
Of mighty realms whilome the nurse, of wit the chosen home?

'How poor they dwell within the tomb, the dumb and voiceless dead,
In some small corner of the earth, a sod above their head,
Mere naked shades! Thrice wretched men! why do they not behold
How day is dwindling after day, how soon their years are told?
Yestreen is passed, the day before has left no trace in sight;
To-day is reckoned but a span in yonder realms of night.
Swift as the twinkling of an eye, I come and drag away
My victim to the grave, and all without compassion slay.
Beauty I quench, nor lovely face can draw from me a tear;
To the meek I show no mercy, and the proud I do not fear.
Who shun me, them I overtake; who seek me, them I fly:
Unbidden at the wedding feast a frequent guest am I.
Wretches! what ye would snatch escapes, and flies while scarce embraced;
Your gathered wealth is scattered soon, and what ye build effaced;
Your glory in a moment quenched, your riches like the dust
Dispersed and gone; quick perishes the name for which ye lust;
Left to the mercy of the sea, as 'twere with idle hand
Inscribed upon the sounding shore, or in the drifting sand.'

'Thee have I chosen,' Murmures, noblest and worthiest,
Of orators most skilled and famed, of virtuous men the best;
Thee have I chosen, that thy name my labours might adorn,
And to thy ears full echo of thy own deserts be borne.
For howsoe'er exalted, thou dost rise before my view,
By so much do I know thee kind, and good and patient too.
Far, far art thou from haughty mien, the proud world's atmosphere,
That gloom from whence no warmth is born, nor light is sent to cheer,
But smoke and vapour dank and thick fill all the region drear.
Be thou the guide of all my way, that I may 'scape the blast
Of wintry storm, and safely reach the longed-for bourne at last.
Let tempest rage, let winds arise, let billows roar and swell,
Yet while I keep before my eyes, that face I love so well,
My one, my guiding star, no rocks shall ever work me harm;
No breakers then shall touch me, nor stormy waves alarm.
But if the greeting which I bring shall haply chance to be
More worthy of my rash resolve than it is worthy thee,
Oh, blame my fortune for the fault, and not my will, I pray.
My heart would ever fain be borne on soaring wings away,
But Fortune casts it to the ground, and clips the pinions spread
To raise me high as Helicon to some tall mountain's head;
Even as they begin their flight and skim above the ground;
Barren desire remains, as when I first was outward bound.
And now in place of all she weened and hoped and showed and taught,
Moving my soul to lofty flight upon the wings of thought,
She builds me castles in the sand, and gardens in the air;
And what by night I meditate, day finds no longer there.'

This last line seems suggested by the Sophoclean verse—

εἴ τι νὺξ ἀφῇ, τοῦτ' ἐπ' ἦμαρ ἔρχεται.

The next writer we shall notice is Franciscus Scuphos, born in Cydon in Crete, and educated in Italy, in 1669 professor at the Greek school in Venice, author of a work on Rhetoric 1681, from which we quote the following example to show how completely the rhetoric of the ancients continues to live in the oratory of modern Greece:—

Μὲ τὸ σχῆμα τῆς δεήσεως θέλω παρακαλέσει τὸν ἐλευθερωτὴν τοῦ Κόσμου Χριστὸν, νὰ ἐλευθερώσῃ μιὰν φορὰν τὸ ἑλληνικὸν γένος ἀπὸ τὴν δουλείαν τῶν Ἀγαρηνῶν, καὶ ἀπὸ τὰς χείρας τοῦ Ὀτομανικοῦ Βριάρεως. Φθάνει, κριτὰ δικαιώτατε, φθάνει! Ἕως πότε οἱ τρισάθλιοι Ἕλληνες ἔχουσι νὰ εὑρίσκωνται εἰς τὰ δεσμὰ τῆς δουλείας, καὶ μὲ ὑπερήφανον πόδα νὰ τοὺς πατῇ τὸν λαιμὸν ὁ βάρβαρος Θράκης; ἕως πότε γένος τόσον ἔνδοξον καὶ εὐγενικὸν νὰ προσκυνᾷ ἐπάνω εἰς βασιλικὸν θρόνον ἕνα ἄθεον τουλουπάνι, καὶ ᾗ χώραις ἐκείναις εἰς ταῖς ὁποίαις ἀνατέλλει ὁ ὁρατὸς ἥλιος, καὶ εἰς ἀνθρωπίνην μορφὴν ἀνέτειλας καὶ ἐσὺ ὁ ἀόρατος, ἀπὸ ἥμισυ φεγγάρι νὰ βασιλεύωνται; Ἆ, ἐνθυμήσου, σὲ παρακαλῶ, πῶς εἶσαι ὄχι μόνον κριτὴς, ἀμὴ καὶ πατὴρ, καὶ πῶς παιδεύεις, ἀμὴ δὲν θανατόνεις τὰ τέκνα σου· ὅθεν ἂν ἴσως καὶ ἡ ἁμαρτίαις τῶν Ἑλλήνων ἐπαρακίνησαν τὴν δικαίαν ὀργήν σου, ἂν ἴσως καὶ εἰς τὴν κάμινον τῆς ἰδίας τῶν ἀνομίας σοῦ ἐχάλκευσαν τὰ ἀστροπελέκια, διὰ νὰ τοὺς ἀφανίσῃς ἀπὸ τὸ προσωπὸν τῆς οἰκοιμένης, ἐσὺ ὁποῦ εἶσαι ὅλος εὐσπλαγχνία, συγχώρησαι καὶ σβῦσαι ἐκεῖνα εἰς τὸ πέλαγος τῆς ἀπείρου σου ἐλεημοσύνης. Ἐνθυμήσου, θεάνθρωπε Ἰησοῦ, πῶς τὸ ἑλληνικὸν γένος ἐστάθη τὸ πρῶτον, ὁποῦ ἄνοιξε ταῖς ἀγκάλαις, διὰ νὰ δεχθῇ τὸ θεῖόν σου εὐαγγέλιον· τὸ πρῶτον ὁποῦ ἔῤῥιξε χαμαὶ τὰ εἴδωλα, καὶ κρεμάμενον εἰς ἕνα ξύλον σὲ ἐπροσκύνησεν ὡς θεόν· τὸ πρῶτον, ὁποῦ ἀντιστάθη τῶν τυράννων, ὁποῦ μὲ τόσα καὶ τόσα βάσανα ἐγύρευαν νὰ ξεῤῥιζώσουν ἀπὸ τὸν κόσμον τὴν πίστιν, καὶ ἀπὸ ταῖς καρδίαις τῶν χριστιανῶν τὸ θεῖόν σου ὄνομα· μὲ τοὺς ἰδρῶτας τῶν Ἑλλήνων ηὔξανε, Χριστέ μου, εἰς ὅλην τὴν οἰκουμένην ἡ ἐκκλησία σου· οἱ Ἕλληνες τὴν ἐπλούτησαν μὲ τοὺς θησαυροὺς τῆς σοφίας, τοῦτοι καὶ μὲ τὴν γλῶσσαν, καὶ μὲ τὸν κάλαμον, μὲ τὴν ἰδίαν ζωὴν τὴν διαφέντευσαν [defenderunt] τρέχοντες μὲ ἄπειρον μεγαλοψυχίαν καὶ εἰς ταῖς φυλακαῖς, καὶ εἰς ταῖς μάστιγαις, καὶ εἰς τοὺς τροχοὺς καὶ εἰς ταῖς ἐξορίαις, καὶ εἰς ταῖς φλόγαις καὶ εἰς ταῖς πίσσαις, μόνον διὰ νὰ σβύσουν τὴν πλάνην, διὰ νὰ ξαπλώσουν τὴν πίστιν, διὰ νὰ σὲ κηρύξουν θεάνθρωπον, καὶ διὰ νὰ λάμψῃ ὅπου λάμπει ὁ ἥλιος, τοῦ σταυροῦ ἡ δόξα καὶ τὸ μυστήριον· ὅθεν, ὡς εὔσπλαγχνος, μὲ τὴν θεϊκήν σου παντοδυναμίαν κάμε νὰ φύγουν τὸν ζυγὸν τέτοιας βαρβαρικῆς αἰχμαλωσίας· ὡς φιλόδωρος καὶ πλουσιοπάροχος ἀνταποδότης, ἀνοίγοντας τοὺς θησαυροὺς τῶν θείων σου χαρίτων, ὕψωσαι πάλιν εἰς τὴν προτέραν δόξαν τὸ γένος, καὶ, ἀπὸ τὴν κοπρίαν, εἰς τὴν ὁποίαν κάθεται, δός του τὸ σκῆπτρον καὶ τὸ βασίλειον. Ναὶ, σὲ παρακαλῶ μὰ τὸ χαῖρε ἐκεῖνο, ὁποῦ ἔφερε τὴν χαρὰν εἰς τὸν κόσμον· μὰ τὴν θείαν σου ἐκείνην ἐνσάρκωσιν, εἰς τὴν ὁποίαν ὄντας Θεὸς, ἐγίνηκες ἄνθρωπος, διὰ νὰ φανῇς μὲ τοὺς ἀνθρώπους φιλάνθρωπος· μὰ τὸ βάπτισμα, ὁποῦ μᾶς ἔπλυνε ἀπὸ τὴν ἁμαρτίαν· μὰ τὸν σταυρὸν ὁποῦ μᾶς ἄνοιξε τὸν παράδεισον, μὰ τὸν θάνατον ὁποῦ μᾶς ἔδωκε τὴν ζωήν. καὶ μὰ τὴν ἔνδοξον ἐκείνην ἔγερσιν, ὁποῦ μᾶς ἀνέβασε εἰς τὰ οὐράνια. Καὶ ἂν ἴσως καὶ ᾗ φωναῖς τούταις δὲν σὲ παρακινοῦσιν εἰς σπλάγχνος, ἃς σὲ παρακινήσουν τὰ δάκρυα, ὁποῦ μοῦ τρέχουν ἀπὸ τὰ ὄμματα, καὶ ἐὰν δὲν φθάνουν καὶ ταῦτα, ἢ φωναῖς, ἢ παρακάλεσαις τῶν ἁγίων σου, ὁποῦ ἀπὸ ὅλα τὰ μέρη τῆς τρισαθλίας Ἑλλάδος φωνάζουσι. Φωνάζει ἀπὸ τὴν Κρήτην ὁ Ἀνδρέας, καὶ σὲ παρακαλεῖ νὰ ἐξολοθρεύσῃς τοὺς Ἀγαρηνοὺς λύκους ἀπ' ἐκεῖνο τὸ Βασίλειον, εἰς τὸ ὁποῖον ἐποίμανε τῆς χριστωνύμου σου ποίμνης τὰ πρόβατα· φωνάζει ἀπὸ τὴν Πόλιν ἕνας Χρυσόστομος, καὶ σὲ παρακαλεῖ νὰ μὴν κυριεύεται ἀπὸ τοὺς ἐχθροὺς τοῦ Υἱοῦ ἐκείνη ἡ χώρα, ὁποῦ μίαν φορὰν ἀφιερώθη τῆς Μητρὸς καὶ Παρθένου· φωνάζει ἡ Αἰκατερίνα, καὶ δείχνοντά σου τὸν τροχὸν, εἰς τὸν ὁποῖον ἐμαρτύρησε, σὲ παρακαλεῖ ὁ τροχὸς πάλι νὰ γυρίσῃ τῆς τύχης διὰ τὴν Ἀλεξάνδρειαν· φωνάζουσιν οἱ Ἰγνάτιοι ἀπὸ τὴν Ἀντιόχειαν, οἱ Πολύκαρποι ἀπὸ τὴν Σμύρνην, οἱ Διονύσιοι ἀπὸ τὰς Ἀθήνας, οἱ Σπυρίδωνες ἀπὸ τὴν Κύπρον, καὶ δείχνοντάς σου τοὺς λέοντας ὁποῦ τοὺς ἐξέσχισαν, ταῖς φλόγαις ὁποῦ τοὺς ἔκαυσαν, τὰ σίδερα ὁποῦ τοὺς ἐθέρισαν, ἐλπίζουσι ἀπὸ τὴν ἄκραν σου εὐσπλαγχνίαν τῶν ἑλληνικῶν πόλεων καὶ ὅλης τῆς Ἑλλάδος τὴν ἀπολύτρωσιν.

Vincentius Kornaros, author of a popular poem in the Cretan dialect, entitled 'Erotocritus,' is generally reckoned as an author of the eighteenth century, for his work was first published at Venice in 1756. It appears, however, that he was born in Sitia in Crete in the year 1620. The opening lines of his 'Erotocritus' are well worth quoting:—

Τοῦ κύκλου τὰ γυρίσματα ποῦ ἀναιβοκαταιβαίνουν,
Καὶ τοῦ τροχοῦ π' ὥραις ψηλὰ, κ' ὥραις στὰ βάθη πηαίνουν,
Καὶ τοῦ καιροῦ τὰ πράγματα, ποῦ ἀνάπαυμὸ δὲν ἔχουν
Μὰ στὸ καλὸ κεὶς τὸ κακὸ περιπατοῦν καὶ τρέχουν.
Καὶ τῶν ἀρμάτων ἡ ταραχαὶς, αἱ χρήταις καὶ τὰ βάρη,
Τοῦ ἔρωτος ἡ ἐμπόρεσες καὶ τῆς φιλιᾶς ἡ χάρι,
Αὐτάνα μ' ἐκινήσασι τὴν σήμερον ἡμέραν
Ν' ἀναθηβάλω καὶ νὰ'πῶ τὰ κάμαν καὶ τὰ φέραν.

'The ups and downs of fortune's wheel, whose ceaseless circling motion
Now scales the heights of heaven above, now sounds the depths of ocean,
With all the changing things of time, whose current resting never,
For worse, for better, fast or slow, is stealing on for ever:
The troublous din of armed hosts, war's train of want and sadness,
The ways and means of desperate love, the charm of friendship's gladness:
These things have moved me to recount, and publish as I may,
The fortunes and the deeds of men while it is called to-day.'

In the eighteenth century we are met by the names of Kosmas the Aetolian, an educational and religious missionary, who founded schools throughout the length and breadth of Greece, and Rhegas of Pherae, the great forerunner of Greek independence. Countenanced by Pasbánoglus, the Bey of Venidi, whose friendship he had gained by saving his life when threatened by Mavrogenes, governor of Wallachia, he did all he could to incite the Greeks to rebellion, and addressed appeals to the European Courts to obtain a promise of their assistance in case of insurrection. He was finally betrayed to the Turks at Belgrade by the Austrian Government, and put to death by them on the spot. His two war-songs, beginning Δεῦτε παῖδες τῶν Ἑλλήνων and Ὡς πότε παλληκάρια νὰ ζοῦμεν 'στὰ στενά, contributed in no small degree to fire the Greeks with that enthusiasm for liberty which soon resulted in the insurrection: but though full of spirit and fervour, they are remarkably wanting in a sense of poetic fitness, and abound with sudden bursts of prosaic bathos which destroy in great measure their effect: e.g.,—

> Ὁ νόμος σας προστάζει
> Νὰ βάλετε φωτιὰ
> Νὰ κάψτε τὴν ἁρμάδα
> Τοῦ Καπιτὰν-πασᾶ. (!)

Rhegas is honourably distinguished, among the many glorious patriots of modern Greece, as being the only one who seemed to understand that the faith of Islam was entitled to any respect. Religious bigotry mars the patriotism of almost every other Greek, and of the larger number of Philhellenes with whom I have come in contact.

In illustration of Rhegas' religious tolerance I quote Perrhaebus, who represents him as thus addressing Pasbánoglus:—

> Ἐὰν ἐγώ, βέη, ἔσωσα τὴν ζωήν σου ἀπὸ τὸν θάνατον, τοῦτο ἦτο χρέος μου, διότι δοξάζω ὅτι ἕνας Θεὸς ἔπλασεν ὅλον τὸν κόσμον, ὥστε εἴμεθα πλάσματα καὶ τέκνα ἑνὸς πατρός, καὶ ἑπομένως ἀδελφοί· φέρω ὡς παράδειγμα τὸ ἑξῆς· ὅταν εἰς πατὴρ γεννήσῃ καθ᾽ ὑπόθεσιν πολλοὺς υἱούς, καὶ ὁ μὲν ἐξ αὐτῶν γένῃ δερβίσης, ἄλλος πραγματευτής, ἄλλος ψωμοπώλης, καὶ ἄλλοι μεταχειρισθῶσιν ἄλλα ἐπαγγέλματα, δύνανται οὗτοι νἀρνηθῶσι τὸν πατέρα των, καὶ τὴν ἀδελφοσύνην των, ἕνεκα τῆς διαφορᾶς τῶν ἐπαγγελμάτων; δικαιοῦνται ἆρα ἐνώπιον τοῦ Θεοῦ διὰ τοῦτο νὰ ἀποστρέφεται καὶ κατατρέχῃ ὁ εἷς τὸν ἄλλον, ἐνῷ ὁ πατὴρ αὐτῶν ἀγαπᾷ ὅλους ἐπίσης; Ἐὰν σὺ καυχᾶσαι ὅτι ἡ Ὀθωμανικὴ πίστις εἶναι καλλιτέρα ἀφ᾽ ὅλας, καὶ ἐγὼ πάλιν φρονῶ ὅτι ἡ ἰδική μου ὑπερβαίνει ὅλας, κατὰ τοῦτο σφάλλομεν καὶ οἱ δύο φιλονεικοῦντες, διότι ὁ Θεός, ὡς κοινὸς πατήρ, μᾶς διατάττει νὰ ἤμεθα εἰλικρινεῖς, δίκαιοι, φιλάνθρωποι, καὶ νὰ ἀγαπῶμεν τοὺς ὑπηκόους,

καὶ νὰ μὴ καταδικάζωμεν αὐτοὺς ἀνόμως ὡς τὰ ἄλογα ζῶα, καθ' ὅσον δὲ ἀφορᾷ εἰς τὰ θρησκευτικὰ, ἡμεῖς δὲν ἔχομεν ἐξουσίαν νὰ ἐξετάζωμεν καὶ διαφιλονεικῶμεν ὅσα ἀνήκουν εἰς τὸν Θεόν· ἡμεῖς οὔτε εἴδομεν, οὔτε ἠκούσαμεν, οὔτε εἰς κανὲν βιβλίον εὕρομεν γεγραμμένον, ὅτι ὁ Θεὸς ἐπαίδευσε τὸν δεῖνα διότι ἦτο Τοῦρκος, ἢ τὸν δεῖνα διότι ἦτο χριστιανὸς, ἢ τὸν δεῖνα διότι ἦτο ἡλιοσεληνολάτρης κ.τ.λ. Βλέπομεν ὅμως καὶ ἀκούομεν, καὶ εἰς τὰ βιβλία εὑρίσκομεν γεγραμμένον, ὅτι ὁ Θεὸς ἐπαίδευσε καὶ παιδεύει πάντοτε τοὺς τυραννοῦντας τὸ πλάσμα του, τοὺς ἀδελφούς των.

Speaking of the Sultan he uses the remarkable expression, ἐξέκλινε ἀπὸ τὸν δρόμον τοῦ Θεοῦ, καὶ (as if synonymous) τὰς ἐντολὰς τοῦ Κορανίου.

That we may see side by side with this religious large-heartedness its natural counterpart, a deadly intolerance of tyranny, we will here give the oath which was administered by Rhegas to all his confederates:—

Ὦ βασιλεῦ τοῦ κόσμου, ὁρκίζομαι εἰς σέ,
Στὴν γνώμην τῶν τυράννων νὰ μὴν ἐλθῶ ποτέ·
Μήτε νὰ τοὺς δουλεύσω, μήτε νὰ πλανεθῶ,
Εἰς τὰ ταξίματά των νὰ μὴ παραδοθῶ·
Ἐνόσῳ ζῶ 's τὸν κόσμον, ὁ μόνος μου σκοπὸς
Τοῦ νὰ τοὺς ἀφανίσω νὰ ἦναι σταθερός·
Πιστὸς εἰς τὴν πατρίδα συντρίβω τὸν ζυγόν,
Κι' ἀχώριστος νὰ ζήσω ἀπὸ τὸν στρατηγόν.
Κ' ἂν παραβῶ τὸν ὅρκον, ν' ἀστράψῃ ὁ οὐρανός,
Καὶ νὰ μὲ κατακαύσῃ, νὰ γέν' ὡσὰν καπνός.

In 1777 was born at Larissa, in Thessaly, Constantine Cumas, author of a great number of geographical, mathematical, and philosophical works: for the sake of its Platonic spirit I give the following extract:—

Ἀλλ' εἶναι, πρὸς Διὸς, φρόνιμος τέκτων ὅστις ἀγοράζει σκεπάρνιον καὶ πριόνιον τὰ ὁποῖα ἐμποδίζονται ἀπὸ τὴν χρύσωσιν καὶ τοὺς ἄλλους στολισμούς νὰ ἐκπληρώσωσι τὰ ἴδια αὐτῶν ἔργα, ἤγουν τὸ ἓν νὰ πελεκᾷ, τὸ δὲ ἕτερον νὰ πριονίζῃ; ἀπαράλλακτα πάσχει, νομίζω, ὅστις διὰ νὰ στολίσῃ τὴν γλῶσσαν μὲ γενικὰς ἀπολύτους καὶ δοτικὰς καὶ χωρὶς ἀνάγκην λέξεις ἀσυνειθίστους, κινδυνεύει νὰ τὴν καταστήσῃ ἀκατάληπτον εἰς τοὺς ἀκούοντας ἢ ἀναγινώσκοντας.

The greatest name that appears at the end of the eighteenth century is that of Adamantios Coraes, the great patriot and linguistic reformer, and one of the most celebrated *literati* of Europe.

It is quite a mistake to suppose that Coraes produced any revolution in the language of modern Greece, or that it is an artificial dialect resuscitated from the grave. The modern Greek of newspapers, novels, sermons, &c., is not half so artificial or pedantic as the writings of the Atticists of the paracme, or even as the Greek of Chrysostom and other fathers of the Eastern Church. All that Coraes did was to set an example to his countrymen in regard to style and the choice of words, which they were not slow to follow. His reform was a very simple one: he proposed to use the classical terminations, wherever these were not altogether obsolete, in preference to those which prevailed in the mouths of the common people; and in addition to this, to banish as far as possible all the foreign words which had crept into the language, and substitute Greek words, often new compounds, in their place.

Coraes was born in Smyrna on April 27, 1748, studied in Amsterdam for six years, and for another six in France, at Montpellier, where he received the degree of Doctor of Medicine. In 1788 he came to Paris, and was there during the Revolution. Here he spent the greater part of his life. Here he wrote letters to his countrymen, encouraging them in the struggle for freedom, to which Rhegas was already instigating them; and here he pursued those literary dies which have established his fame as an European ιolar.

His published works are as follows :—

La Médecine Clinique. Montpellier, 1787 (μετάφρασις ἐκ τοῦ γερμανικοῦ τοῦ Selle).

Introduction à l'étude de la Nature et de la Médecine. Ibid.

Catéchisme Orthodoxe Russe (from the German of Plato, Archbishop of Moscow).

Vade-mecum du Médecin. Montpellier (from the English).

Esquisse d'une Histoire de la Médecine. Paris, 1767 (from the English).

Pyretologiae Synopsis. Montpellier, 1786.

Ἀδελφικὴ διδασκαλία, an answer to Πατρικὴ δικασκαλία, a forgery of the Turkish Government, published under the name of Anthimus, Patriarch of Jerusalem, for the purpose of allaying the tumultuary tendencies of the Greek subjects of the Porte.

Les Caractères de Théophraste. 1799.

Traité d'Hippocrate, des airs, des eaux et des lieux. Paris, 1806.

Ibid., second edition, with Greek Title. 1816.

Βεκκαρίου περὶ ἀδικημάτων καὶ ποινῶν. Paris, 1802, 1823.

Σάλπισμα πολεμιστήριον. Paris, 1803. (On the death of Rhegas.)

Ἡλιοδώρου Αἰθιοπικὰ βιβλία δέκα. Paris, 1804. In two volumes.

Lettre du Docteur Coray sur le testament secret des Athéniens, dont parle Dinarque dans la harangue contre Demosthènes.

Διάλογος δύο Γραικῶν κατοίκων τῆς Βενετίας. 1805. Καὶ ἐν Ὕδρᾳ, 1825.

Πρόδρομος Ἑλληνικῆς βιβλιοθήκης. 1809–1827.

Ἑλληνικὴ βιβλιοθήκη. Paris, 1807–1835. 15 vols. (consisting of editions of classical authors, with notes).
Πάρεργα Ἑλλ. βιβλιοθήκης. 1809–1827. 9 vols.
Ἰλιάδος ῥαψωδίαι Δ. 1811–1820.
Διατριβὴ αὐτοσχέδιος περὶ τοῦ περιβοήτου δόγματος τῶν σκεπτικῶν φιλοσόφων Νόμῳ καλόν, Νόμῳ κακόν.
Ἄτακτα. Paris, 1818–1825. 2 vols.
Συνέκδημος ἱερατικός. 1831.
Σύνοψις ἱερᾶς Κατηχήσεως.
Αὐτοβιογραφία. 1833.

Besides numberless articles in the 'Logios Hermes,' a Greek periodical published in Vienna, on philological and political subjects.

On his death he left his library and MSS. to the Gymnasium at Chios, the birthplace of his ancestors. His unpublished works are more numerous, if not more voluminous, than those which have been given to the world. Besides this, the margins of many of his books are crowded with notes in his handwriting.

Few countries, none certainly save Germany, can show such a literary Hercules as Adamantios Coraes, the second Leo Allatius of Greece. Would that some enterprising compatriot would undertake the complete publication of all his works.

As contemporaries of Coraes we may mention, out of many literary men of no mean deserts, Constantine Oekonomos, whose turgid style formed as striking a contrast to the simplicity of Coraes as did, on the other hand, the abandoned vernacular of Jakobos Rhizos Nerulos, the unsparing satirist of the 'Logios Hermes' and its promulgators.

I give three short extracts to illustrate the above remark, taken respectively from the Αὐτοβιογραφία of Coraes, the treatise Περὶ προφορᾶς of Oekonomos, and the Κορακιστικά, a satirical comedy of Nerulos, in which I need hardly say the Κόρακες are the followers of Coraes:—

Ὅστις ἱστορεῖ τὸν ἴδιον βίον χρεωστεῖ νὰ σημειώσῃ καὶ τὰ κατορθώματα καὶ τὰ ἁμαρτήματα τῆς ζωῆς του, μὲ τόσην ἀκρίβειαν ὥστε μήτε τὰ πρῶτα νὰ μεγαλύνῃ, μήτε τὰ δεύτερα νὰ σμικρύνῃ ἢ νὰ σιωπᾷ παντάπασι· πρᾶγμα δυσκολώτατον διὰ τὴν ἔμφυτον εἰς ὅλους ἡμᾶς φιλαυτίαν. Ὅστις ἀμφιβάλλει περὶ τούτου, ἂς κάμῃ τὴν πεῖραν νὰ χαράξῃ δύο μόνον στίχους τῆς βιογραφίας του καὶ θέλει καταλάβει τὴν δυσκολίαν.—*Coraes*, Αὐτοβιογραφία.

Τὸ περὶ γνησίας τῶν ἑλληνικῶν γραμμάτων προφορᾶς πολύκροτον πρόβλημα πρὸ τρίων ἤδη αἰώνων εἰς τὴν Εὐρώπην ἀναφυέν, ὑπῆρξε πολλάκις εἰς πολλοὺς πολλῶν καὶ μεγάλων συζητήσεων ὑπόθεσις.— *Oekonomos*, Περὶ προφορᾶς.

The studied rhythm and inflated style is worthy of a Prodikus.

Εἶναι δύο χρόνια τώρα ὁποῦ ὁ πατέρας μου ἀρρωστεῖ ἀπ' ἐν ἀλλόκοτο πάθος τὸ νὰ ὁμιλῇ κορακιστικά, καὶ ἄλλο δὲν κάμνει παρὰ νὰ σκαλίζῃ λεξικὰ, νὰ πλάττῃ λέξαις ἀνήκουσταις καὶ παράξεναις, νὰ διαβάζῃ κἄτι διαβολόχαρτα τυπωμένα, ὁποῦ τὰ ὀνομάζουν Λόγιον Ἑρμῆ καὶ νὰ γράφῃ καὶ νὰ λαλῇ μιὰ γλῶσσα, ὁποῦ τὴν δημιουργεῖ ὁ ἴδιος. Τί νὰ κάμω; γιὰ νὰ τὸν ὑποχρεώσω, βιάζω τὸν ἑαυτόν μου νὰ μάθω αὐταῖς ταῖς ἀηδέστατες φλυαρίας, καὶ μ' ὅλον ὁποῦ δὲν γυρνᾷ ἡ γλῶσσά μου 's αὐτὰ τὰ καταραμένα κορακιστικά, μ' ὅλον τοῦτο, ἐπειδὴ καὶ τὰ λατρεύει, βιάζομαι κ'ἐγὼ νὰ τὸν ὁμιλῶ τῇ γλῶσσᾳ του, καὶ εἰς κάθε λέξι 'δικήτου ὁποῦ ἤθελα προφέρει, μὲ δίδει τὴν εὐχή του.—*Nerulos*, Κορακιστικά.

Modern Greece has produced but few authoresses: of these Angelica Palle, chiefly known by her ode on the 'Death of Lord Byron,' which I shall here quote, belongs to the beginning of the nineteenth century.

1.

Τοὺς λαμπροὺς ὕμνους τῆς νίκης ἀφίνων
Κλαυθμῶν ἠχεῖ ἡρώων ὁ στρατός·
Πικρῶς λυποῦντ' αἱ ψυχαὶ τῶν Ἑλλήνων,
Τ' ἀκούει μακρόθεν καὶ χαίρει ὁ ἐχθρός.

2.

Ὁ φίλος ἦλθε· πλὴν μόλις τὸν εἶδον
Σκάπτουν κλαίοντες τὸν τάφον αὐτοῦ,
Ἰδοῦ τὸ τέλος ἐνδόξων ἐλπίδων,
Καὶ τὸ τρόπαιον θανάτου σκληροῦ.

3.

Ἦλθε νὰ ἐμπνεύσῃ ὡς ἄλλος Τυρταῖος
Εἰς κάθε στῆθος πολέμων ὁρμήν·
Πλὴν, φεῦ, ὁ Βάρδος ἐλπίσας ματαίως
Ἰδοῦ μένει εἰς αἰώνιον σιωπήν.

4.

Ὡς δένδρον κεῖτ' ὁπ' ἐκόσμει μεγάλως
Τὴν κορυφὴν μουσικοῦ Παρνασσοῦ·
Νῦν πρὸ ποδῶν φθείρουσά του τὸ κάλλος
Πνοὴ τὸ ἔρριψ'· ἀνέμου σφοδροῦ

5.

Ἑλλὰς ! ἐὰν τὸ σῶμα του ἡ Ἀγγλία
Νὰ φέρῃ εἰς μνῆμα ζητᾷ πατρικόν·
Εἰπὲ, Μουσῶν ὦ μητέρα γλυκεῖα,
Εἶναι τέκνον μου ὁ υἱὸς τῶν Μουσῶν.

6.

Καταφρονῶν τῶν ἐρώτων τοὺς θρήνους,
Ἡδονῆς μὴν ἀκούων τὴν φωνήν,
Ἐζήτει ἐδὼ ἡρώων τοὺς κινδύνους,
Τάφον ἂς ἔχῃ ἡρώων 'ς τὴν γῆν.

Angelica Palle compares very favourably indeed with Felicia Hemans.

The metre is one peculiarly liable to run into jingle, from

which it is only preserved by the retarding effect of a judicious irregularity in the word accent, and the frequent substitution of single syllables lengthened by τονή for the trochees which form the first part of the dactyls.

The great lyrical poet of Greece is, however, Athanasios Christopulos, who was born at Kastoria, in Macedonia, in 1772, and who died in Moldavia, where he held the office of judge, in 1847. He is sometimes called the modern Anacreon, but is too original a poet to need any such metonym. Unfortunately, his undoubted genius was consecrated chiefly to the glory of the wine-bottle, yet he wrote some love-songs of exquisite tenderness and beauty, which have been copied without acknowledgment by various modern poets. Consciously or unconsciously, the 'Nightingale' of Christopulos is certainly at the foundation of the 'Swallow' of Tennyson. Inasmuch as the nightingale sings, and the swallow only twitters, I confess I prefer the Greek to the English poet in this particular case.

For four of the following examples I am indebted to C. C. Felton's 'Selections from Modern Greek Writers.'

OLD AGE.

Νὰ ἡ τρίχες σου ἀρχίζουν,
'Αθανάσιε ν' ἀσπρίζουν !
   Νὰ δακρύων ἐποχή !
Νὰ σὲ λέγει καὶ ὁ Ἔρως,
Φίλε πλέον εἶσαι γέρος,
   'Σ τὸ ἑξῆς καλὴ ψυχή.
Τὴ νεότητα χαιρέτα,
Τὰ φιλήματ' ἄφησέ τα,
   Ξέχασέ τα παρευθύς,
Καὶ ἀρχίνα μὲ ὑγεία
Τὰ πικρὰ τὰ γερατεῖα
   'Σ τὸ ἑξῆς νὰ τὰ γευθῆς.

Δὲν σὲ πιάνουν τὰ λουλούδια,
Δὲν σὲ πρέπουν τὰ τραγούδια,
 Πῆγ' ἐκεῖνος ὁ καιρός·
Τώρα τάφος πλησιάζει,
Τώρα θάνατος φωνάζει,
 Τώρα Χάρος λυπηρός !
Ὅθεν πλέον ἑτοιμάσου,
Ῥῆξε ὅλα τὰ καλά σου,
 Πὲ τὸν κόσμον ΕΧΕ ΓΕΙΑ !
Καὶ τὰ δάκρυα βάστα μόνον
Εἰς τὴν λύπην κ' εἰς τὸν πόνον
 Μιὰ μικρὴ παρηγοριά !

ANSWER TO THE PRECEDING.

Πᾶ ! ἡ τρίχες μ' ἂν ἀσπρίζουν
Μήπως τάχατε πικρίζουν ;
 Τί ἔχ' ἡ ἄσπρη τους βαφή ;
Τοιγὰρ τ' ἄσπρο θανατόνει ;
Ἡ φιλῶντας ἀγκυλόνει
 Τὰ χειλάκια 's τὴν ἀφή ;
Τὸ τραντάφυλλό μας, πρῶτον,
Τὸ λουλούδι τῶν Ἐρώτων
 Εἶναι ἄσπρο καθαρό·
Καὶ τὸ κόκκινο ἡ φύσις
Τὸ συγκέρασεν ἐπίσης
 Μ' ἕνα χρῶμ' ἀσπρουδερό.
Ἡ μυρτιὰ τῆς Ἀφροδίτης
Εἰς τὸ πράσινο κλαδί της,
 Μέσ' 's τὰ φύλλα τὰ χλωὰ
Ὅλα κάτασπρα, σὰν χιόνι,
Τὰ λουλούδια τῆς φυτρόνει
 Τ' ἀνθηρά, καὶ τρυφερά.

Καὶ ὁ Δίας ὁ μεγάλος
Γιὰ τῆς Λήδας του τὸ κάλλος
    Κύκνος γίνκε μιὰ φορά.
Ν' ἀποδείξ᾽ εἰς κάθε μέρος,
Ἄσπραις τρίχαις θελ᾽ ὁ Ἔρως,
    Σὰν τοῦ κύκνου τὰ φτερά.

Τὸ λοιπὸν κέγ᾽ ὅσο θέλει,
Ἂς ἀσπρίζω δὲν μὲ μέλει,
    Παντελῶς δὲν μὲ λυπᾷ·
Ὅτι ὅσο παντ᾽ ἀσπρίζω,
Τόσο πλέον νοστιμίζω,
    Τοσ᾽ ὁ ἔρως μ᾽ ἀγαπᾷ.

LOVER'S LONGING.

Ἂς γένουμουν καθρέφτης!
    Νὰ βλέπεσαι 's ἐμένα,
Κ' ἐγὼ νὰ βλέπω πάντα
    Τὸ κάλλος σου, κ᾽ ἐσένα.
Ἂς γένουμουν χτενάκι!
    Σιγὰ σιγὰ ν᾽ ἀρχίζω
Νὰ σχίζω τὰ μαλλιά σου,
    Νὰ σ᾽ τὰ συχνοχτενίζω!
Ἂς ἤμουν ἀεράκης!
    Καὶ ὅλος νὰ κινήσω
'Σ τὰ στήθη σου νὰ πέσω,
    Γλυκὰ νὰ τὰ φυσήσω.
Ἂς ἤμουν τέλος ὕπνος!
    Νὰ ἔρχωμαι τὸ βράδυ,
Νὰ δένω τὰ γλυκά σου
    Ματάκια 's τὸ σκοτάδι.

THE NIGHTINGALE.

Κίν' ἀηδονάκι μου καλό,
Κίνα καὶ πάγε 'στὸ γιαλό
 Τὴν ἀκριβὴ ποῦ ξεύρεις,
 Νὰ πᾷς νὰ μὲ τὴν εὕρῃς·
Καὶ σὰν τὴν βρῇς καὶ τὴν ἰδῇς
Ἀρχίνα κεῖ νὰ κελαδῇς,
 Γλυκὰ γλυκὰ μὲ χάρι
 Νὰ σκύψῃ νὰ σε πάρῃ
Ἄν σ' ἐρωτήσῃ τί 'σ' ἐσύ;
Καὶ ποιός σὲ στέλνει ἀπ' τὸ νησί;
 Εἰπὲ, πῶς εἶμαι δῶρο
 Πουλὶ στεναγμοφόρο!
Πῶς ὁ ἀφέντης μου ἐδῶ
Μὲ στέλνει νὰ σὲ τραγουδῶ·
 Τὰ πάθη μου νὰ κλαίγω
 Μὲ μέλος νὰ σ' τὰ λέγω.
Ὕστερα σκύψε ταπεινά
Καὶ λάλησέ την σιγανά,
 Καὶ ἄρκισ' την 'ς τὰ κάλλη
 Στὸν κόρφο νὰ σε βάλῃ·
Ἄχ ἀηδονάκι μ' δὲν βαστῶ
Θὰ σὲ τὸ πῶ, Εἶσαι πιστό;
 Ἐπίβουλο μὴ γένῃς
 Στὸν κῆπον ποῦ ἐμπαίνεις.

TRANSLATION OF 'THE NIGHTINGALE.'

'Fly, nightingale, to yonder shore;
Fly, fly, what need I tell thee more:
 Go find me out my dearest,
 Go, if my prayer thou hearest.
And when my dearest thou hast found,
Begin to sing thy sweetest sound,
 That she may stoop and take thee,
 And her companion make thee.

And if she then shall make demand,
Who sent thee from the island strand,
    Say, "Hither come I flying,
    A bird of saddest sighing;
My master sends me for a gift,
That I in song my voice may lift
    To tell how he doth languish,
    And warble all his anguish."
Then like a suppliant appear,
And whisper softly in her ear,
    And plight thy master's duty,
    Swearing by all her beauty.
Placed in the garden of her breast—
Ah nightingale, I cannot rest,
    Uneasy fears dismay me,
    Lest there thou shouldst betray me.'

BACCHI LAUDES.

"Οταν πίνω τὸ κρασάκι
'Στὸ χρυσό μου ποτηράκι
Καὶ ὁ νοῦς μου ζαλισθῇ·
Τότ' ἀρχίζω καὶ χορεύω,
Καὶ γελῶ καὶ χωρατεύω,
Κή ζωή μ' εὐχαριστεῖ.

Τότε παύουν ἡ φροντίδες
Τότε σβύνουν ἡ ἐλπίδες
Τότε φεύγουν οἱ καπνοί.
Κή καρδιά μου γαληνίζει,
Καὶ τὸ στῆθός μου ἀρχίζει
Ν' ἀνασαίνῃ, ν' ἀναπνῇ·
Γιὰ τὸν κόσμον δὲν μὲ μέλει,
'Ας γυρίζῃ, ὅπως θέλει,
Τὸ κρασάκι μου νὰ ζῇ.
'Η κανάτα νὰ μὴ στύψῃ,
'Απ' τὸ πλάγι νὰ μὴ λείψῃ,
Ν' ἀποθάνωμε μαζί.

Ὅσο ἔχω τοῦτον, τοῦτον
Τὸν ἀκένωτόν μου πλοῦτον,
Κόσο πίνω καὶ ῥουφῶ·
Ὅλα σκύβαλα τὰ ἔχω,
Εἰς κάνένα δὲν προσέχω,
Καὶ κάνένα δὲν ψηφῶ.

From these examples it will be seen that Christopulos adopted the language of the common people in literary composition. He had a theory that the vernacular was nothing but Aeolo-Doric, and that it ought so to be called, and, as Mr. Sophocles emphatically observes, 'it was called Aeolo-Doric.' After which I think nothing further can be said on the subject; except it be that Christopulos was the author of an 'Aeolo-Doric' Grammar, and several other works, translations, &c., in the same dialect.

Before proceeding to our contemporaries in Greek literature I will say a few words on the popular poetry, the nameless and numberless ballads, which after all are the pride of modern as of ancient Greece.

However glorious and unparalleled the Iliad and the Odyssee may be, as works of genius, yet the mind that brought them forth remains a great unknown, and in their origin and first publication they were just as much ballads as the popular poetry of Greece.

It has been already frequently remarked how curiously the old mythology of Greece survives in the popular superstitions, and yet at the same time how strangely it is modified. Charon for example, as in the following poem, appears rather as the Hermes Pompeios than the genuine Charon of the ancients.

CHARON AND THE GHOSTS.

Τί είναι μαύρα τὰ βουνά, καὶ στέκουν βουρκωμένα;
Μήν' ἄνεμος τὰ πολεμᾷ; μήνα βροχὴ τὰ δέρνει;
Κ' οὐδ' ἄνεμος τὰ πολεμᾷ, κ' οὐδὲ βροχὴ τὰ δέρνει
Μόνε διαβαίν' ὁ Χάροντας μὲ τοὺς ἀπεθαμμένους·
Σέρνει τοὺς νιοὺς ἀπὸ ἐμπροστά, τοὺς γέροντας κατόπι,
Τὰ τρυφερὰ παιδόπουλα 's τὴν σέλλ' ἀρραδιασμένα.
Παρακαλοῦν οἱ γέροντες, κ' οἱ νέοι γονατίζουν·
'Χάρε μου, κόνεψ' εἰς χωριό, κόνεψ' εἰς κρύα βρύσι,
Νὰ πιοῦν οἱ γέροντες νερό, κ' οἱ νιοὶ νὰ λιθαρίσουν,
Καὶ τὰ μικρὰ παιδόπουλα νὰ μάσουν λουλουδάκια.'—
'Κ' οὐδ' εἰς χωριὸ κονεύω γώ, κ' οὐδὲ εἰς κρύα βρύσι·
Έρχοντ' ἡ μάννες γιὰ νερό, γνωρίζουν τὰ παιδιά των·
Γνωρίζονται τ' ἀνδρόγυνα, καὶ χωρισμὸ δὲν ἔχουν.'

Of the so-called Klephtic Ballads, the finest with which I am acquainted is

THE BURIAL OF DEMOS.

Ὁ ἥλιος ἐβασίλευε, κ' ὁ Δῆμος διατάζει·
'Σύρτε, παιδιά μου, 's τὸ νερόν, ψωμὶ νὰ φάτ' ἀπόψε.
Καὶ σύ, Λαμπράκη μ' ἀνεψιέ, κάθου ἐδῶ κοντά μου·
Νά! τ' ἄρματά μου φόρεσε, νὰ ἦσαι καπιτάνος·
Καὶ σεῖς, παιδιά μου, πάρτε τὸ ἔρημο σπαθί μου,
Πράσινα κόψετε κλαδιά, στρῶστέ μου νὰ καθίσω,
Καὶ φέρτε τὸν πνευματικὸ νὰ μ' ἐξομολογήσῃ·
Νὰ τὸν εἰπῶ τὰ κρίματά ποῦ ἔχω καμωμένα,
Τριάντα χρόνι' ἁμαρτωλός, κ' εἴκοσι πέντε κλέφτης·
Καὶ τώρα μ' ἦρθε θάνατος, καὶ θέλω ν' ἀπαιθάνω.
Κάμετε τὸ κιβούρι μου πλατύ, ψηλὸ νὰ γένῃ,
Νὰ στέκ' ὀρθὸς νὰ πολεμῶ, καὶ δίπλα νὰ γεμίζω.
Κ' ἀπὸ τὸ μέρος τὸ δεξὶ ἀφῆστε παραθύρι,
Τὰ χελιδόνια νὰ 'ρχωνται, τὴν ἄνοιξιν νὰ φέρουν,
Καὶ τ' ἀηδόνια τὸν καλὸν Μάϊ νὰ μὲ μαθαίνουν.'

I offer the following as a nearly literal translation:—

The sun was falling from his throne when Demos thus commanded:
'Oh! children, get you to the stream, to eat your bread at even;
And thou, Lambrakes, kinsman mine, come near and sit beside me;
There, take the armour which was mine, and be like me a captain.
And ye, my children, take in charge the sword by me forsaken;
Cut branches from the greenwood tree, and spread a couch to rest me.
Go fetch me now the priest of God, that he may come and shrive me,
For I would tell him all the sins that I have ere committed,
While thirty years a man-at-arms, one score and five a robber.
And now to take me death has come, and I for death am ready.
Then make my tomb on every side right broad, and high above me,
That I may upright stand to fight, and stoop to load my musket:
And on the right hand side, I pray, leave me a little window,
Where swallows in the early year may bring the springtime with them,
And of the merry month of May the nightingales may tell me.'

As a fitting accompaniment to this I would cite another beautiful ballad, entitled

Ἡ ΒΟΗ ΤΟΥ ΜΝΗΜΑΤΟΣ.

Σάββατον ὅλον πίναμε, τὴν κυριακ' ὁλημέραν,
Καὶ τὴν δευτέραν τὸ πουρνὸν [πρωί] ἐσώθη τὸ κρασί μας.
Ὁ καπετάνος μ' ἔστειλε νὰ πάω κρασὶ νὰ φέρω.
Ξένος ἐγὼ καὶ ἄμαθος δὲν ἤξευρα τὸν δρόμον,
Κἐπῆρα στράταις ξώστραταις καὶ ξένα μονοπάτια.
Τὸ μονοπάτι μ' ἔβγαλε σὲ μιὰν ψηλὴν ῥαχοῦλαν·
Ἧταν γεμάτη μνήματα ὅλ' ἀπὸ πολληκάρια.
Ἕν μνῆμα ἦταν μοναχὸν ξέχωρον 'πὸ τὰ ἄλλα·
Δὲν εἶδα, καὶ τὸ πάτησα ἀπάνω 'στὸ κεφάλι·
Βοὴν ἀκούω καὶ βροντὴν ἀπὸ τὸν κάτω κόσμον.
Τί ἔχεις μνῆμα καὶ βογγᾶς καὶ βαρυαναστενάζεις;
Μήνα τὸ χῶμα σοῦ βαρεῖ, μήνα ἡ μαύρη πλάκα;
Οὐδὲ τὸ χῶμα μοῦ βαρεῖ, οὐδὲ ἡ μαύρη πλάκα,

Μόν' τόχω μάραν κ' έντροπὴν κ' ἕναν καῦμὸν μεγάλον
Τὸ πῶς με καταφρόνησες, μὲ πάτησες 'σ τὸ κεφάλι·
Τάχα δὲν ἤμουν κ' ἐγὼ νέος; δὲν ἤμουν παλληκάρι;
Δὲν ἐπερπάτησα ἐγὼ τὴν νύκτα μὲ φεγγάρι;

The following is given to show how the notion of the consciousness and, as it were, suppressed vitality of the dead is further connected with the old superstition of daemons or genii, which belongs not only to Greece, but to Eastern belief generally, as we see in the 'Arabian Nights.' In modern Greece the στοιχεῖον seems always of a malevolent disposition; and that that was the case in the early ages of Christianity we may infer from the use of δαιμόνιον in the New Testament. Sad to say, this superstition has been known to result in human sacrifice, as in the case of the Bridge of Arta, which, according to the popular ballad, could not be built securely until the little daughter of the masterbuilder had been sacrificed to the genius of the place, by being thrown down and buried in the stones, which were to form the foundation of the structure.

Do we not find traces of this dark superstition, which, like other dark superstitions, the Greeks seem to have borrowed from the East, in Joshua's curse pronounced over Jericho (Josh. vi. 26)? 'Cursed be the man before the Lord, that riseth up and buildeth this city Jericho: he shall lay the foundation thereof in his firstborn, and in his youngest son shall he set up the gates thereof.' See the fulfilment of this curse in 1 Kings xvi. 34. And is it not a significant fact that the story of the 'temptation' of Abraham to offer up Isaac is associated with Mount Moriah, one of the hills upon which, according to tradition, Jerusalem was built?

ΤΟΥ ΜΟΥΣΙΚΟΥ ΚΑΙ ΤΟΥ ΣΤΟΙΧΕΙΟΥ.

Ἐψὲς χιόνι ψιχάδισε κ' ὁ Ἰάννης ἐτραγούδα,
Τόσον τραγούδιε γλυκὰ καὶ νόστιμα κοιλάδει,

Τοῦ πῆρ' ἀέρας τὴν φωνὴν 'σ τοῦ Δράκοντος τὴν φέρει.
Ἐβγῆκ' ὁ Δράκος κ' εἶπέ τον, Ἰάννη, θὲ νὰ σὲ φάγω,
Γιατί Δράκο, γιατί θεριό, γιατί θὰ μὲ σκοτώσῃς;
Γιατί διαβαίνεις πάρωρα καὶ τραγουδεῖς πανοῦργα·
Ξυπνᾶς τ' ἀηδόνι' ἀπ' ταῖς φωλιαῖς καὶ τὰ πουλιὰ 'π' τοὺς κάμπους.
Ξυπνᾶς κ' ἐμὲ τὸν Δράκοντα μὲ τὴν Δρακόντισσά μου,
Ἄφες μὲ Δράκο νὰ διαβῶ, ἄφες μὲ νὰ περάσω·
Τράπεζαν ἔχ' ὁ βασιλεᾶς καὶ μ' ἔχει καλεσμένον·
Μ' ἔχει γιὰ πρῶτον μουσικὸν πρῶτον τραγουδιστήν του.

The forms Δράκος nom., δράκοντος gen., and δράκο voc., seem to show that δράκος is not a metaplastic form, but rather a relic of the original form δράκοντ, of which another modern form is δράκοντας, obtained by the insertion of a vowel to facilitate pronunciation.

We will conclude these examples of the popular poetry of Greece with two more pieces, the first illustrative of the personification of Death as Χάρος:—

Λεβέντης ἐροβόλαεν ἀπὸ τὰ κορφοβούνια,
Εἶχε τὸ φέσι του στραβὰ καὶ τὰ μαλλιὰ κλωσμένα·
Καὶ Χάρος τὸν ἀγνάντευεν ἀπὸ ψιλὴν ῥαχοῦλαν,
Καὶ εἰς στενὸν κατέβηκε κ' ἐκεῖ τὸν καρτεροῦσε·
Λεβέντη πόθεν ἔρχεσαι; λεβέντη ποῦ πηγαίνεις;
Ἀπὸ τὰ πρᾶτα ἔρχομαι, σ' τὸ σπῆτί μου πηγαίνω·
Πάγω νὰ πάρω τὸ ψωμὶ, κ' ὀπίσω νὰ γυρίσω.
Κέμενα μ' ἔστειλ' ὁ Θεὸς νὰ πάρω τὴν ψυχήν σου.
Ἄφσε με Χάρε, ἄφσε με, παρακαλῶ νὰ ζήσω,
Ἔχω γυναῖκα πάρα νέαν καὶ δὲν τῆς πρέπει χήρα·
Ἂν περπατήσῃ γλίγωρα, λέγουν πῶς θέλει ἄνδρα,
Κἂν περπατήσῃ ἤσυχα, λέγουν πῶς καμαρόνει,
Ἔχω παιδιὰ ἀνήλικα καὶ ὀρφαν' ἀπομνήσκουν·
Κὸ Χάρος δὲν τὸν ἤκουσε, καὶ ἤθελε νὰ τὸν πάρῃ·
Χάρε σὰν ἀποφάσισες καὶ θέλεις νὰ μὲ πάρῃς

Γιὰ ἔλα νὰ παλέψωμε σε μαρμαρέν' ἁλῶνι·
Κἂν μὲ νικήσῃς Χάρε μου, μοῦ παίρνεις τὴν ψυχήν μου,
Κἂν σὲ νικήσω πάλ' ἐγὼ πήγαινε 's τὸ καλόν σου.
Ἐπῆγαν καὶ ἐπάλεψαν ἀπ' τὸ πρωΐ ὡς τὸ γεῦμα,
Καὶ τοῦ κοντὰ 'σ τὸ δειλινὸν τὸν καταβάν' ὁ Χάρος.

The following lines, sung from house to house at the approach of spring, by children, are plainly a remnant of the χελιδόνισμα of the ancients:—

Χελιδόνα ἔρχεται
Ἀπ' τὴν ἄσπραν θάλασσαν.
Κάθησε καὶ λάλησε·
Μάρτι, μάρτι μου καλέ,
Καὶ φλεβάρη φλιβερέ·
Κἂν χιονίζεις, κἂν ποντίζεις,
Πάλε ἄνοιξιν μυρίζεις.

Before closing this chapter, a few words are due to our contemporaries. The writings of many modern Greek prose authors, as for instance the Ἱστορία τῆς Ἑλληνικῆς ἐπαναστάσεως by Spyridon Tricupes, and the Πάπισσα Ἰωάννα of Roïdes, are well known in England, and have been reviewed in some of our leading journals. Professor Asopios is well known by his Εἰσαγωγὴ εἰς Πίνδαρον, and Professor Damalas by his Περὶ ἀρχῶν. Papparregopulos' history of Greece is remarkable for its clear and simple style, and the unstudied purity of its language. I shall content myself with laying before the reader a few specimens of verse from the pens of living or but lately deceased poets.

A. R. Rangabes, late Greek Ambassador in Paris, is known not only as a scholar and archaeologist, but also as a poet. In his lighter moods, as a satirist, he recalls to our minds something of the great Greek comedian whom it is not unfair to suppose he imitates:—

Καὶ τάχα ποίους λόγους ἰσχυροὺς, σοφοὺς,
προτείνετε ; 's αὐτὸν τὸν ἀνεμόμυλον
ποῦ βάφετε, ἀσπρίζετε, κτενίζετε,
σγουραίνετε καὶ λάθος ὀνομάζετε
σεῖς αἱ γυναῖκες κεφαλὴν, νὰ μάθωμεν
δὲν ἠμποροῦμεν ποῖος ἄνεμος φυσᾷ ;

Τοῦ κόσμου τοῦ ὑπουργικοῦ τὸν Ἄτλαντα
ἂς ψάλῃ πᾶν στόμα·
τὴν εὐγενῆ του κορυφὴν φιλόδοξος
ἀνάπτει φαγοῦρα.
Τίς οἶδε δάφναι ἂν φυτρόνουν εἰς αὐτὴν;
ἢ ἔντομα βόσκουν;
Εἶν' Αἴτνα ἡ καρδία κή κοιλία του
φοβοῦ τὰς ἐκρήξεις.

A. Ἂν κατορθώσῃς νὰ μὲ κάμῃς ὑπουργόν
χρειάζεται παιδεία ἴσως; ἂν αὐτὸ,
ὁμολογῶ πῶς δὲν τὴν ἔχω.—B. ὄχι δά!
Καιρὸς δὲν εἶναι ὁποῦ εἶδα ὑπουργὸν,
κ' ἐκράτει τὸ κονδύλι του ὡς δίκελλαν
κ' ἔσκαπτεν ὑπογραφὴν, καὶ ὡμοίαζαν
τὰ γράμματά του κακοήθειαι μυιῶν.

So much for the politics of Athens. The newspaper editor Sphecias describes himself as the editor of the 'Eatanswill Gazette' might have done:—

Πῶς εἶναι πλὴν ἐνόμιζα
εἰς τὰς Ἀθήνας φύλλα περισσότερα
ἐφημερίδων παρὰ φύλλα πράσινα.
A. Εἶνε πολλὰ, ἀλλ' οὐκ ἐν τῷ πολλῷ τὸ εὖ.
Τὸ φύλλον μου εἶνε καυτήριον ὀξύ, ...
κή ὕβρις μου εἶνε γυμνὴ καὶ ἀναιδὴς,
εἶν' ἔχιδνα, εἶν' ἐμπρηστήριος δαυλός.
μ' αὐτὸν φωτίζω τὸν Ἑλληνικὸν λαὸν

διδάσκων τὰ ῥητὰ καὶ τὰ ἀπόρρητα. . . . .
Εἰς τῆς ὀργῆς μου, ἄνθρωπε, τὸ φύσημα
ξερριζωμένη θὲ νὰ πέσ' ἡ νέα σου
ὑπόληψις, αὐτὴ ποῦ κατεκράτησες.

The power of Russia is thus finely described:—

Ὁ γίγας τῆς ἰσχύος μας ἔχων στρωμνὴν τοὺς παγετούς,
τὴν δύσιν καὶ ἀνατολὴν συνέχ' εἰς τὰς ἀγκάλας του.
Ἀδάμας εἰς τὸ στέμμα του τοῦ Πόλου λάμπει ὁ ἀστήρ·
πατεῖ κ' ὑπὸ τὸ βῆμα του σχίζοντ' οἱ πάγοι τοῦ Οὐράλ·
κ' εἶν' ἡ πνοὴ τοῦ στήθους του ὑπερβορεία θύελλα.

The following appear from the headings to be founded on German originals:—

I. ΠΕΡΙΣΤΕΡΑ.

Σκοπὸς; *Sag' an o lieber Vogel mein.*

Ποῦ μ' ἁπλωμένα τὰ πτερὰ
πετᾶς λευκὴ περιστερά,
ὅτ' ἐφ' ἡμῶν
βαρὺς χειμὼν
τοὺς πάγους φέρει τοῦ βορρᾶ;

'Ὅπου ἡ ἄνοιξις γελᾷ,
καὶ αὖραι πνέουν ἀπαλὰ
ἐκεῖ πετῶ
τὸ φῶς ζητῶ
ζητῶ τὰ ἄνθη τὰ πολλά.'

Πτηνὸν μὴ φεύγῃς, δειλιῶν
πῶς μᾶς κατέλαβε χειμών.
Θερμὸν, θερμὸν
ἐντὸς ἡμῶν
θάλπει τὸ πῦρ τῶν καρδιῶν.

'Θερμὴ καρδία φιλικὴ
πάλλει παντοῦ. Δὲν μοὶ ἀρκεῖ,'
μᾶς ἀπαντᾷ,
γοργὴ πετᾷ
κεἰς ξένας στέγας μετοικεῖ.

II. ΝΥΚΤΕΡΙΝΟΝ.

Σκοπὸς; *Leise fliehen meine Lieder.*

Μὴν κοιμᾶσαι, ἡ σελήνη
λάμπει ἀργυρᾶ,
καὶ τὴν κόμην της ἐκτείνει
εἰς στιλπνὰ νερά.

"Εβγα· νὰ ἰδῇς· εἰς φύλλα
εἰς τὸ φῶς χρυσᾶ
λαρύγγιζ' ἡ Φιλομήλα
ᾆσμα ὡς τὰ σά.

"Ακουσον τί ψάλλ' ἡ γλῶσσα
ἡ μαγευτική.
Σὺ τὸ φῶς, καὶ σὺ ἡ ζῶσα
εἶσαι μουσική.

Τὸ πᾶν πλῆρες ἁρμονίας
καὶ θερμῶν παλμῶν.
Ἐλθέ, κἔνθουν ἐκ καρδίας
ἔγειρον ψαλμόν.

"Ανοιξον ὡραῖα χείλη,
νὰ σκιρτήσ' ἡ γῆ·
καὶ ἐντός μου ν' ἀνατείλῃ
πάμφωτος αὐγή.

Αἱ ψυχαί μας δέ, ὡς τόνος
μέλους συμφωνῶν,
"Αφες ν' ἀναβοῦν συγχρόνως
εἰς τὸν οὐρανόν.

A very popular poet in Greece is Zalacostas, who has been dead some ten years or more, a voluminous translator from Italian poets, and as an original writer full of power and imagination, though rather unequal in felicity. He has the merit, if merit it be, of introducing a vast variety of new metres into modern Greek versification. He would appear to have passed the greater part of his life in conversation with the manes of Greek heroes and martyrs, indignant at the degradation of their country.

The following may serve as an example:—

> Εἰς τὸν τύμβον ἐκεῖνον πλησίον,
> ἠνεώχθη μὲ πάταγον χάσμα·
> καὶ τῆς γῆς ἐκ τῶν σπλάγχνων τῶν κρύων
> ἐτινάχθη δεκάπηχυ φάσμα.
> Ἀ ! δὲν ἦτο τοῦ νοῦ μου ἀπάτη,
> μήτε φροῦδον τοῦ φόβου μου πλάσμα.
>
> Βλοσυρὸν περιέστρεφε 'μάτι,
> καὶ λαμπάδα φλογῶν διαπύρων
> μὲ τὴν ἄσαρκα χεῖρα ἐκράτει,
> Ἐθερμάνθη ἐπ' ἄμετρον γύρον
> ὁ αἰθὴρ καὶ ἡ γῆ καὶ οἱ λίθοι,
> καὶ ἡ κόνις αὐτὴ τῶν μαρτύρων.
>
> *   *   *   *   *
>
> Τοὺς γενναίους μας μάρτυρας εἶδα
> ὅσοι ἔπεσον πίστεως φίλοι
> διὰ μίαν θανόντες πατρίδα.
> Κατηφεῖς, σκυθρωποὶ καὶ ὀργίλοι
> κατεδείκνυον μέλη θλασμένα
> καὶ πληγῶν διαχαίνοντα χείλη.

Aristoteles Valaorites writes for the common people in vernacular Romaic.

Ὁ Βρυκόλακας, 'The Vampire,' is thus described, or rather

addressed by the widow of the deceased Thanases Vagias, a notorious wretch:—

> Πές μου τί στέκεσαι Θανάση, ὀρθός,
> Βουβὸς σὰ λείψανο 'στὰ μάτια ἐμπρός;
> Γιατί, Θανάση μου, βγαίνεις τὸ βράδυ;
> Ὕπνος γιὰ σένανε δὲν εἶν' 'στὸν Ἅδη;
>
> Τώρα περάσανε χρόνοι πολλοί·
> Βαθειὰ σ'ἐρρίξανε μέσα 'στὴ γῆ.
> Φεύγα σπλαχνίσου με. Θὰ κοιμηθῶ,
> Ἄφες με ἥσυχη νἀναπαυθῶ.......
>
> Στάσου μακρύτερα......Γιατί μὲ σκιάζεις;
> Θανάση τί ἔκαμα καὶ μὲ τρομάζεις;
> Πῶς εἶσαι πράσινος! μυρίζεις χῶμα·
> Πές μου, δὲν ἔλυωσες, Θανάση, ἀκόμα;

Notice here the imperative *πές* for *εἰπές*, and compare *ἄφες*, &c. This is another relic of the verbs in μι.

I will conclude this chapter with two anonymous fragments of Greek popular songs. For the German rendering of the first, which is more successful than the English, I am indebted to my friend Herr Julius Henning, of Athens:—

> Πάντα νά 'μεθα μαζὺ,
> Τί μεγάλη εὐτυχία!
> Τί πικρὸς ὁ χωρισμὸς,
> Τί μεγάλη δυστυχία!
> μακρὰν 'πὸ σὲ, ψυχὴ,
> Τί τὴν θέλω; τί τὴν θέλω τὴν ζωή;
>
> Δακτυλίδ' ἀπὸ μαλλιὰ
> μόν' ἀνάμνησις μοῦ μένει.

"Αλλο δὲν παρηγορεῖ,
Αὐτὸ μένει καὶ μαραίνει......
Μακρὰν ἀπὸ σέ, ψυχή,
Τί τὴν θέλω; δὲν τὴν θέλω τὴν ζωή!

'Ever to abide with thee
Were the height of purest bliss;
But the bitter, cruel parting,
Where is grief to match with this?
When I am far from thee,
What is life, ah, what is life to me?

'One memorial still is left,
A ring from thy fair tresses braided;
Nothing else my soul can cheer.
This remains, but I am faded:
And thus forsaken here,
How can I, nay, I cannot live a life so drear.'

'Stets vereint mit dir zu sein
Wäre Himmelsseligkeit:
Ach du bitteres böses Scheiden!
Ewig flieht das Glück mich weit:
Was, Geliebte, fern von dir
Frommet wohl, ja frommet wohl das Leben mir?

'Nur aus Locken noch ein Ring
Bleibet als Erinnerung mir:
Andrer Trost ist nicht zu finden;
Dieser bleibt, ich bleiche schier.
Was, Geliebte, fern von dir
Frommet, nein es frommet nicht das Leben mir.'

I know nothing in any language more beautiful of its kind than the following, with which I gladly close a long and laborious but not ungrateful task :—

Εἰς τὸ ῥεῦμα τῆς ζωῆς μου
Διὰ τί νὰ σ' ἀπαντήσω;
Δι' ἐμὲ ἀφ' οὗ δὲν ἦσο
Διατί νὰ σὲ ἰδῶ;......

Καὶ μὲ ἔκαμες ἀπαύστως
Στεναγμοὺς νὰ ὑποφέρω,
Καὶ γελᾷς διότι κλαίω,
Διὰ σὲ καὶ θρηνωδῶ.

Στέρξε, κάμε ἢ νὰ ζήσω
Ἢ νὰ παύσῃ ἡ πνοή μου·
Ἴσως, ἴσως, στὴν θανήν μου
Πλέον μεταμεληθῇς.

* * * *

Δὲν ζητῶ, οἱ στεναγμοί μου
Τὴν καρδίαν σου ν' ἑλκύσουν·
Θέλω μόνον, ὅταν σβύσουν
Τῆς ζωῆς μου αἱ στιγμαί,
Ἕνα στεναγμὸν θρηνώδη
Ὡς χαιρετισμὸν ν' ἀφήσῃς,
Κεἰς τὸν τάφον μου νὰ χύσῃς
Ἓν σου δάκρυ δι' ἐμέ.

I have attempted the following German translation, finding it beyond my powers to render the sense and metre in English:—

> An dem Strome meines Lebens
> Ach wozu dir noch begegnen?
> Da ich liebe dich vergebens
> O warum dich wiedersehn?
>
> Dir, Erbarmungslose, gelten
> Unaufhörlich meine Seufzer,
> Und du lachest, weil ich weine,
> Und verhöhnst mein bitt'res Flehn.
>
> Ach, genug! nun lass mich leben,
> Oder sterben doch im Frieden;
> Ja vielleicht wenn ich geschieden,
> Wirst du deinen Hohn bereun.
>
> * * * *

Nicht will ich dass meine Seufzer
Ein so kaltes Herz bewegen;
Nur dass wenn sich nicht mehr regen
Meines Odems matte Züg',
Eine jammervolle Klage
Du zum Abschied nach mir sendest,
Und an meinem Grabe spendest
Eine Thräne noch für mich.

APPENDIX I.

On the Greek of the Gospels of St. John and St. Luke.

I MUST now hasten to redeem a promise, made at the commencement of this work, by indicating, in however brief and cursory a manner, what kind of light may be derived from the study of modern Greek with regard to the respective ages of documents of disputed authenticity. I shall confine my remarks principally to the Gospels of St. John and St. Luke, only premising that the following is thrown out merely as a kind of forerunner to a work which I hope one day to accomplish, and which, if its ideal is ever realized, will consist of a comparison of the Greek of the various books of the Septuagint, apocryphal or otherwise, and of those of the New Testament, with a view to determining how far the evidence of language confirms or weakens, and how far it is an adequate criterion of, the results of modern research.

For the present, I would remark in the outset that several cautions must be borne in mind in attempting to weigh evidence of this kind. In the first place, it is obviously not enough to count up a number of modernisms in two documents, and balancing the number found in the one against the number found in the other, at once draw the hasty conclusion that a majority of modernisms proves a later origin. For many other questions have to be taken into consideration, and above all that most important one, is the style of the authors such that they admit of this simple comparison? Is there evidence of artifice and pedantry, such as would lead us to expect the *avoidance* of modernisms? are there signs, as in most of the Fathers, of a straining after archaic expressions? And if so, in what degree? For there are degrees of pedantry on the one hand, and degrees of familiarity on the other. Plato is more popular in his phraseology than Thucydides, Aristotle often more so than Plato.

Then, again, the frequent occurrence of a single modernism is more significant than the occasional occurrence of many; and again, there are some modernisms which are far more striking and unquestionable instances than others.

Such are some of the considerations to be borne in mind in applying the test of language as an evidence of the antiquity of documents; to which we may add another and very obvious one—namely, the limits which the slow growth of language sets to any accuracy in determining the age of any writing by the light of style and diction alone. Thirty years is a scarcely appreciable interval, but a hundred years, or even two generations, may make a very marked difference.

Let us now approach the subject a little more in the concrete.

The first thing that strikes us is that the Greek of the New Testament, however popular, familiar, and simple, is by no means so vulgar, so nearly a vernacular, as that of the Septuagint. We miss with few exceptions, and those to be found chiefly in the Apocalypse, forms like εἶδα, ἐλέγοσαν, ἐλάβοσαν, πίσε for πίσον, &c., all of which we know must have existed in the age of the New Testament, just because they have been preserved in modern Greek, sometimes in a slightly altered shape, up to the present day. What then may we generally conclude with respect to the Greek of the New Testament as a whole? We answer, that while it was familiar and popular it was not vernacular; it adopted the homely expressions, but did not as a rule let itself down to the grammatical level of the common people, in which respect it may be compared to the style of a popular modern Greek newspaper, which is familiar enough to be readily intelligible, but not enough so to be vulgar; neither altogether the spoken language of the common people, nor yet by a long way the book-language of the learned.

But when we come to compare the books of the New Testament among themselves, we do not find them exactly the same in style; there is a certain striving after semi-classical words and expressions in Luke and the Acts which we miss in other parts, while the Epistles may be looked upon, for the most part, as such simple utterances of the feelings called forth by the occasions on which they were written, that, *a priori*, we should expect the use of more familiar expressions in them than in other writings of the New Testament. If therefore we find πάντοτε for ἀεί, and καθεῖς for ἕκαστος, in St. Paul's Epistles, this does not argue their late date with anything like the force that the occurrence of the same words possesses in St. John, where the theological speculative style would naturally lead us to look for an avoidance of too familiar expressions; and therefore their presence in St. John's Gospel argues that, in the time when it was written, these same familiar expressions had risen to the level of book-language, and were no longer confined to conversation.

Now let us notice briefly what are the most striking

modernisms in the fourth Gospel, and see whether they can be reasonably accounted for except on the hypothesis of a very much later origin than that of the first two Gospels.

The most significant fact which lies on the surface of St. John's Gospel is the immense frequency of certain modernisms. For example, πιάζω (modern Greek πιάνω, ἐπίασα) occurs, not sometimes but invariably, for συλλαμβάνω. Now there is no doubt that πιάζω occurs in the Septuagint in the modern Greek sense, but then the Septuagint was much nearer the vernacular of the time; but its *frequent* occurrence in the fourth Gospel shows it must have been written at a time when πιάζω had become the recognized word for συλλαμβάνω, and that moreover in a more cultivated style than that which the Septuagint represents. And who can help noticing that where the fourth Gospel says πιάζω, those of Matthew and Mark say κρατῶ or συλλαμβάνω? And yet the style of Matthew and Mark is not more refined or elevated, but less so, than that of St. John. Again, St. John says ὀψάριον for ἰχθύς: compare John vi. 9 with Matthew xiv. 15, Mark vi. 35. Now no one denies that ὀψάριον is as old as Aristophanes, but he uses it as intentionally quoting the vernacular, while the fourth Evangelist employs it as the natural word. But more striking still is the use of τρώγω for ἐσθίω, not in a colloquial, but in the most solemn and mysterious connection possible: ὁ τρώγων μου τὴν σάρκα, καὶ πίνων μου τὸ αἷμα, ἔχει ζωὴν αἰώνιον, ὁ τρώγων με, κἀκεῖνος ζήσεται δι' ἐμέ, ὁ τρώγων μου τὴν σάρκα καὶ πίνων μου τὸ αἷμα, ἐν ἐμοὶ μένει καὶ ἐγὼ ἐν αὐτῷ, ὁ τρώγων τοῦτον τὸν ἄρτον ζήσεται εἰς τὸν αἰῶνα. Here τρώγω is invariably, and ἐσθίω not once, used as the present, answering to φάγω. In modern Greek τρώγω is the only present of φάγω in use. In Polybius, indeed, we have δύο τρώγομεν ἀδελφοί, but this is quoted as a proverb, a familiar colloquial expression, just as *fressen* and *saufen* are

APPENDIX I.

vulgarly used in German for *essen* and *trinken*. It is therefore an exceptional usage, which goes to prove the point which we desire to settle, namely, that τρώγω as applied to a human being in the sense of simply *eating*, did not establish itself in the written language until the time of St. John. But I shall perhaps be told that in chap. xiii. St. John quotes the Septuagint, Psalm xli. 9, thus, ὁ τρώγων μετ' ἐμοῦ τὸν ἄρτον, ἐπῆρεν ἐπ' ἐμὲ τὴν πτέρναν αὐτοῦ. Let us see whether this is a quotation. Let us turn to the passage in question, and what do we find? That St. John has actually been at the pains of translating ἐσθίων into τρώγων, thereby proving beyond the possibility of a doubt that he deliberately preferred τρώγων to ἐσθίων, as more familiar and more intelligible. Again, how constantly, and indeed almost invariably, does St. John use ὑπάγω for εἶμι where St. Matthew and Mark frequently use βαίνω, πορεύομαι, &c., and with whom ὑπάγω is of comparatively rare occurrence. Again, the use of θεωρῶ, the modern Greek θωρῶ, as simply equivalent to βλέπω, is characteristic of St. John, and to some extent of St. Luke. Notice too the continued recurrence of πιστεύω εἰς in St. John instead of πιστεύω with the dative.

We will now give a brief view of the remaining modernisms in St. John, and challenge any one to produce a like array from either St. Mark or St. Matthew:—

Εἰς τὸν κόλπον τοῦ πατρὸς: οὗ ἐγὼ οὐκ εἶμι ἄξιος ἵνα λύσω αὐτοῦ τὸν ἱμάντα τοῦ ὑποδήματος, where *one* of these genitives must stand for a dative; observe that Matthew says ἄξιος βαστάσαι, not ἵνα βαστάσω. Πρῶτός μου ἦν, compare in modern Greek μόνος μου, ποτέ μου, whereas in classical Greek this kind of relation is expressed by the dative, e. g. ἰδίᾳ αὐτῷ διαφέρει in Thucydides; ὡσεὶ for ὡς, modern Greek ὡσάν; ποῦ μένεις, τί μὲ δέρεις, both familiar modern Greek phrases; ὑποκάτω τῆς συκῆς; φέρετε in an aorist sense, as in modern Greek, where the present is φέρνω; the continual use of ἄρτι for νῦν; the frequency of diminutives, as φραγέλλιον, ὀψάριον, ψωμίον (modern Greek equivalent of ἄρτος), ὠτίον, &c.; ποῦ ὑπάγει for ποῖ εἶσι; the frequent use of periphrastic perfect passives, ἦν ἀπεσταλμένος, ἐγένετο ἀπεσταλμένος, ἀπεσταλμένος εἰμί, ἦν βεβλημένος, &c.; ἐπάνω πάντων for ἐπὶ πᾶσι, ἐπὶ with the accusative implying rest; ἀφῆκε τὴν Ἰουδαίαν, in the modern sense, instead of ἀνεχώρησεν ἀπὸ; ἐκαθέζετο; προσκυνῶ, used now with the dative, now with the accusative; συνάγει καρπόν, modern Greek συνάζει καρπόν; the frequent use of κόπος, a common modern Greek word; the frequency of such forms as λαλιά, ἀνθρακιά; vernacular forms, as the accent itself shows, though with some analogy (e. g. στρατιὰ) in classical Greek. In modern Greek as spoken by the common people the termination ία regularly appears as ιά; the fourth Evangelist says also σκοτία for σκότος, preferring the form in ία with the modern Greeks, who say σκοτιά, δροσιά, φωτιά, for σκότος, δρόσος, φῶς;—ὅλος frequently for πᾶς, as in modern Greek; ἀφ᾽ ἑαυτοῦ for ἐφ᾽ ἑαυτοῦ; the far more frequent use of ἵνα with the subjunctive; the comparative rareness of the aorist participle, and frequency of the copulative καὶ; for example (one instance out of many), ἐγερθεὶς ἆρον σου τὴν κλίνην, Matthew; ἔγειραι ἆρον, St. John. Here too observe St. John uses the modern κράββατον (κρεββάτιον); St. Matthew says ἐγερθεὶς ἀπῆλθε, St. John ἦρε τὸν κράββατον αὐτοῦ καὶ περιεπάτει;—ἀπ᾽ ἐμαυτοῦ for ἐπ᾽ ἐμαυτοῦ; εἰς ὃν ἠλπίκατε, παιδάριον ἕν, for παιδίον without ἕν; πλοιάριον for πλοῖον, and πλοῖον for ναῦς; ἐχορτάσθητε, a common modern Greek word; the frequent repetition of αὐτοῦ, αὐτόν, and the loss of all distinction between αὐτὸν and αὑτόν; πῶς οὗτος γράμματα οἶδε, modern Greek πῶς οὗτος γράμματ᾽ ἠξεύρει; εἷς καθεῖς, one by one; ἤνοιξε side by side with ἀνέωξε; μηδένα for οὐδένα; εἰς τὰ ὀπίσω; ὀπίσω ἐμοῦ for μετὰ ἐμέ; κόσμος for ὄχλος; διὰ μέσου αὐτῶν for δι᾽ αὐτῶν; ἔγνωκαν for ἐγνώκασι, cf. modern Greek εὕρηκαν; σκορπίζω, διασκορπίζω, προσφάγιον, βαστάζω, passim for φέρω; ὑπάγεις ἐκεῖ

APPENDIX I.

for ἐκεῖσε; ἐξυπνίσω, γεμίζω, ἐγγίζω; ἔπεσεν εἰς τοὺς πόδας αὐτοῦ instead of ἔπεσεν αὐτῷ πρὸ πόδων; ἐτάραξεν ἑαυτὸν, ἐφανέρωσεν ἑαυτόν, showing that the middle voice is on the wane; εὐχαριστῶ for χάριν οἶδα; ὀνάριον, τὰ ἱμάτια; ὅπου ὑπάγω for ὅποι εἰμι; μοναὶ πολλαί, *many dwelling-places* (μονὴ is modern and Byzantine Greek for a monastery;) ἐμφανίζειν; καὶ αὐτοὶ ἔλαβον for οἱ δὲ ἔλαβον; βάλε in the sense of 'put;' ψῦχος ἦν, in modern Greek ψῦχος ἦτο; ἔστι συνήθεια ὑμῖν for εἰώθατε, in modern Greek συνήθειά σας εἶναι; ὀφείλει ἀποθανεῖν; παρασκευὴ without the article as a proper name, so in modern Greek παρασκευὴ = Friday; τῇ μιᾷ τῶν σαββάτων, so in modern Greek τῇ μιᾷ τοῦ Ἀπριλίου; εἰς τὰ δεξιὰ μέρη τοῦ πλοίου.

Many of these modernisms occur in the other Gospels; but it is the frequency of their occurrence, the comparative regularity and consistency in the usage, and above all the presence of certain special modernisms of a very marked character, which make it impossible, I think, for any dispassionate reader to avoid the conclusion that the fourth Gospel must have been composed at least two, or perhaps three, generations later than either the first or the second.

As to the Revelation of St. John, it can scarcely be compared with the Gospel, for it approaches much nearer the vernacular, and is so wild and barbarous in its grammar, that it is hard to believe it was written by one perfectly at home in the Greek language. Therefore the very striking modernisms in it, as κολλούριον ἔγχρισον τοὺς ὀφθαλμούς σου, in modern Greek κολλούριον ἔγχρισε τοὺς ὀφθαλμούς σου, in ancient κολλύριον ἔγχρισον τοῖς ὀφθαλμοῖς σου, or, better, κολλυρίῳ ἐγχρῖσαι τοὺς ὀφθαλμούς; ζεστὸς for θερμός, δώσῃ for δῷ, δώσουσι for δώσωσι, and that for δῶσι, ἐστάθη for ἔστη, &c., do not enable us to assert on philological grounds the later origin of the Apocalypse, while the matter and spirit of the book point rather to an earlier period.

The Epistles of John, at least the first Epistle, which alone gives fair scope for judging, closely resembles the Gospel in phraseology, but it is a kind of resemblance that looks like imitation.

A few words on the Gospel according to St. Luke. This, we have already observed, betrays a certain pedantry of style. There is a would-be classical ring about such phrases as ἀνατάξασθαι διήγησιν, ἵνα ἐπιγνῷς περὶ ὧν κατηχήθης τὴν ἀσφάλειαν, ἔδοξε κἀμοὶ παρηκολουθηκότι ἄνωθεν πᾶσιν ἀκριβῶς, which shows an effort to struggle against the common familiar style of writing prevailing among the early Christians, who were mostly, as St. Paul says, ἰδιῶται τῷ λόγῳ. All the more striking therefore are the modernisms in St. Luke, which are continually cropping up in the midst of his most ambitious attempts, even when the effort is most sustained, as in the introduction to the Gospel. For example, τῶν πεπληροφορημένων, which probably means 'those things of which information has been given,' πληροφορῶ meaning in modern Greek like εἰδοποιῶ, *to inform*. Again, ἐξ ἐφημερίας Ἀβία is an extremely modern expression, and hardly intelligible till we know that in modern Greek ἐφημέριος means a priest. Notwithstanding all his Atticizing tendencies, Luke exceeds all but St. John in modernisms, and some of these are of a very startling character. For instance, ἐν αὐτῇ τῇ ὥρᾳ, *in that hour ;* in modern Greek εἰς αὐτὴν τὴν ὥραν.

St. Matthew, St. Mark, St. John, all have αὐτὸς used without the article as equivalent to οὗτος or ἐκεῖνος, but only St. Luke, as far as I have discovered, uses it with the article and a noun in this sense. Nor does any other use even αὐτός, especially with καί, so persistently as a simple demonstrative or personal pronoun. Other remarkable modernisms are εὐλαβὴς for εὐσεβής, μηδὲν for οὐδέν, πλὴν for ἀλλὰ passim, προσέρρηξεν for προσέπεσε ; cf. modern Greek ῥήχνω = ῥίπτω ; τὸ ῥῆγμα τῆς οἰκίας for ἡ πτῶσις ; ἄφες ἐκβάλω he shares with St. Matthew ; ὁ μικρότερος for ὁ ἐλάχιστος, περισσότερον for πλέον, are modern Greek; so too are μήτε—μήτε for οὔτε—οὔτε; ἱματισμένον; the very frequent use of ὅλος for πᾶς; the employment of ὑπῆρχε, ὑπάρχει (common to St. Luke and St. John) as simply equivalent to ἦν, ἐστί; πορεύου εἰς εἰρήνην for ἐν εἰρήνῃ; θέλεις εἴπωμεν; κατὰ συγκυρίαν (in modern Greek also κατὰ συντυχίαν); ἔφθασεν for *arrived* simply; ὀπτασία for *vision*. Εἰς ἔτη πολλά, xii. 19, is a regular form of congratulation in Greece at the present day. The phrase 'rich toward God' is hard; we should rather say 'rich in God,' taking εἰς as equivalent to ἐν. Ποίᾳ ὥρᾳ for τίνι ὥρᾳ is modern Greek. ὁ καύσων is also modern Greek. Εὐφραίνομαι, of 'festive enjoyment,' is used in exactly the same connection in three places in St. Luke as in the modern Greek drinking-song:—

> Ἐ χοῦ ἐλᾶστε,
> Φέρτε κεράστε·
> Βάλτε νὰ πιοῦμε,
> Νὰ εὐφρανθοῦμε.

The phrase εὐφραινόμενος καθ' ἡμέραν λαμπρῶς has a modern ring in it which is quite astounding to one familiar with colloquial Greek. We have, again, εἰς τὴν κοίτην for ἐν τῇ κοίτῃ. Ὀδυνᾶσαι, φάγεσαι καὶ πίεσαι are startling modern forms, coming as they do so close together. Ἀνάπεσαι is clearly a false spelling for ἀνάπεσε, chap. xvii. 7, as there could be no meaning in the middle. Διὰ μέσου Σαμαρείας καὶ Γαλιλαίας, μετὰ παρατηρήσεως, *with observation*, a singularly modern phrase, σταθεὶς for στᾶς, δυσκόλως for χαλεπῶς, τρυμαλιᾶς, cf. ἀνθρακιά, &c., καιρὸς for χρόνος, ἐγγίζειν, ἐπάνω for ἐπί, παιδεύσω = *castigabo*, ἰσχύω passim for δύναμαι, τὸ πῶς παραδῷ, εὐκαιρίαν, χρείαν ἔχομεν, διϊσχυρίζετο, ἐνώπιον αὐτοῦ, ὡμίλουν for ἐλάλουν, συζητεῖν, εὐλογῶ, ψηλαφῶ = simple ψαύω, are other modernisms of St. Luke. Ἔκρυβε is an interesting form because condemned by Phrynichus, who, if the German critics be right, was almost a contemporary of the writer of this Gospel.

APPENDIX I.

There can be little doubt that the Acts of the Apostles belongs to an age as late as the Gospel according to St. Luke, if not later. There is much general similarity in the language, notwithstanding the difference in the spirit and tendency of the whole; but one phrase claims our especial notice, as a very decided modernism not found elsewhere in the New Testament. This is the word γεύσασθαι used in the sense not of 'to taste,' but 'to eat,' in fact 'to dine;' ἐγένετο πρόσπεινος καὶ ἤθελε γεύσασθαι. In modern Greek γεῦμα is *dinner*, γεύομαι, *to dine;* προγεύομαι, *to breakfast;* τὸ ἀπόγευμα, *the afternoon*.

I need not remind those who are acquainted with the critical investigations of Baur, Schwegler, and Hilgenfeld, that the conclusions to which a purely philological examination seems likely to lead us are the same to which they have arrived on other grounds, grounds quite strong enough in themselves, but still not so readily admitted by most, that they can altogether afford to dispense with even such evidence as the present, which, while not altogether as conclusive as some might desire, is yet, as I think even this meagre sketch has shown, not mere fancy or guess-work, but subject to definite rules; and capable of leading to definite results. Above all, I think it is an advantage when a question of this kind can be removed for a moment from the heated arena of theological strife, and looked upon in the clear 'dry light' of the passionless science of philology.

APPENDIX II.

A Short Lexilogus, containing a few of such words in modern and ancient Greek as seem to derive additional light by comparison.

Ἄβαλε, or ἃ βάλε, Callim. Fr. 455, Anth. P. 7. 699, and βάλε, Alcman. Fr. 2, is said to be equivalent in meaning to εἴθε, εἴθ' ὤφελε, &c., and seems to be an imperative from βάλλω. That βαλέ, or βάλε, should mean 'grant' is not at all unnatural, but what an abundant confirmation of this theory is it to find in modern Greek·the derivative form βολεῖ = *licet*.

Ἀγάπη, ἀγανός, Ἄγαβος. The probable radical identity of these words has been noticed above. The modern Greek ἀγαντικός, or ἀγαφτικός = ἐρωτικός, seems to make this etymology still more likely.

Ἀγγέλλω. The derivation of this word can hardly be any other than ἀνα-κέλλω; κέλλω being used in the sense of κέλομαι, and possibly identical in root with τέλλω in ἐπιτέλλω. At any rate the root of the second half of the word is (as Professor Max Müller informs me) *gar-*, which appears in κέλομαι, κέλαδος, and καλέω; and as the form γελ- is not found elsewhere in Greek, I think we must assume that the γ is the result of the contact of κ with the nasal.

Ἄγουρος. This is the modern Greek form of ἄωρος. The interest attaching to it consists in the fact that it implies a form γώρα for ὥρα, which is precisely what the cognate forms *yáre* in Zend, *jahr* in German, &c., would lead us to expect.

Ἀγροικῶ. This word would mean, if found in ancient Greek, 'to be boorish, rude, or ignorant;' in modern Greek, on the other hand, it means to know, e. g.

Καὶ ὅσοι τοῦ πολέμου τὴν τέχνην ἀγροικοῦν.
War Song of Rhegas.

Here the signification which usage has sanctioned seems to be the very reverse of the original. Perhaps we have an intermediate stage in the ἀγροικόσοφος, 'coarsely wise,' of Philo, and the ἄγροικος σοφία of Plato's Phaedrus, 299 E. We too talk of being 'rough and ready.' What if we should have in the history of this word the record of the popular prejudice against philosophy, as a useless unpractical study which we have described in the Republic of Plato?

Is it not as though the honest farmer said, ὑμεῖς μὲν φιλοσοφεῖτε, ἐγὼ δὲ ἀγροικῶ, i.e. 'while you are star-gazing I am working in my farm.' To such a man φιλοσοφία is 'the would-be-wisdom,' ἀγροικία 'useful knowledge.'

This accords very well with the usage of ἀγροικῶ, which means to know an art, rather than a science; as in the example quoted above. There was, moreover, very likely a sense of irony in this use of ἀγροικῶ, as though it were, 'I am the boor, as you philosophers call me.' With regard to the transitive use of ἀγροικῶ in the example cited above, I thankfully adopt Professor Max Müller's suggestion, that it may originally have meant 'to cultivate,' comparing οἰκονομῶ.

Ἀλέτρι is modern Greek for ἄροτρον. Does not this go far to establish the original identity of the roots ἀρο- and ἀλε- or ἀλεϝ-? Petavius, *Uranolog.* p. 258, calls the constellation

Orion ἀλετροπόδιον. In modern Greek ἀλετροπόδιον is neither more nor less than a ploughshare. Its aptitude as applied to the constellation in question is striking.

Ἀμή, a modern Greek word for 'but,' 'however,' should I think be written ἀμῆ or ἀμῇ, which in classical Greek is hardly found save in the compound ἀμηγέπη = ὁπωσοῦν. The meanings, 'in some way or another,' and 'anyhow,' 'however,' are very nearly allied.

Ἄξιος is from ἄγω, according to Liddell and Scott; whether in the sense of 'that which weighs' or 'that which is esteemed.'
This derivation prepares us to recognise in μοναξιά, modern Greek for 'solitude,' i. e. μοναξία (cf. στρατιὰ for στρατία, &c.), the etymology μοναγ-σία; in μονὰξ or μονάξ, Od. ii. 417, μονάγ-ς; and in μονάζω, μονάγιῶ = 'I live lonely,' 'I lead a lonely life.' It seems very likely that the termination -άζω is often to be thus explained, as standing for an original -άγω. So we have πειράζω, 'to lead an attempt,' i. e. to attack, tempt, or tease, of which the aorist is in modern Greek ἐπείραξα; pointing to an original πειράγω, just as συνάγω is in modern Greek συνάζω, aor. ἐσύναξα.

Ἀράδα, metaplastic for ἀράς. This word throws light on ἀραδέω = κινέω, cited by Hesychius. The word ἀράδα in modern Greek means 'turn,' 'order,' 'row.'

Βάρβαρος, probably connected with the Sanscrit *bárbaras*, *várvaras*, which according to Bopp = *stultus*, and with the Latin *balbus*, *balbutio*. The modern Greek βέρβερος, 'stammering,' βερβερίζω, 'to stammer,' is a striking and obvious confirmation of this etymology.

Βαστάζω. This is a very interesting word, because its etymology involves so many others; and also because, while it occurs in almost every Greek writer from the age of

Homer to that of the New Testament, we only find its derivation in modern Greek. Βαστάζω is plainly a compound standing for βαστὰ ἄγω, as we may see from βάσταγμα, βαστακτός, and the modern (really most ancient) Greek aorist ἐβάσταξα. Βαστὰ ἄγω can mean nothing else than 'I bear burdens.' But what is the etymology of βαστά? We have the answer in modern Greek, in which βάζω means 'I put,' and in sense = βάλλω. Βαστὰ means, accordingly, burdens, loads, things placed on the back of the horse, mule, or ass. A word of cognate meaning is βάνω, which leads us to connect βαίνω, βάνω, βάζω, and βιβάζω.

Assuming, as I think we may, that this is the radical signification of the ancient βάζω in the Homeric, ἀνεμώλια βάζεις, πεπνυμένα βάζεις, &c., we have a striking analogy in the word λέγω, which originally meant 'to put,' the English *lay* and the German *legen* being doubtless from the same root. Here belong ἐμπάζομαι, modern Greek ἐμπάζομαι or ἐμβάζομαι, with the simple verb βάζομαι εἴς τι = *curae mihi est*, i.e. 'I put myself into it.' With βάζομαι, ἐμπάζομαι, cf. πατέω, ἐμβατέω, and in modern Greek βαίνω, ἐμπαίνω. For the phonetic law on which such changes depend, see p. 37.

Βδάλλω means, in ancient Greek, 'to milk.' I more than suspect this is a vulgar corruption, taken from the mouth of the common people, of ἐκβάλλω, the modern Greek βγάλλω, which is by metathesis for ἐγβάλλω. Βγάλλω αἷμα means 'I bleed,' and βγάλλομαι αἷμα, 'I am bled.' So βγάλλω γάλα, 'I milk,' and βγάλλομαι γάλα, 'I yield milk.' Compare βόες βδάλλονται γάλα, Arist. H. A. 3, 21, 2. The etymology of βδέω from ἐκ-βέω, 'I put forth,' βέω being the transitive of βέομαι, 'I go;' βδέλλα, i.e. 'the vomiter,' from βδέλλω, i.e. ἐκβέλλω for ἐκβάλλω, whence also βδελύσσω, is more than probable.

Βεκός, or βέκκος, which Herodotus says is Phrygian, Hipponax Cyprian, for 'bread,' should be compared with the Albanian δοῦκα, which also means 'bread.' Here too belong, as Professor Max Müller reminds me, the German *backen*, *Gebäck*, the English *bake*.

Γελανὴς and γαλήνη are said to be connected. The Doric form γαλανός means, in ancient Greek, 'calm,' of the sea, in modern, 'blue,' of the sky.

Γέρινος is another form for γύρινος; compare in modern Greek γύρνω and γέρνω = γύρω.

Γιερδάνι for γιερδάνιον means, according to Passow, in the Glossary appended to his 'Carmina popularia Graeciae recentioris,' *aquatile*. He rightly connects it with ἀρδαίνω. Are the names Jordan (supposing it be Indogermanic) and Ἰάρδανος not connected with the same root? This seems likely. We must not, however, forget that the γι- in γιερδάνι may stand for δι-, i. e. διά.

Γλήγορα, γρήγορα, ἐγρήγορα or ὀγλήγορα; a neuter plural, used adverbially from γρήγορος (connected with ἐγείρω, ἐγρήγορα). The word γρήγορος, though found only in modern Greek, plainly existed in the age of the Septuagint, as is proved by the word γρηγορῶ, which is equivalent in force to γρήγορός εἰμι.

Γλίσχρος, ὀλισθαίνω, ὀλισθηρός. That these words are connected seems probable from the modern Greek γλιστράω, γλιστρέω, 'to slide,' γλιστερός = ὀλισθηρός.

Γοργώ. This word is explained by Liddell and Scott to mean 'the Grim One.' The mediaeval and modern meaning of γοργὸς is simply 'swift.' Xenophon uses γοργὸς of 'spirited horses,' and Eustathius of 'a concise style.' Is not γοργὸς connected with ἐγείρω, standing for γοριός? See on p. 116 χωργὰ for χωριά.

Διάφορον in modern Greek = κέρδος, τὰ διάφορα = τόκος: compare Thuc. iv. 86.

'Εκπαθαίνομαι, Clem. Al. 231, receives abundant illustration from the modern formations, παθαίνω for πάσχω, μαθαίνω for μανθάνω, τυχαίνω for τυγχάνω, αποθαίνω for ἀποθνήσκω, κ. τ. λ.

Εὐρώεις, εὐρώς. Are not these words connected with the modern Greek βρώμη, βρωμάω, *stench*, *stink*? If ἄρωμα be, as Pott suspects, connected with the Sanscrit *ghrá*, 'to smell,' that too must stand for an original γρῶμα or βρῶμα.

Ζάβα, *lorica*, a modern Greek word. Does not this mean, 'that which goes across,' i. e. Διάβα. Τὸ ἀνάβα, τὸ κατάβα occur in the sense of ἀνάβασις and κατάβασις. So too Ζαβὸς seems to be formed from διαβά-, and to mean that which 'slants' or 'goes across,' as a diagonal. Its derivative meaning, 'silly,' 'strange,' 'foolish,' may well be illustrated by the English 'queer,' compared with the German *quer*. A similar etymology is suggested for ζάρος, ζάρον, ζαρόω = 'wrinkle,' 'furrow,' 'to wrinkle,' 'to furrow,' where we can hardly fail to detect the etymology δι-άρος, δι-άρον, δι-αρόω.

Θανὴ is modern Greek for θάνατος, which is, however, equally common. Θανὴ is plainly a more primitive form, and is implied in ἡμίθανος, θανεῖν, &c.; θάνατος, like κάματος, being a derivative, and adjectival or participial rather than substantival in form, as we see in ἀθάνατος; cf. κάματος, ἀκάματος.

Ἰ. This, the nominative of ἰ, ἴν, or ἴν, appears in modern Greek as the masculine article. 'In some parts of Greece,' says Mr. Sophocles (Modern Greek Grammar, p. 65), 'the uneducated use ἡ for ὁ, as ἡ δάσκαλος, ἡ ἄνδρας.' But he adds, 'This peculiarity does not extend beyond the nominative singular.' Surely that is a most significant fact, and proves beyond dispute that this ἡ (or ἰ as I should write it) is certainly not the feminine article used ignorantly for the masculine. Add to this the fact that in Albanian ἰ or ἰ appears

APPENDIX II. 195

as the masculine nominative of the definite article, and there is scarcely any room for doubt as to the identity of the modern and ancient ἱ.

Ἱνατὶ is common in the New Testament and Septuagint for διατί; we have no example of this in modern Greek, but ἱνατιάζω means 'to be obstinate;' which, if the word be of Greek derivation at all, must mean 'to keep asking why?'

Κάρσιος. Hesychius and Suidas give this form, but we only find the forms ἐγκάρσιος, ἐπικάρσιος in classical writers. It is therefore interesting in modern Greek to meet with καρσὶ = ἐναντίον.

Κλαίω. Is not this connected with κράζω? The modern Greek κλαύω, κλαύγω, Cretan κραύω, compared with κραυγή, seem to render this more likely than not. We should think too of the German *klagen* and our *cry*.

Κόκκαλος means 'the kernel of a pine-cone,' κοκκάλια, 'land-snails.' In modern Greek τὰ κόκκαλα stands for τὰ ὀστᾶ. With regard to the association of ideas, compare ὀστοῦν, ὄστρακον, and ὀστρακὶς = κόκκαλος.

Κόλαξ. Does not this word mean 'one who sucks like a leech,' perhaps connected with κόλλα, κολλάω? The compound βρου-κόλαξ, βρυκόλαξ, in modern Greek means 'a blood-sucker,' 'a vampire.' Βροῦς, according to Hesychius, = πιεῖν; and βρῦν εἰπεῖν, Ar. Nub. 1382 = 'to cry for drink.' The flatterer is called κόλαξ because he is a parasite.

Κοντὰ in modern Greek means 'near.' What is its derivation? If Donaldson (New Cratylus, p. 349, 3rd edit.) is right in regarding κα-τὰ as a compound of κα = κεν and the suffix τα, then, as he points out, there must have been a form κεντά. In this case κοντὰ may very well be another form of κεντά, the change of ο and ε being, as we have seen, almost

O 2

a matter of course in Greek. From κοντά = 'by,' or 'near,' we get the adjective κοντός, short, which occurs already in Byzantine Greek, and κοντεύω, 'to approach;' also κοντάκιον, 'a breviary.'

Κρύος, κρύσταλλος, κρυερός. In modern Greek κρύος, κρύα, κρύον is the common word for ψυχρός.

Λυκόφως, ἀμφιλύκη, λεύσσω, γλαύσσω. With these should be compared the modern Greek γλυκοφέγγει, γλυκοχαράζει, 'it dawns.'

Μά. In modern Greek this word is used both in a negative and positive sense: as in the formulas μὰ τὸν σταυρόν, and μὰ τὸ ναί, which latter form of affirmation or negation appears to be a relic of heathen times, the obvious derivation being μὰ τὸ ναίον, ναίον being a diminutive for ναόν. Μὰ is also used in formulas of supplication, as σὲ παρακαλῶ μὰ τὸν θεὸν for πρὸς τοῦ θεοῦ. Donaldson considers μὰ as another form of μή, and connects both with μέ, ἐμέ, considering *mere subjectivity* to be the primary notion. He also connects μὴ with μήν, and the whole series with με in με-τά. Now it is certainly interesting, and seems to be significant, that in modern Greek we have μὴν for μή, and μὲ in the sense of 'with,' for μετά. This leads us to the further inference that μὴν is really for μή-να, just as ἢν appears to be for *éna*, Sanscrit. Now μήνα is actually found in modern Greek as an interrogative particle.

This leads us to consider the force of να, which Donaldson everywhere regards as denoting remoteness from the speaker. As a termination he finds it in ἀνά, ἵνα, and ἢν, but nowhere as a separate word. But in modern Greek we have νὰ as an independent word in what, if Donaldson be right, is its most primary form and signification. Νὰ means 'see there,' *voilà*, νά το, *le voilà*. It is also used (like νη in τύνη)

APPENDIX II. 197

as a strengthening demonstrative suffix, e. g. αὐτάνα; and once, if not twice, though modified in the second place, in the forms ἐμέναντ, ἐσέναντ.

In the vulgar, but we cannot doubt extremely ancient, forms αὐτῆνος, αὐτοῦνος, αὐτόνος = αὐτός, αὐτήνη = αὐτή, αὐτόνων = αὐτῶν, &c., we find this *objective* particle ν- inserted in the middle of a word. Ἀνὰ occurs in modern as in ancient Greek for the shorter ἀ privative, e. g. ἀνάβαθος, ἀναμελῶ, for ἄβαθος, ἀμελῶ.

Μαλόνω means, in modern Greek, 'to fight.' The root is a very common one, which, according to Professor Max Müller, we have under a great variety of forms; which may be referred however to two main heads, namely *mar-* or *mal-* as their respective starting-points. The original sense is to grind or crush. From it we get, among other words, *mrínámi* Sanscrit, μάρναμαι Greek, and I suspect also μῶλος, as well as the modern Greek μαλόνω, and μαλερὸς, which means 'quarrelsome.' *Mola* and μύλος are from the same root; and, it need hardly be added, the English 'mill,' which in its secondary and vulgar employment bears the same sense as μαλόνω.

Μηγαρή, τίγαρη, τίγαρ, i. e. μὴ γὰρ ᾖ, τί γὰρ ᾖ, τίγαρ, equivalent in sense to μῶν, μή. The force of the several particles is very plain, and is preserved intact, although the particles themselves are for the most part obsolete in modern Greek. Γὰρ = γε ἆρ is equivalent to 'why then,' μὴ has the force of 'do not imagine,' and ᾖ = 'or,' introducing the following verb: so μηγαρὴ ἔρχεται = 'surely then he is not coming—[or] is he?' In German the form of expression is very common, and μηγαρὴ ἔρχεται might be almost literally translated thus, *Er wird ja denn nicht kommen, oder?* Similarly τίγαρη would mean 'What then?' or 'Is it really so?' The forms μηγαρή, τίγαρη are interesting, inasmuch as they preserve the old conjunction γὰρ which is elsewhere supplanted by διότι.

Μνήσκω and μναίσκω are modern Greek forms for μένω. Compare θνήσκω and the Doric θναίσκω in ancient Greek.

'Ορούσε, ὄρουσε. Perhaps both ways of accenting this word are allowable. 'Ορούσε would then be an imperfect from the root ὀρο-, as in modern Greek ἐχρυσοῦσε from χρυσόω (χρυσόω), while ὄρουσε would be a first aorist from ὀρούω. In modern Greek we seem to have a derivative form ὀρούω in γιουρούσιον, i. e. διορούσιον = ὅρμημα, 'a sally.'

Πέδιλον and πέταλον. These appear to be but different forms of the same word, when we know that πέταλον in modern Greek is the regular word for a horse-shoe. We may compare πέδαυρος and πέταυρος. The Ionic form of πέταλον is πέτηλον, for which πέτιλον, πέδιλον, would be a natural iotacism.

Πέρνημι, περάω. I am inclined to connect both these words by means of the modern Greek περνάω, which has the sense of the latter.

Ποῦ, που. This word is always written as a proclitic ποῦ, never as an enclitic που, in modern Greek; but this can hardly be more than a matter of writing, for its use as a qualifying particle is very similar to its classical employment, though more restricted. It is chiefly used in such exclamations as the following: δυστυχὴς ποῦ εἶναι, i. e. 'unhappy man that he is,' or τί δυστυχὴς ποῦ εἶναι, 'how unhappy is he.' Here it seems a connecting particle, like the French que, as 'que paresseux que vous êtes.' And is it not also a connecting particle in ancient Greek, e. g. in τάχα που, ἴσως που, εἰ που, ἐάν που, ὅτε που? Just so we say 'if that' in old English. Does not this help us to understand how ποῦ has come to be used in modern Greek as an indeclinable relative? Let us see whether we have not at least something which looks very like this vulgar usage in the colloquial language of Aristophanes. In the 'Knights,' line 203, the ἀλλαντοπώλης puts the question—

τί δ' ἀγκυλοχήλης ἐστίν;

to which the answer is—

αὐτό που λέγει,
ὅτι ἀγκύλαις ταῖς χερσὶν ἁρπάζων φέρει.

Here Adolph von Velsen (Aristophanis Equites, Leipzig, 1869) reads τοῦτό που λέγει, being offended at αὐτός used apparently as a simple demonstrative. Mr. W. G. Clark (Journal of Philology, vol. ii. p. 314) retains the reading of the MSS., but translates 'The thing speaks for itself;' in which case, I presume, the που must be translated 'I take it.' But surely this is a very stilted expression for so colloquial a style. With regard to the meaning of αὐτό, there are innumerable instances where it plainly means simply 'that,' even in classical Greek; as, for example, αὐτὸ οὐκ εἴρηται, ὃ μάλιστα ἔδει, Plat. Rep. 362 d; and αὐτὸ ἂν ἔφη τὸ δέον εἴη, Xen. An. 4. 7, 7; where to say with Liddell and Scott that τοῦτο or ἐκεῖνο is understood, is very like begging the question. In the New Testament αὐτός meets us at every turn in the sense of οὗτος or ἐκεῖνος, and indeed it is almost a necessary demonstrative, inasmuch as it holds a middle position between οὗτος and ἐκεῖνος, just as αὐτοῦ, in modern and ancient Greek, holds a middle place between ὧδε and ἐκεῖ.

Now in modern Greek the sense of αὐτό που λέγει, or, as we should prefer to write it, αὐτὸ ποῦ λέγει, would be very simple indeed, and suit the passage exactly.

The question is, 'What does ἀγκυλοχήλης mean?' and the answer is, 'Just what it says;' αὐτὸ ποῦ λέγει. Surely this is better than, 'I imagine it speaks for itself.'

Αὐτὸ ποῦ λέγεις is a very common phrase in modern Greek;

so common, that I have known and conversed with people who invariably prefaced their remarks by this singular expression. It means 'as you say,' and implies either that the speaker's words have been suggested by some remark which the person addressed has let fall, or that he reckons at any rate on your agreement with what he says.

Στοιχεῖον. This word means, as stated on page 94, a ghost or demon among the modern Greeks. Yet that is hardly a sufficient definition of the word. Στοιχεῖον is, according to the popular belief, the principle of life or spiritual power which lies concealed in every natural object, animate or inanimate. For a very striking and singularly felicitous explanation of the origin of this superstition, see an essay 'On the Origin of Animal Worship' &c., in the 'Fortnightly Review' for May 1, 1870, by Mr. Herbert Spencer, who, regarding the belief in the continued existence of an active personality after death as the origin of all religious belief, supposes that the names of natural objects, as 'mountain,' 'bear,' 'lion,' &c., were first applied to the living in default of abstract names, in order to indicate height, shagginess, fierceness, and so forth; that such metaphors were perpetuated in patronymics; that succeeding generations, ignorant of the origin of the metaphor, interpreted it as literal fact, and supposed that they were really descended from mountains, bears, or lions: hence arose the belief that that other self, which continued to exist when the body was dead, and needed to be propitiated, was to be looked for in animate or inanimate natural objects. The belief in monsters would arise from compound patronymics, such as would be formed when, for instance, 'a chief, nicknamed the Wolf, carries away from an adjacent tribe a wife who is remembered either under the animal name of her tribe, or as a woman.'

APPENDIX II.

Unite with this once universally prevalent superstition, the preserving power of the Greek's poetic and vivid imagination, and we seem at once to understand the secret of Greek mythology and of Greek superstition. The Christian dogma has succeeded to a great extent in supplanting the first, but it has left the second almost untouched.

The νηρεΐδες, or water nymphs, still survive as ναραΐδες or νεραΐδες among the modern Greeks; while Χάρων, though deprived of his boat and his office of ferryman, conducts the souls of the dead to Ἅδης on horseback. But in no respect is the belief of ancient Greece more faithfully preserved than in regard to the δαίμονες or στοιχεῖα, the personified powers of Nature. According to the Greek belief, anything may become a στοιχεῖον, from a rock or a river to a bird or a beast. Often this στοιχεῖον is conceived of, like the ancient δαίμων, as the spirit of some departed hero, with whose actions during life this or that natural object has been especially associated. Sometimes, on the other hand, and this is still more common, the powers of nature are personified without being identified with any particular human being. Achilles conversing with his horses, or with the river Scamander, is exactly the kind of thing which meets us at every turn in popular modern Greek poetry. The question which we have now to ask is, How old is the signification which the modern Greeks give to στοιχεῖον, and how did it arise? What is really the force of στοιχεῖον? In the first place, we must most decidedly differ from Liddell and Scott, who regard it as a diminutive of στοῖχος, 'a row,' and leave us to infer that because στοῖχος means 'a row of poles' (or indeed of anything else), that therefore the so-called diminutive στοιχεῖον might mean 'a little pole;' hence they give as the original meaning of στοιχεῖον, the upright rod which throws its shadow on the sundial. But στοῖχος would not give us στοιχεῖον as a diminutive, but στοιχίον, just as τοῖχος gives us τοιχίον; -εῖον is never used as a diminutive termination. It may cause surprise that, believing as we do in the general identity of the modern and ancient pronunciation of the Greek language, we should have so much difficulty in accepting an etymology which would simply require us to regard εἰ as another way of writing ι; but here the modern Greek language itself enters a most emphatic protest against confusing a short ι with the diphthongal εἰ, or even with ῑ. Had στοιχεῖον stood for στοιχίον, it is a matter of absolute certainty, which no one acquainted with the principles of modern Greek etymology could doubt for a moment, that its Romaic form would have been στοιχί. But this is not the case. It appears as στοιχειό, just as μνημεῖον appears as μνημειό, and the final o is never lost; ειον and ιον regularly preserve the o, ιον as regularly loses it in modern Greek. Στοιχεῖον then is no diminutive form of στοῖχος, as it cannot stand for στοιχίον. Nor, if it were, could it mean a little rod; it would rather mean a little row.

There is no doubt about the derivation of στοιχεῖον; it must come, like στοῖχος, from στείχω, which although only found in the derivative sense of 'directing one's steps,' 'proceeding,' may have meant originally 'to arrange.' Hence we see its connection with στίχος and στοχάζομαι. Bearing in mind the force of the termination, we see that as τὸ μνημεῖον means 'that which reminds,' 'memorial;' so στοιχεῖον might mean 'that which arranges,' 'marks out,' 'points.' The στοιχεῖον of the sundial was the intelligent part of it, compared to a human being who observes the progress of the sun in the heavens, and hence called also γνώμων. Or, to get the meaning still more simply from στείχω, may not στοιχεῖον have signified 'that which moves?' referring of course to the shadow of the upright rod, rather than the rod itself. That στοιχεῖον really had this meaning appears from the phrase δεκάπουν στοιχεῖον, i. e. supper time when the shadow was ten feet long. In any case, the idea of regular, intentional, intelligent motion indicative of intelligence is contained in the word στείχω and στοιχεῖον; and it was of course the shadow to which life and intelligence were attributed. There must have been something awfully mysterious in the regular progression of that shadow across the dial, even to the inventor who had some dim perception of natural cause and effect; but how much more to the ordinary man who had none. That little upright rod, he observed with amazement, had a shadow like his own, a second self; and this second self was far more knowing (γνώμων) than the little rod which always stood still in the same place.

Then he would soon observe that rocks and trees and animals had also their στοιχεῖα; and στοιχεῖον would naturally become with him a name for that living or moving personality which he seemed to find connected with, and hidden behind all natural objects. Do we not now understand why σκιά is used of the spirits of the departed? and, what is still more remarkable, how it is that we have inherited the word *gnome*, plainly connected with γνώμων, in the sense of spirit or genie? Σκιάζω, σκιάζομαι, meaning in modern Greek respectively 'to frighten,' 'to fear,' and the masculine derivative σκιός or ἴσκιος, from σκιά, are sufficient indications of the appalling sense of personality with which the Greeks still continue to regard shadows.

But now, how are we to connect this meaning of στοιχεῖον with the Platonic and subsequent philosophic usage of the word in the sense of 'element?' This is not very difficult. The shadow, the στοιχεῖον, was the mysterious hidden self, the inner personality of all things, shrinking away almost to nothing in broad noonday, and slowly but regularly creeping out as the sun approached the horizon. Therefore to the popular mind, and more or less even to themselves, the inquiry of the physical philosophers after the beginnings of all things was a kind of necromancy, a search for ghosts.

Hence it is that for a long time the Ionic philosophers had no difficulty in enduing their στοιχεῖα or ἀρχαὶ with life and motion, or rather they were unable to conceive of them as divested of these attributes of personality. It belonged naturally to Plato, the great popularizer of philosophy, to adopt the people's word στοιχεῖον, and give it a philosophical meaning, thus combating in friendly guise the ἔνεροι καὶ ἀλίβαντες (Rep. 387 c) of the popular superstition. What a fine conception do we here obtain of the struggle between Greek enlightenment and Greek superstition. To get at the bottom of these στοιχεῖα, these dreadful phantoms, to penetrate to their ῥιζώματα with Empedocles, and show, as he thought he could, that there were but four of them after all; this was, as the physical philosophers vainly hoped, to 'rob the grave of victory, and take the sting from death.'

The word στοιχεῖα, as applied by Plato to the letters of the alphabet, indicated originally not the signs, but the 'living voices,' the souls, so to speak, of the letters, just as *litterae* and *elementa litterarum* were distinguished by the Latin grammarians. That this word στοιχεῖον would inevitably connect itself in Plato's mind with his doctrine of ideas, is seen at once, and the full force of his polemical attitude towards the popular belief appears when we consider that the στοιχεῖα of the common people were the antipodes of his own. Shadows were with him the least real, with them the most real, of all appearances. His στοιχεῖα were ideas, theirs were shadows and reflections.

It was the very essence of the popular notion of στοιχεῖον that it should exist independently of the object which first suggested it. So bears and rams were soon found in the sky among the stars, where their outlines were fancifully traced. Hence we have the signs of the Zodiac also called στοιχεῖα (Diog. L. vi. 102). Hence, too, στοιχεῖα is used by ecclesiastical writers, and by Manetho especially, of the heavenly bodies. Most striking and conclusive is St. Paul's use of the word στοιχεῖα in phrases like τὰ στοιχεῖα τοῦ κόσμου (Gal. iv. 3, &c.; Col. ii. 8, 20). Baur (Christenthum der drei ersten Jahrhunderte, p. 49) and Hilgenfeld (Galaterbrief, p. 66, Das Urchristenthum und seine neuesten Bearbeitungen : Zeitschrift für wissenschaftliche Theologie, erster Jahrgang, Heft i. p. 99) expressly attribute this sense to St. Paul's words, and Hilgenfeld quotes Philo Judaeus (De Humanitate, § 3, p. 387; De Parentibus Colendis, § 9, ed. Tauchn. v. p. 62; De Vita Contemplativa, § 1, p. 472), the Clementine Homilies (x. 9. 25), and even a Sibylline fragment anterior to the time of Christ (Orac. Sibyll. iii. 80, ed. Friedl.), in support of this view. How too, he pertinently asks, could St. Paul speak of the στοιχεῖα τοῦ κόσμου as the guardians or tutors of mankind before Christ, and of their being enslaved or in bondage under them, and how could he so directly oppose them to Christ unless he attributed to them a real personality? That St. Paul means especially the heavenly powers by στοιχεῖα τοῦ κόσμου is plain from the connection in which he places them with the observance of 'days and months and times and years.' How vivid his realization of the conflict between Christ and the στοιχεῖα τοῦ κόσμου may be seen from Ephesians vi. 12: Ὅτι οὐκ ἔστιν ἡμῖν ἡ πάλη πρὸς αἷμα καὶ σάρκα, ἀλλὰ πρὸς τὰς ἀρχὰς (observe that ἀρχή is a synonym for στοιχεῖον), πρὸς τὰς ἐξουσίας, πρὸς τοὺς κοσμοκράτορας τοῦ σκότους τοῦ αἰῶνος τούτου, πρὸς τὰ πνευματικὰ τῆς πονηρίας ἐν τοῖς ἐπουρανίοις.

We are now in a position to understand how στοιχειόω in Byzantine Greek comes to mean 'to enchant,' and στοιχειόνω, 'to haunt,' στοιχειάζω, 'to be haunted,' in modern Greek.

Τυτθὸς and τίτθη. There is every reason to believe, with Liddell and Scott, that these two forms are etymologically connected. The change of υ and ι, as well as the change of accent, is perfectly regular. An exact analogy as regards the meaning is supplied by the modern Greek βᾶια, 'nurse,' which we cannot but regard as connected with βαιός, 'little.'

Φθάνω. In modern Greek, φθάνω means simply 'I arrive,' 'I come;' τὸ φθάσιμον, 'the arrival.' It means, however, also 'to be in time for,' as ἔφθασα τὸ ἀτμόπλοιον, 'I caught the steamer:' this is, however, its transitive sense. The ordinary, absolute employment of φθάνω in classical Greek is represented in modern Greek by the compound προφθάνω. The modern usage of φθάνω approaches most nearly to the ancient in the phrase φθάνει, 'it is enough.' Yet the fact that the compound προφθάνω is used by Aeschylus, Aristophanes, and Euripides, is proof enough that φθάνω might mean in ancient Greek simply 'I arrive,' 'I come,' 'I reach' (i.e. my destination), otherwise προφθάνω would be a pleonasm. The non-recognition of this, in modern Greek the common, and, as we believe, even in ancient Greek the original meaning of φθάνω, has caused much difficulty to the commentators on Thuc. III. 49. 3, καὶ τριήρη εὐθὺς ἄλλην ἀπέστελλον κατὰ σπουδὴν, ὅπως μὴ, φθασάσης τῆς δευτέρας, εὕρωσι διεφθαρμένην τὴν πόλιν: where we have only to disabuse our minds of the prejudice that φθασάσης must mean 'having *first* arrived,' translating simply, 'lest, *on the arrival* of the second, they should find the city destroyed,' and all is clear.

Χάω. This root appears in the modern χάνω, 'to lose,' and in χατῆρι (from χατέω) = πόθος.

Ψηλαφῶ. Liddell and Scott derive this word from 'ψάω, ψάλλω, ψαθάλλω, ψαλάσσω, the -αφάω being a mere termination.' But even mere terminations must have some meaning, and we will endeavour to suggest a more plausible and complete etymology for ψηλαφῶ than one which barely explains one half of the word.

To begin with what is most obvious: ἀφάω, Il. vi. 322,

APPENDIX II. 207

θώρηκα καὶ ἀγκύλα τόξ' ἀφόωντα, is derived simply enough from ἀφή, and means 'to touch,' or 'to feel:' therefore ψηλ-αφάω means plainly, to touch or feel in a particular manner, and implies an adjective ψηλός, with a corresponding adverb ψηλῶς or ψηλά. But ψηλός, so written, is not found. We know, however, by the derivation of ψιλός from ψάω, that this word is merely an iotacism for ψηλός, and ought so to be written: cf. ἀπατηλός, from ἀπατάω. Now what does ψιλός or ψηλός according to its derivation mean? One significa-tion is no doubt 'rubbed bare,' but an equally natural one, and the prevailing one in modern Greek, is 'rubbed fine,' used, for instance, of tobacco that has become powdery from keeping, or of small coin. To distinguish this meaning from the classical, as preserving most faithfully the etymology from ψάω, we may, if we like, write the word ψῃλός when used in this sense. Hence we have, as a matter of course, ψηλοκοπῶ, 'to split hairs,' 'to mince matters;' ψῃλο-σοφῶ, 'to be over-subtle,' no doubt a play upon φιλοσοφῶ; ψῃλογράφω, 'to write fine;' ψῃλοτραγουδῶ, 'to sing gently;' and an infinite number besides, for the modern Greek language has an unlimited licence in multiplying such compounds. Who, then, can resist the conclusion that ψηλαφάω means 'to touch lightly,' 'to feel about one,' like the German *herumtappen*. Its usage in ancient Greek bears out this etymology most strikingly. Xenophon, Eq. 2. 4, uses it in the sense of 'stroking,' Latin *palpare*. In Aristophanes, Pax 691, we have ἐν σκότῳ ψηλαφᾶν τὰ πράγματα: comp. Eccl. 315, and Plato, Phaed. 99 b. In Odyssee ix. 416, we have it used of the blind Cyclops:—

> Κύκλωψ δὲ στενάχων τε καὶ ὠδίνων ὀδύνῃσιν,
> Χερσὶ ψηλαφόων, ἀπὸ μὲν λίθον εἷλε θυράων,
> Αὐτὸς δ' εἰνὶ θύρῃσι καθίζετο χεῖρε πετάσσας
> Εἴ τινά που μετ' ὄεσσι λάβοι στείχοντα θύραζε.

Compare also Acts xvii. 27, ζητεῖν τὸν Κύριον, εἰ ἄρα ψηλαφήσειαν αὐτὸν καὶ εὕροιεν.

Ψηλάφησις is used by Plutarch in the sense of 'tickling,' and the essential condition of tickling is, as we know, a light touch.

This is one of those cases where a knowledge of modern Greek enables us to pronounce with certainty for a derivation which it would seem has not so much as suggested itself to philologers who have not made modern Greek their study. It is one of those extremely simple and obvious etymologies which, when once observed, make us wonder how they could have so long lain hidden.

Ψηφίζω. In modern Greek, ψηφάω means not 'to vote,' but 'to care for' or 'regard;' apparently from ψῆφος, in the sense of *cipher*, as we say, 'to reck not,' 'reckless,' &c.

INDEX

OF

GREEK AND ALBANIAN WORDS.

ἄβαλε, p. 189.
ἀββᾶς, 107.
ἀβδέλλα, 12.
ἀβληχρὸς, 12.
ἀβράγω, 119.
ἀβράμυλον, 12.
ἀβρότανον, 12.
ἀβρύον, 12.
ἀγαπάει, 72.
ἀγάπη, ἀγαυτικὸς, Ἄγαβος, ἀγαυὸς, 29, 104, 189.
ἀγγέλλω, 189.
ἀγγίζω, 12.
ἄγγος, ἄγκος, 29.
ἀγέρωχος, 81.
ἀγκάθι, 31.
ἀγκούλα, 20.
ἄγκουρα, 20.
ἄγουρα, 122.
ἄγουρος, 189.
ἀγροικῶ, 190.
ἀδανὰ, 114.
ἀδερφός, 36.
ἄδεσθαι, 28.
ἀετὲ, 118.
ἄθε, 113.
ἀθία, ἀθί, 123.
αἰ ἀν, 25.
αἴγα, αἴγαν, 71, 74, 75.
αἰεὶ, 12.
αἰὲν, αἰὲς, 77.
αἰετὸς, 12.

Αἰόλου, 45.
αἰπὺς, 25.
αἰώνιος, 105.
αἰώρα, 25.
ἀκολουθῶ, 103.
ἀκμὴ, ἀκμὴν, 35, 102.
ἀκούεις, 116.
ἀλάκαιραις, 143.
ἀλέθω, 36.
ἀλείβω, 30.
ἀλειμμάτιον, 26.
ἀλέτρι, 190.
ἀλετροπόδιον, 190.
ἀληθης, 117.
ἀλλάξιμον, -ατος, 108.
ἀλλ' ἱμάτιον, 26.
ἄλογον, 93.
Ἄλυ, 108.
ἀλύφαντος, 35.
ἄλφιτον, 36.
ἅμα, 12.
ἀμαιμάκετος, 25.
Ἀμαλὲκ, 30.
ἁμαρτία, 102.
ἀμβλακίσκω, 37.
Ἀμβρακία, 37.
ἄμβων, 107.
ἀμέλγω, 35.
ἀμέργω, 35.
ἄμεσος πρότασις, 99.
ἀμὴ, ἀμῇ, 190.
ἀμολγῷ, 35.
ἀμόργη, 20, 35.

ἄμον, 113.
ἀνάβαθος, 196.
ἀνάθεμα, 15.
ἀναθυμίασις, 93.
ἀναιβαίνω, 12.
ἀνάλυσις, 93.
ἀνάμεσον, 89.
ἄνδετέ, 136.
ἀνελύπητη, 144.
ἄνθε, 36, 120.
ἄνι, 137.
ἀνοιγοσφάλισμα, 144.
ἀντίσπασμα, 103.
ἄξιος, 191.
ἄπειρον, 93.
ἀπεκρίθη, 79.
Ἀπέλλων, 24.
ἀπὸ, 102, 104.
ἀποκότησα, 146.
ἀπὸ μακρόθεν, 105.
Ἄραβας, 74.
ἀρά γε, 99.
ἀρδδα, 191.
ἀραίωσις, 93.
Ἀραπιὰ, 30.
ἄρδεμεν, 129.
ἀρετὴ, 96.
Ἄρη, 71.
ἄρθτ, 130.
ἀρίζηλος, 118.
ἀρμαθιὰ, 12.
ἄρματα, 106.
ἀρματωλὸς, 106.

INDEX.

ἀρόω, 191.
ἄρτι, 183.
ἀρχέως, 107.
ἀρχή, 93.
ἄρωμα, 193.
ἆs, 103, 107.
ἀσᾶι, 133.
ἀσκαλώπας, 74.
ἄσπακ, 132.
ἀστάχυ, 12.
ἀσταφὶς, 12.
ἀστεροπή, 12.
ἀτάρ, 131.
ἀτὲ-δερά, 132.
ἀτιὲ, 132.
ἀτμόπλοιον, ἀτμόπλουν, 27.
αὐγὸν, 31.
αὐτάνα, 196.
αὐτίον, 24.
αὖτις, 38.
αὐτοῦνος, 196.
αὐτὸς, Ϝατὸς, 132.
αὔω, 29.
ἄφες, 103, 186.
ἀφ' οὗ, 40.
ἀψ, 24.
ἄψῦ, 134.

βάγγα, 24.
βάζω, 192.
βάϊα, βαιὸς, 205.
βάλε, 185.
βαλίκιος, 29.
βαλτὸς, 83.
βάνω, 192.
βάρβαρος, 191.
Βαριωνᾶ, 24.
βασιλέαν, 74.
βασιλέας, 71, 74.
βασιλεύει, 92.
βασιλὲϜς, 143.
βασίλισσα, 106.
βαστάζω, βαστὰ, 184, 192.
βατεῖν, 30.
βαυκάλιον, 24.
βάχος, 115.
βγάλλω, 192.
βδάλλω, 192.

βδέλλα, βδελύσσω, 192.
βδέω, 192.
βείκατι, 29.
βεκὸς, βέκκος, 192.
βελόνα, 12.
βέλτερος, βελτὸς, 83.
βεμβρὰς, 30.
βέρεθρον, 11.
βὲτ, 131.
βέφυρα, 29.
βέω, 192.
βῆ, βῆ, 18.
βῆμα, 16.
βιβάζω, 192.
βιέδιν, 132.
Βιλαρᾶς, 30.
Βίλιππος, 30.
βλέφω, 31.
βλησκοῦνι, 30.
βόθρος, 12.
βοΐ, βοηθεῖν, 16.
βολεῖ, 189.
βόλομαι, 45.
βότσχυ, 118.
βούλει, βούλῃ, 15.
βουνὶν, 115.
βοῦρκος, 29.
βράχος, 29.
βρὲ, 37.
Βρεκεκεκὲξ, 19.
βρέχει, 103.
βρίζα, 29.
βρίθω, βαρύθω, 22.
βρόχη, 117.
βρυκόλαξ, 195.
βρόμη, 193.
βύβλος, βίβλος, 22.
βυζάω, 30.
βύθος, 12.
βυτίνη, 30.
Βωκάλιον, 24.

γὰ, 119.
γάζα, 30.
γαὶ, 118.
γαῖα, 30.
γαῖμα, 31.
γαλάζιος, 133.
γαλανὸς, 33.
γὰρ, 96, 197.

γαργαλέων, 29.
γέφυρα, 29.
γδοῦπος, 187.
γδυμναὶς, γδύω, 144.
γελανὴς, 117.
γελάσιμον, 80, 105, 1
γέλλω, 189.
γέλων, 73.
γεμίζω, 105.
γεράκιν, 109.
γέρινος, 193.
γέρνω, 193.
γέροντς, 74.
γερὸς, 32.
γεύσασθαι, 188.
γέφυρα, 32.
γῆ, 145.
γηγενὴς, 16.
γιὰ, 32.
γιαίνω, 32.
γιάκιον, 32.
γιαμὰ, 145.
γιαδότε, 135.
γιατρὸς, 31.
γίγας, 16.
γίννος, 30.
γιουρούσιον, 198.
γιώκω, 32.
γλακῶ, 31.
γλάρος, 31.
γλέπω, 29.
γλέφαρον, 29.
γλέφσω, λεύσσω, 31.
γλήγορα, 193.
γλιστραίνω, 193.
γλίσχρος, 193.
γλυκοφέγγει, 31.
γνέθω, 31.
γνώμων, 202.
γνωρίω, 117.
Γόμορρα, 30.
γοργὸς, 193.
γούλια, 31.
γοῦν, 20.
γουναῖκα, 118.
γοῦπα, 29.
γούργουρας, 29.
γράμματα οἶδε, 184.
γράφορ, 121.
γραφούμενε, 121.

INDEX.

γραφουρένι, 121.
γραφτέ, 121.
γραψίματα, 81.
γράψιμον, 81.
γρήγορος, 193.
γρούσσα, 119.
γρώμα, 193.
γυαλον, 32.
γών, 20.

δά, 114.
Δαβίδ, 29.
δαγκάνω, 31.
δαίμων, 94, 201.
δάνουν, 130.
δάρκυα, 31.
δάτυλο, 119.
δέ, δέν, 144.
δείχνω, 118.
δενούμενε, 118.
δένω, 72.
δέξου, 79.
δέον, 132.
δέρεις, 183.
δετέ, 135.
Δεύς, 31.
δεύω, 24.
δέχομαι, δέκομαι, 38.
δέψω, 24.
Δήμας, 16.
Δημήτηρ, 16.
δημιουργός, 98.
διάβα, 194.
διάβολος, 105.
διαθήκη, 16.
διαίνω, 32.
διαίφυρα, 32.
διάκιον, 32.
διάλεκτος κοινή, 115.
διαμέσου, 184.
διά νά, 89.
διδρος, 194.
δίαιτα, 12.
διατάζω, 83.
διαφέντευσαν, 149.
διάφορον, 193.
Δίδυμος, 16.
δίδω, διδόνω, 116.
διερός, 32.
διισχυρίζετο, 187.

δικαιοδοσία, 103.
δίκαιον, διαίόν, 26.
δίκλοπος, 113.
δίλι, 132.
διορισμός, 97.
δίου, 119.
δισιγνάτος, 15.
δίττ, 129.
διώκω, 32.
διώχνω, 118.
δόνω, 116.
δόξας, δόξαις, 71, 78, 82.
δουκάνη, 20.
δράκος, 168.
δροσιά, 184.
δύί, 132, 135.
δύνω, 72.
δώση, 185.

έάν, 25.
έαυτόν, 97, 132.
έγαμήκα, 122.
έγγίξω, 103, 185.
έγνοιαις, 143.
έγνωκαν, 184.
έγών, 30.
έδέ, 110, 130.
έδέχθη, 79.
έδολιούσα, 76.
έδόντες, 13.
έδώ, 103.
έδωκα, 80.
έεεεν, 77.
έειξεν, 118.
έζρου, 127.
έθηκα, 80.
είθε, 87.
είβω, 116.
είδικός, 97.
ειερέος, 106.
είλω, 26.
είμαι, 71, 108.
είναι, είνε, 79, 108.
είντας, είντα, 117.
είρην, 26.
ειρώνεια, 97.
είς, 103, 187.
είσαι, 71, 108.
είχασι, 118.
είχνω, 118.

έκάνου, 110, 123.
έκείνος, 13.
έκι, 122.
έκπαθαίνομαι, 193.
έκρυβε, 187.
έκω, 118.
έλα, 115.
έλάκτισε, 17.
έλεγα, 72, 83.
έλεξες, 72, 83.
έλέχθηκα, 72, 80.
έλληνος, 113.
Έλυμπος, 24.
έμα, 122.
έμάς, 71.
έμβατέω, 37.
έμβόλιμος, 30.
έμε, 134.
έμένα, 71, 78.
έμέρα, 18.
Έμμανουήλ, 17.
έμπάζομαι, βάζομαι, 192.
έμπαίνω, 37.
έμποίκα, 122, 123.
έμπορος, 36.
έμφανίζειν, 185.
έναύω, 28.
ένδελέχεια, 37.
ένδον, 37.
ένδόσθια, 37.
ένθεύτεν, 38.
ένθσχε, 119.
ένόησες, 119.
ένοιξε, 118.
έντερα, 36.
έντερι, 127.
έντεύθεν, 38.
έντός, 37.
έντύνω, 37, 72.
ένώπιον, 187.
έξαπίνης, έξαίφνης, 118.
έξάτμισις, 93.
έξομόργνυμι, 35.
έξυπνίσω, 93.
έπάνω, 103, 184, 187.
έπήβολος, 16.
έπιστήμη, 97.
έπίστεψα, 24.
έπτάί, 109.
έπωκαν, 106.

P 2

ἔρθομαι, ἔρδα, ἔρδεμ, 36, 130.
ἐριμήτα, 19.
ἔριν, 74.
ἔρκομαι, 118.
ἔρος, ἔρον, 74.
ἔρσην, 11.
ἔρως, 104.
ἔσα, 122.
ἐσὲ, 13.
ἐσεῖς, 71.
ἐσένα, 71, 78.
ἔεδι, 117.
ἔσο, 79, 82, 107.
ἐσοῦ, 120, 125.
ἐστάθη, 185.
ἐστάθην, 103.
ἐσὺ, 13.
ἔτεινερε, 121.
ἐτοιμάζω, 103.
ἔτος, 29, 132.
εὐγενὸς, 104.
εὕδω, 102.
εὔθυμος, 24.
εὐθὺς, 24.
εὐκαιρίαν, 187.
εὐλαβὴς, 186.
εὐλογῶ, 187.
εὕρηκαν, 106.
Εὐροκλύδων, 21.
εὐτυχὴς, 23.
εὐφραινόμενος, 187.
εὐχαριστία, 23.
εὐχαριστῶ, 103, 106.
ἐφ' ἔτος, 39, 132.
ἐφθὸς, 37.
ἐψὲ, 13.
ἔψω, 24.
ἐῶ, 107.
ἑώρα, 25.
ἑώρακαν, 106.

ζάβα, 194.
Ζάβαλης, 33.
ζαβὸς, 194.
ζάλον, 33.
ζαρίφης, 33.
ζάρος, 194.
ζὲ, 119.
ζεῖος, 119.
ζεστὸς, 185.
Ζεὺς, 33.
ζητάει, 12.
ζία, 120.
ζῶος, 119.
ζμερδαλέος, ζμῆγμα, ζμικρὸς, ζμινύη, Ζμύρνα, 33.
ζορκάδιον, 31.
ζόρξ, 31.
ζουφάλα, 120.
ζωθριον, 12, 106.

ἤ, 71.
ἤν, 197.
ἡγούμενος, 103.
ἤγραφα, 117.
ἠδὲ, 16, 130.
Ἠλὶ, 30.
ἤλκυσε, 107.
ἠμβλακον, 37.
ἤμβρατον, 12.
ἤμουν, 72.
ἤμπλακον, 37.
ἤνθον, 35.
ἠξεύρω, 105, 184.
ἤπια, 117.
ἤρθα, 36.
ἤρξατο, 111.
ἤρχα, 116.
ἠρώτησα, 14.
ηὔθυμος, 24.
ηὗρον, 14.
ηὐτύχει, 45.

θὰ, 87, 88, 90, 130.
θαγατέρα, 114.
θᾶν, 130.
θανὴ, 194, 175.
θάξ, 130.
θὲ, 87.
θεῖος, 119.
θέλει νὰ, 87.
θέλεις εἴπωμεν, 187.
θέλω νὰ, 87.
θένω, θείνω, θῖνα, 24.
θέου, 120, 122.
θέσις, 94.
θέω, 24.
θεωρῶ, 183.

θηκάριον, 32.
θιγγάνω, 31.
θλιμμένος, 72.
θλῖψις, 105.
θὺμ, 129.
θόνα, 129.
θόνι, 129.
θοστε, 130.
θραμμένος, 72.
θρίγγος, 87.
θυμούκου, 120.
θῶμα, 24.
θῶν, 129.
θωριὰ, 143.
θωρῶ, 144, 183.
θῶδιν, 130.
θῶτ, 129.

Ἰ, 194.
ἰαίνω, 32.
ἰάκιον, 32.
ἰακχὴ, 38.
ἰατρὸς, 31.
ἴγγι, 121.
ἰγῆ, ἴγιν, 127.
ἴγκιαῖ, 121.
ἰδὲ, 16.
ἴδιον, 103.
ἰδοῦ, 104.
ἱερὸς, 32.
ἰθὺς, 24.
ἱκάνω, 119.
ἰκμάω, ἰκμὰς, 35.
ἵκωσι, 107.
ἴλη, 26.
ἴλλω, 26.
ἱμάτια, 103.
ἱμέρα, 18.
ἵνα, 89, 104, 109.
ἱνατὶ, ἱνατιάζω, 194.
ἴννι, 122.
ἴννος, 30.
ἴντας, ἴντα, 117.
ἰουμῶν, ἰουμῶν, 125.
ἱπὲρ, 22.
ἴρην, 26.
Ἰφθιμος, 4.
ἴψος, 22.
ἰὼ, ἰὸν, ἰώνγα, 116.

INDEX. 213

'κ, 114.
κά, 115, 130.
καθελς, 104.
καθέλου, 118.
καθέλου, 103.
καθισταίνω, 12.
καθέλου, 97, 118.
καί, τε, 25.
καιδνὸς, 25.
καίριος, 34.
καιρὸς, 109.
καῦρος, 118.
κακορρίζικοι, 144.
καλὰ, 146.
καλαύρωψ, 24.
κάλος, 118.
καλῶς, 110.
κάμ, 130.
κάμιλος, 17.
κάμποσος, 89.
κὰν, 109.
κανεὶς, 99.
καπνὲ, 119.
καρκέσι, 39.
καρσὶ, 195.
καστελλωμένος, 108.
καταβόθρα, 12.
καταιβαίνω, 12.
κάτέρ, 135.
πατέχω, 105.
κατοικῶ, 103.
Καύκωνες, 20.
καυχᾶσαι, 78.
κάψις, 24.
κὲ, 25, 88, 115.
κεῖνος, 34.
κέλομαι, 189.
κερίον, 15.
κὲς, 115.
κέτὲ, 134.
κεφαλᾶς, 71.
κῖ, 130.
κιάμονν, 144.
κιάνω, 199.
κιβοῦρι, 20.
κιθὼν, 40.
κιμοῦ, 124.
κίμων, 34.
κίνδυνος, 21.
κινέω, 34.

κὶς, 34.
κλαίω, κράζω, 195.
κλέϝος, 23.
κλεὶς, κλῆς, 15.
κλειτὸς, κλυτὸς, κλητὸς, 15, 22.
κνῖσα, τζίκνα, 145.
κοιμῶμαι, 103.
κοινὴ διάλεκτος, 21, 101.
κοίρανος, 34.
κόκκαλος, κόκκαλα, 195.
κοκώνη, 35.
κόλαξ, 195.
κόλασις, 105.
κολλούρα, 20.
κολλούριον, 185.
κοντὰ, 195, κόντα, 118.
κοπάδι, 108.
κοπέλα, 35.
κορακιστικὰ, 157.
κοράσιον, 106.
κουρϝὲνια, 131.
κορόμηλο, κορόμπλο, 37.
κορύσσω, 37.
κότσυφος, 37, 118.
κοῦε, 119.
κουλλὸς, 20.
κοὔνδὲρ, 138.
κουτάλιον, 20, 83.
κουφὸς, 15.
κρεββάτιον, 12.
κριάρι, 118.
κρίε, 199.
κρουνὸς, κρήνη, 33.
κρύβω, 106, 187.
κρύος, 195.
κρυφυκάμωμα, 141.
κρύε, 132.
κτουπῶ, 119.
κύθρα, 40.
κύκλος, 12.
Κύπρος, 21.
κύριος, 103.
Κχονδιστὰν, 38.
κώκα, 35.
κώλε, 123.
Κῶς, 71.

λάζομαι, 29.
λάμνω, 116.

λάρος, 31.
λαύρος, λάβρος, 24.
λεγάμενος, 72.
λέγεσαι, 72.
λέγονταs, 72.
λέγουν, λέγουνε, 72.
λέξε, 72, 78.
λέξον, 72, 78.
λεύσσω, 31.
λέω, 30.
ληστὴς, 16.
λιγυρὸς, 22.
λιθάριον, 106.
λίος, 30, 116.
Λιουσίας, 21, 121.
λογῆς, 89.
λοιμὸς, λιμὸς, 28.
λοιπὸν. 97, 104.
λυκόφως, 31, 196.
λυσέμεναι, λύσουμουν, 129.

μὰ, 196.
μάγουλον, 115.
μαζῆ, 89.
μαιμάω, 25.
μαϊμοῦ, 7.
μαλερὸς, 197.
μάλιστα, 99.
μαλόνω, 197.
μαξίλας, 115.
Μάρτης, 71.
μβρὲ, μπρὲ, 37.
μδαλαφάκε, 131.
μδὲ, μδὶ, 135.
μὲ, 109, 133, 196.
με, μέγε, μέγετ, 133.
μεάλος, 115.
μέγεθος, 41, 46.
μεθαύριον, 39.
μέλισσα, 118.
μελίσδω, 32.
μελίσσιν, 116.
μεμβρὰς, 30.
μερικὸς, 97.
μερίον, 15.
Μεσαϝουρία, 116.
μέσα εἰς, 106.
μετὰ, 107.
μετανοιῶ, 105.

μηγαρί, 197.
μὴν, μήνα, 96, 196.
μιᾶ, 185.
μίκον, 131.
μικρή, 12.
μίγ, 135, 136.
μλοῖον, 116.
μοιρογράφημα, 146.
μόλυβδος, μόλιβος, 21.
μοναξία, 191.
μόναχά τωνε, 143.
μονή, 185.
μονογενῆ, 73.
μοῦ, μοί, 83.
μούδε, 215.
μουνάξ, 191.
μοῦνος, 45.
μοῦργα, 20.
μο ρμίγγι, 20.
μουρμουρίζω, 20.
Μοῦσα, μοῖσα, 27.
μουχτερὸς, 20.
μπούζουνας, 33.
μύγα, 31.
μυζάω, 30.
μυκάομαι, μηκάομαι, 22.
μύσος, μῖσος, 22.
μύσταξ, μάσταξ, 12.
μωρὲ, 37.
Μῶρος, μαῦρος, 24.
μῶς δάψε, 131.

νά, 87, 196.
νάνδιετ, 135, 136.
ναραῖδες, νερεῖδες, 200.
νδιέκιν, 131.
νὲ, νέξε, νά, 133.
νέμικουν, 131.
νερὸν, νέρον, νηρὸν, 106, 118.
νέφος, γνέφος, 31.
νήθω, γνέθω, 31.
νῆστις, νήστης, 14.
νὶ, 120, 126, 135, 136.
νιάτι, 137.
νίβγω, 33.
νίζετ, 135.
νιοῦτα, 119.
νοάω, 83.
νόμο, 119.

νυκτὸς ἀμολγῷ, 35.
νύχα, 119.

ξενιτεύειν, 106.
ξερὸς, ξηρὸς, 15.

ὄγκος, ὄγγος, 36.
ὀδυνᾶσαι, 187.
ὀδύνη, ὠδὶν, 22.
οἶ, 97.
οἰνάριν, 115.
οἶος, 27.
ὀλεύθερος, 118.
ὀλίος, 116.
ὅλος, ὅλων, 103, 184, 187.
ὅλως, 97.
ὁλοσωματωμένη, 141.
ὀμαδεῖ, 31.
ὁ μικρότερος, 186.
ὅμορφος, 118.
ὀνάριον, 185.
ὀνείρατα, 80, 81.
ὀνεχώρησε, 12.
ὄντα, ὄντε, 117.
ὄντας, 72.
ὄνυξ, 12.
ὄνω, 12.
ὀξύβαφον, 21.
ὄξω, 13.
ὅπου, 185.
ὀπτὸς, 38.
ὀπφὶς, 38.
ὄρεξις, 99.
ὄρνιχα, ὄρνιχος, 33.
ὀροῦσε, 197.
ὅτι, 97.
ὅτοιμος, 118.
οὐδάφτ, 132.
οὐδάνουν, 133.
οὐδείφτουε, 131.
οὐδουκ, 131.
οὐλόμενος, 20.
οὖν, 20.
οὐπεργιάτουν, 133.
οὐρανόδρομος, 141.
οὐρανὸς, 103.
οὐσιώδης, 99.
ὄχθη, 38.
ὄχι δὰ, 115.

παιδὶν, 116.
πάντοτε, 181.
παράδειγμα, 99.
παραὶ, 12.
παράκλητος, 16.
παραπλήσιον, 103.
Πάρις, 71.
πᾶσα, 144.
πάσχα, 119.
πατέρας, 71.
πέδιλον, πέταλον, 198.
πεντικὸς, 118.
πὲρ, 135.
περγιάτουν, 133.
περιπατᾶτε, 12.
περισσότερον, 104, 186.
περιστάσεις, 104.
Πέρσες, 109.
πέσε, 135, 181.
πιάνω, πιαίνω, πιάζω, 12, 81.
πιέζω, πιάζω, 118.
πίεσαι, 187.
πιστεύω εἰς, 183.
πίστις, πύστις, 22.
πίστις, 103.
πλάκα, 109.
πλέγω, 11, 23, 29.
πλὴν, 103.
πληροφορῶ, 186.
πλήσια, 144.
πνῆμα, 116.
ποδεδίζω, 115.
ποῖος, 89.
πόκε, πόκα, 34.
πόρεσχε, 120.
πόστιν, 115.
ποτὲ μου, 183.
που, ποῦ, 184, 198.
ποῦα, 120.
ποὺλ, ποῦλος, πῶλος, 132.
ποῦ μένεις, 183.
πραγ-, 37.
πραγματικῶς, 104.
πρᾶμα, 30.
πράτη, 117.
πρέϊ, 135.
πρῆστις, πρίστης, 16.
προσέρρηξεν, 186.

INDEX.

πρόσκομμα, 113.
πρότασις, 99.
προύατα, 120.
προύκα, 27.
πύαλον, πύελον, 118.
πύκνωσις, 93.
πύλας, 22.
πυρπολημένος, 108.
πυτίνη, 30.
πῶς δὲν, 99.

ῥαχοῦλα, 29.
ῥὲ, 132.
ῥέζω, 11, 23, 29.
ῥέξομεν, 116.
ῥεπάνι, ῥαφάνιον, 12.
ῥῆγμα, ῥήχνω, 186.
ῥίζα, βρίζα, 29.
ῥιζικὸν, 144.
ῥοδοκόκκινος, 141.
ῥύγχος, ῥῖς, 22.
ῥύπτω, ῥίπτω, 22.
ῥῶς, 129.

σὰ, 131, 145.
σάμερε, 127.
σαρανταργὰ, 116.
σᾶς, 71, 109.
σάγατ, 131.
σὲ, 'σ, σὲμούνδετ, 132.
σέβας, 29.
Σεβῆρος, 29.
σέβομαι, σεύομαι, 29.
σεῖς, 71.
σιτέριν, 118.
σκάφος, 12.
σκελὶς, σχελὶς, 39.
Σκηπίων, σκίπων, 16.
σκιάζω, 203.
σκίζω, 39.
σκιλβόω, 34.
σκόλασμα, 29.
σκολειὸ, 39.
σκοτία, 184.
σκοτόνω, 92.
σκυλάκιον, 116.
σκύφος, 12.
σμίξιμον, 80.
σοβέω, 29.
σουπιαῖς, 83.

σουσάμι, 83.
σταθεὶς, 187.
σταθερὸς, 106.
στάσου, 79.
στάτε, 135.
στέπη, 131.
στέρξε, 176.
στήλη, στῦλος, 22.
στήριγξ, στύραξ, 22.
στίχοι πολιτικοὶ, 110.
στοιχεῖον, 93, 99, 200.
στρογγυλομορφοπήγουνος, 141.
συγκυρίαν, 187.
συζητεῖν, 187.
σύζυγε, 22.
συντηροῦσι, 143.
σφογγέριν, 118.
σχῆμα, 94.
σωματούργησες, 141.

τὰ, 133, = ἃ, 115, 145.
τάνδε, 134.
τάξις, 94.
ταρβύζω, ταρβέω, τραβέω, 116.
Ταρτησσὸς, 16.
τάσσω, 37.
ταυτὸν, 116.
τὲ, 129, 133.
τέκνη, 118.
τέκνυς, 107.
τεμ-άτ, 134.
τέμε, 134.
τέτσαρες, 118.
τέγε, τέγετ, 133.
τζαγγάρια, 108.
τζὶ, τζὲς, 121.
τζίκνα, κνίσα, 145.
τζουμᾶς, 108.
τὴ, τὴμ, 75.
τῆνος, 34.
τί, 120, 133.
τί λογῆς, 89.
τιέτρι, 137.
τιμ-έτ, 134.
τιοῦ, 121.
τίνας, 117.
τίποτα, 11.
τμῆμα, τμῆγμα, 30.

τοίγαρ, 99.
τον, 116.
τούι, 134.
τοῦμα, 126, 127.
τοὺς = οὓς, 145.
τοῦτον, 116.
τοὔγὲν, 134.
τραγί, 118.
τρὲ, 135.
τρεπνὸς, τερπνὸς, 116.
τροῦπα, 83.
τράγω, 182.
τσούζω, 33.
τσχὶ, 119, 121.
τυκάνη, δουκάνη, 20.
τύραννος, κοίρανος, 34.
τῦς, 27.
τὺτ, 134.
τῶν, 109.
τῶν, τόνὲ, τόνα, 134.
τώρα, 89.
τώρα πλέον, 120.

ὕαλος, 32.
ὑὲ, ὑηνία, 16.
υἱὸς, 28.
ὕλη, 21, 99.
ὕο, 126.
ὑπάγω, 103, 183.
ὑπάρχω, 99, 187.
ὕπατος, 25.
ὑπεύθυνος, 45.
ὑπόδημαν, 111.
ὑποκείμενον, 99.
ὑσεῖς, 115.
ὓτ, 134.
ὕψιστος, ὑψηλὸς, 25.

φάγεσαι, 187.
φαίνεται, 99.
φαίνω, φέγγω, 25.
φέβομαι, φέβγω, 29.
φέρεσαι, 25.
φερίζερε, 127.
φερτὸς, φέρτερος, φέρτοτος, 83.
φεῦξε, 82.
φὴρ, 33.
φηκάριον, 33.
φθάνω, 24, 187.

216 INDEX.

φθίνω, 24.
φιλοσοφία, 196.
φίτρον, φύτρα, 22.
φκειάνω, φτειάνω, 34.
φκυάριον, φτυάριον, 34.
φληνὸς, φλυνὸς, 22.
φλησκοῦνι, 30.
φλίβω, φλιβερὸν, 33.
φλούδιον, 27.
φοβᾶσαι, 12.
φοβέω, 29.
φοζούμενος, 119.
Φοίνιξ, 27.
φορᾷ, 132.
φορέετε, φορεῖτε, 15.
φορέθηνε, 117.
φύζουμεν, φύζω, 119.
φυλάγω, 37.
φύσις, 21.

φυτεύω, φιτύω, 29.

ἧα, 132.
χαίτη, χετὸς, 25.
χάμαι, χάμου, 145.
χαμπλὸς, χαμηλὸς, 37.
ἤάνγρουν, 132.
χάνω, χάω, 206.
χάρις, ἤάρις, 118.
Χάρος, Χάρωντας, 92.
ἤερὶ, 132.
χήρα-ρε, 117.
ἤὶρ, 132.
χιτὼν, 40.
χλαμὺς, 21.
χουλιάριον, 40.
χρηματάω, 117.
χρυσόον, χρυσοῦν, 15.
χύτρα, 40.

χωργὰ, 116.

ψακὰς, ψιχάλα,
ψαυτέριν, 21.
ψὲς, 144.
ψηλαφῶ, 206.
ψηλὸς, ψιλὸς, ψι
206.
ψηφῶ, 208.
ψιμμύθιον, ψιμμὶ
ψοφάει, 92.

ὤβεον, 21.
ὤλαξ, 24.
ὠνομάσθαι, 28.
ὠὸν, 21.
ἔρα, 189.
ὡρᾶκα, 128.
ὠτίον, 24.

BIBLIOLIFE

Old Books Deserve a New Life
www.bibliolife.com

Did you know that you can get most of our titles in our trademark **EasyScript**™ print format? **EasyScript**™ provides readers with a larger than average typeface, for a reading experience that's easier on the eyes.

Did you know that we have an ever-growing collection of books in many languages?

Order online:
www.bibliolife.com/store

Or to exclusively browse our **EasyScript**™ collection:
www.bibliogrande.com

At BiblioLife, we aim to make knowledge more accessible by making thousands of titles available to you – quickly and affordably.

Contact us:
BiblioLife
PO Box 21206
Charleston, SC 29413